ANTHOLOGY IN LAW AND THE SOCIAL SCIENCES

I0642416

Kenneth K. Mwenda
PhD, LLD, DSc(Econ)

ANTHOLOGY IN LAW AND THE SOCIAL SCIENCES

VOLUME - 2

Kenneth K. Mwenda
PhD, LLD, DSc(Econ)

www.africaincanadapress.com

TORONTO, CANADA – 2016

Anthology in Law and the Social Sciences

Kenneth K. Mwenda

http://www.kennethmwenda.com

PUBLISHED BY:

AFRICA IN CANADA PRESS

18A-100 Westmore Drive, Toronto, ON M9V 5C3, CANADA

Tel: 1 (416) 644-1106, Fax: 1 (416) 644-1126

http://www.africaincanadapress.com

AFRICA IN CANADA PRESS is committed to publishing works by authors of African descent in Canada and abroad with excellence.

COVER DESIGN & TYPESETTING BY:

DIAMOND BOOKS

www.diamondbooks.ca

PAPERBACK EDITION -V1 : ISBN: 978-1-988251-10-3 – AFRICA IN CANADA PRESS

PAPERBACK EDITION -V2 : ISBN: 978-1-988251-07-3 – AFRICA IN CANADA PRESS

E-BOOK EDITION : ISBN: 978-1-988357-03-4 – DIAMOND PUBLISHERS

PRINTED IN CANADA

DEDICATION

In loving memory of my father,
Mr. Joseph T. Mwenda Snr.

Your footprints remain indelible. You taught me to think critically about the virtues of honesty, integrity, love, faith and truth. You inspired in your children the values of continuous learning and erudition. You lived an exemplary life, with the highest standards of integrity and moral character. You will always be my greatest role model. And I know that you are up there teaching angels how to love. We miss you always and forever.

"A wise [man] will hear, and will increase learning; and a man of understanding shall attain unto wise counsels: To understand a proverb, and the interpretation; the words of the wise, and their dark sayings. The fear of the LORD is the beginning of knowledge: but fools despise wisdom and instruction."

Proverbs 1:5-7

ACKNOWLEDGEMENT

To my many students and former students worldwide at the various international universities where I have taught, thank you for being promising leaders for the next generation. That a number of my former law students have gone on to become notable Supreme Court judges, Constitutional Court judges, Court of Appeal judges and High Court judges, including an eminent Chief Justice, while others continue to serve as law professors, diplomats and ambassadors, as well as judicial clerks and prominent Cabinet Ministers, is only the beginning of the story. For, there are also those that have held or continue to hold senior positions at the World Bank, the African Development Bank, the Common Market for Eastern and Southern Africa, and many other international organizations. I am truly humbled and grateful to God, Jehovah, Almighty, for all these blessings.

Special thanks also go out to all friends and colleagues (as well as my family members, including my wife and son) who provided comments on the various sayings, musings and metaphors in this book. Their tireless contributions helped to sharpen my views on a number of issues. My other thanks go out to **Africa in Canada Press** for the timely and efficient publication of the book. **Diamond Books - Canada** is also hereby acknowledged for the excellent typesetting work and the preparation of the cover design.

TABLE OF CONTENTS

PART - A

PART - B

PART - C

PREFACE

While this book does not purport or pretend to have all the answers to the many social challenges that we face in life, it certainly does raise some thought-provoking questions for us to think through. I hasten to add, however, that the book is not a work of fiction. Neither is it about motivation like many motivational books that are on the bookshelves today. Rather, it is an example of public intellectualism in Law and the Social Sciences. The book distills complex ideas that are often confined to the academic world into more easily discernible ideas by everyone, including the laity. Such is a cardinal objective of the book – to provoke some critical thinking across a broad spectrum of society on certain topical themes pertaining to Law and the Social Sciences. With an inter- and multi-disciplinary focus, the book cuts across many contemporary themes in the Law and Social Science discourse.

What started out first as a series of short intellectually stimulating and thought-provoking articles published in a number of media outlets in Zambia and elsewhere culminated into the publication of this anthology: that is, a collection of short articles in the Law and Social Science discourse. Over the years, I have made significant contributions to contemporary debate on various political, economic and social issues. Many individuals that have followed my scholarly and public contributions have encouraged me to bring together into a book a collection of some of my well-received media articles. And so, this is how the idea of this book came about. The writing of the book was a response to the increasing and growing demand from the readership. I have included in this book new and updated material whose 'footage' has not been seen before. It has not been an easy path to tread where you sometimes have to raise certain 'unorthodox' and out-of-the-box questions that many folks would rather ignore or pretend not to have some idea about. But avoiding a problem only provides temporary relief for you to face the same problem again tomorrow. So, to avoid facing the same problem the next day, it is best to confront it – like the taking of a bull by the horns!

In putting this book together, I carefully crafted the aforesaid material along the lines of certain themes examined in a number of my media articles. For example, the chapters on religion and the law follow one another in one section of the book. And while the book presents an eclectic taste of the Law and the

Social Science discourse, such that many a reader might find it hard to put the book down once they start reading, a deliberate effort is made to set the discussion in its proper socio-political and socio-economic contexts. Indeed, law does not exist or operate in a vacuum. It must be situated in its proper socio-political and socio-economic contexts. Thus, the book presents a valuable 'Law in Context' contribution. Much of the analyses are made through the prism of the social sciences.

The paperback edition of the book is arranged in **two (2) volumes** whilst the **electronic edition** is **a single publication** containing both Volumes 1 and 2. For those accessing the book as a paperback, you are encouraged to read both Volumes 1 and 2. For those accessing the electronic edition, you are encouraged to read the whole book. In this book, a number of themes pursued are closely interrelated. They cut across intertwined disciplines. Against this background, it would benefit the reader to get a good grasp of both Volumes 1 and 2 of the paperback edition or the whole of the electronic edition. Elsewhere, I have authored several scholarly books and journal articles that are now widely cited in academia and by major policy institutions as well as by the courts of law. The current book is, therefore, not my maiden effort at writing. The reader is encouraged to consult also, if need be, my many scholarly works that are abundantly available in almost all of the world's leading academic libraries.

In this book, I endeavour to stand back from my notable scholarly work of authoring for an academic and intellectual audience. What I propose to do instead is to seek dialogue with a broader section of society, ranging from the most intellectually sophisticated to the least enlightened person. Very often, as scholars, our ideas tend to be detached from the real world, particularly when we use technical language and jargon or other forms of communication that only our fellow intellectuals can understand or decipher. Take, for example, the case of a PhD economist who is in the habbit of using complex mathematical formula to write or report on contemporary economic issues in the media. How useful is such writing and information to the common man on the ground that has little interest in learning about complex mathematical equations?

A notable role of public intellectualism is to stand back from the intimidating language of a technocrat so as to avoid some kind of tunnel-vision where only you, the author, and your fellow technocrats are the ones who can understand what you are talking about. And this is exactly what this book endeavours to do. People from different walks of life will find the book an easy read, whether they are travelling on a train or they are on a long flight. The book will give them a valuable companion. And even though some of the readers may not be in full agreement with some contentious arguments that the author advances in certain parts of the book, many a readers' thoughts are likely to be provoked to some greater degree. That, really, is what matters most. Indeed, it is that stimulation of debate that lies at the centre of this book.

Closely related to the foregoing, although the debate continues on the meaning of the term 'public intellectual', it is not far from a truism that such an individual cannot be pigeon-holed into a dogmatic or single way of expressing and communicating his or her ideas. A public intellectual often transcends the boundaries of academic pedagogy, while avoiding the chasm that divides scientific inquiry and intellectualism from the typical practitioner role of unscientific advocacy. A public intellectual often remains focused on translating complex theoretical and conceptual ideas into easily discernible scientific and objective analyses that even wananchi (*i.e.* the public citizens) can understand. In doing so, the public intellectual should try to communicate and speak the language of the common man, without stifling debate or intimidating the audience with all manner of intellectual sophistry. To that end, the use of metaphors, adages, and illustrations becomes handy in breaking down certain ideas that would ordinarily be seen as too complex for the common man to understand. This book takes such an approach, breaking down complex ideas into easily discernible ideas.

Although some illustrations and examples provided in the book are drawn from specific jurisdictions and localities, a good number of them are of wider application to many other contexts and situations. This is not a book about Africa only or about America and Europe alone. Rather, it is a book about the human condition everywhere in the world. Every single reader will be able to relate to one or more illustrations and arguments contained in the book. For example, while the issue of tribalism is often rife in developing countries, the closely related issue of racism is often rife in the developed Western world. In tackling these issues, the book does so with honesty and critically insightful wit.

As noted above, a good many of chapters in this book have appeared as short articles in the media. However, I have made significant efforts to revise and update these articles, capturing now much of the feedback that has been received from many sections of the readership. The revised articles are set alongside new material that has never been published before. And it is expected that a wide section of society will find the book a valuable read, irrespective of their level of intellectual sophistication or their race, gender, creed or ideological belief.

The analyses, arguments, interpretations and conclusions expressed in this book are entirely those of the author. They do not represent the views of any institution, person or body to which the author is affiliated.

Professor Kenneth K. Mwenda
PhD, LLD, DSc(Econ).

Washington DC, USA.
Tuesday, March 1, 2016

CHAPTER 57

THE INDELIBLE GENIUS OF BOB MARLEY

The date is April 17, 1980. The place is Salisbury, Zimbabwe, now known as Harare. The event is Zimbabwe celebrating its political independence. The celebratory chanting is by the visibly excited people. The clairvoyant wailing on the stage is by Bob Marley and the Wailers. Yes, they are wailing passionately for Africa. The Jamaican Rastaman, Hon. Robert Nesta Marley (Bob Marley), is at hand in Salisbury to perform one of his best performances ever.

Clad in fashionable tight brown leather pants and a matching brown leather waistcoat, with a striped T-shirt inside, Bob takes to the vocals with a passionate cry for his motherland, Africa. Like Che Guevara who had travelled thousands of miles from Latin America to help the Congolese fight for and win independence from the Belgians, Bob had also travelled thousands of miles from the island of Jamaica to witness Zimbabwe's independence. The invitation extended to Bob Marley for this special event reaches its climax as he shares in his Nyabinghi rhythm through the classic, timely and well-written song, "Zimbabwe". The crowd just goes crazy!

And the lyrics of the song are simply marvelous. The Nyabinghi rhythm sets the song's pulse for a testimony to the success of the Zimbabwean revolution. There is also some smoke and fumes in the background, but who cares what type of smoke it is. All that matters here, and what the people care for, is that: "Every man gotta right to decide his own destiny…, And in this judgement there is no partiality. So arm in arms, with arms, we'll fight this little struggle…, Cause that's the only way we can overcome our little trouble. Brother, you're right, you're right…, You're right, you're right, you're so right! We gon' fight (we gon' fight), we'll have to fight (we gon' fight), We gonna fight (we gon' fight), fight for our rights! Natty Dread it in-a (Zimbabwe); Set it up in (Zimbabwe); Mash it up-a in-a Zimbabwe (Zimbabwe); Africans a-liberate (Zimbabwe), yeah."

As if to give prophecy to his African brothers and sisters, Bob Marley continues: "No more internal power struggle; We come together to overcome the little trouble. Soon we'll find out who is the real revolutionary…, 'Cause I don't want my people to be contrary. And, brother, you're right, you're right, You're right, you're right, you're so right! We'll 'ave to fight (we gon' fight), we gonna fight (we gon' fight)… We'll 'ave to fight (we gon' fight), fighting for our rights!... To divide and rule could only tear us apart; In every man chest, mm – there beats a heart. So soon we'll find out who the real revolutionary is; And I don't want my people to be tricked by mercenaries. Brother, you're right, you're right..."

In this month of May, we celebrate the anniversary of the passing of the late Bob Marley at a Miami hospital in the USA. He crossed over on May 11, 1981 at a tender age of only 36 years after succumbing to cancer. But his music lives on, together with that of other great reggae legends like the late Peter Tosh.

In his album, "Rastaman Vibration", Bob Marley left us an indelible musical rendition of the famous 1936 speech of the late Emperor Haile Selassie at the League of Nations in Geneva. The song is titled, "War", and is particularly important as we celebrate African Freedom Day this month on May 25. Bob wails passionately:

"Until the philosophy which holds one race superior and another inferior is finally and permanently discredited and abandoned, everywhere its war – Me say war! That until there no longer be first class and second class citizens of any nation... Until the colour of a man's skin is of no more significance than the colour of his eyes – Me say war! That until the basic human rights are equally guaranteed to all without regard to race – Dis a war. That until that day, the dream of lasting peace, world citizenship, rule of international morality will remain in but a fleeting illusion to be pursued, but never attained – now everywhere is war... war! And until the ignoble and unhappy regimes that hold our brothers in Angola, in Mozambique, South Africa...in sub-human bondage have been toppled, utterly destroyed – well, everywhere is war – Me say war! War in the east, war in the west, war up north, war down south – war... war... rumours of war. And until that day, the African continent will not know peace..., We Africans will fight, we find it necessary. And we know we shall win, as we are confident in the victory of good over evil – good over evil, yeah! Good over evil – good over evil, yeah!"

Indeed, Bob Marley was more than just an ordinary musician. He was a social scientist. Despite his humble educational background, he graduated from the school of hard knocks of self-taught geniuses. Bob was a self-taught man whose sensitivities to the plight of the suffering masses transcended skin-colour, geographical boundaries, nationality and ethnicity. It is no surprise that he was invited to grace the occasion of Zimbabwe's political independence. In summer of 2010, I was privileged to watch a live musical performance by the Wailers in Rockville, Maryland, USA. And Bob's former bandmate, the great bass guitarist, "Family Man", was there doing his magic on the bass guitar. You could actually feel the Bob Marley presence at the concert.

More recently, decades after Bob Marley's passing, news continues to filter through, suggesting that (see C. Thomasos, *The Christian Post* (Online): February 6, 2012): "... although many are familiar with the reggae legend as a Rastafarian, others may be surprised to hear that he was baptized as an Orthodox Christian before his death. Marley was an influential figure in the global expansion of a Rastafarian religious movement through his music. The movement began in 1930s Jamaica, focusing on the worship of former Ethiopian Emperor, Haile Selassie I, whose followers believe him to be a messiah that will lead them into righteousness and prosperity."

Thomasos continues: "Although Marley sang and spoke about being a Rasta, some say he converted to Christianity before his death. Abuna Yesehaq, Archbishop of the Ethiopian Orthodox Church in the Western Hemisphere who died in 2005, admitted that he baptized Marley about one year before his death.

Yesehaq appeared in a 1984 interview with Jamaica Gleaner's Sunday magazine, titled 'Abuna Yesehaq Looks Back on 14 Years of Ministry in Jamaica,' in which he spoke about Marley's desire to become a Christian long before his death. 'Bob was really a good brother, a child of God, regardless of how people looked at him,' Yesehaq said. 'He had a desire to be baptized long ago, but there were people close to him who controlled him and who were aligned to a different aspect of Rastafari. But he came to church regularly.' In the interview, Yesehaq addressed claims that Marley's terminal cancer was the motivation behind his acceptance of Jesus Christ as his personal savior."

Even more intriguing is information from the

Christian Post (*Ibid*), quoting Archbishop Abuna Yesehaq who also conducted the rites for Bob Marley's funeral, that when Bob Marley toured Los Angeles, New York and England he preached the Orthodox faith, and many members in those cities came to the Church because of Bob. Archbishop Yesehaq further observes that: "Many people think he was baptized because he knew he was dying, but that is not so. He did it when there was no longer any pressure on him, and when he was baptized, he hugged his family and wept, they all wept together for about half an hour."

Giving credence to Archbishop Yesehaq's testimony, Judy Mowatt, a reggae and gospel singer who formerly sang backup for Marley in the group I Threes, recalls learning about Marley's conversion to Christianity in an interview with Cross Rhythms radio (see: Christian Post (*Ibid*)). It is reported that Mowatt spoke with her former bandmate and Marley's wife, Rita, about the late musician calling out to Jesus Christ on his death bed. Ms. Mowatt recounts: "When Bob was on his dying bed, his wife Rita called me on the phone and said to me that Bob was in such excruciating pain and he stretched out his hand and said, 'Jesus take me.' I was wondering to myself, 'Why is it that Bob said Jesus and not Selassie'... Then I met a friend of mine and he said his sister, who is a Christian, was a nurse at the hospital where Bob was before he passed on, and she led him to the Lord Jesus Christ. So when Rita saw him saying 'Jesus take me,' he had already received the Lord Jesus Christ in his life."

CHAPTER 58

DISCERNING THE ZEAL AND ZEST FOR THIRD-TERM PRESIDENTIAL BIDS

Many are familiar with the fears of some people that a particular Head of State may decide to extend his or her stay in power beyond the usual two-term limit under the national constitution. Some of these fears are just speculation, especially if they are coming from a desperate opposition party, while others are genuine and should not be dismissed as a mere hunch.

It is often not easy to tell how serious some suspicions are in the absence of strong evidence to suggest that the sitting Head of State is indeed intent on prolonging his or her stay in power. It is usually the impatience of a desperate opposition leader to take-over power from the incumbent that leads to the fabrication of many half-truths and unfounded rumours. Not every Head of State in Africa or elsewhere, though, is intent on prolonging his or her stay in power. Sometimes, it is the cronies to the Head of State, as well as many of those that surround him or benefit directly or indirectly from his Presidency, that end up misleading him to stay on. If they have to tell the President lies that he is popular, they will do so shamelessly, urging him that the people are all behind him. And many political leaders are often blinded by power and thus remain detached from the people on the ground. These leaders rely instead on advice from their close allies, henchmen and cronies. That form of tunnel vision can be quite dangerous. It is very easy to be misled into thinking you are a star or hero by those that are eating from your pocket.

Some political leaders that have attempted to prolong their stay in power have done so for a number of reasons. Chief among them are the following: (a) where, through an insatiable appetite for political power, a President has stepped on too many toes, and has also victimized and hurt so many people, especially those in the opposition, he will be afraid to leave office, fearing for what would happen to him should he leave; (b) where a President's henchmen have done so much damage to the country through perpetrating abuses of human rights, corruption, unlawful detentions, or where they have mistreated so many people in different social settings such that these henchmen and the President both fear that, should the latter vacate office, the henchmen will end up as 'orphans' and thus become politically vulnerable to the retributions and vendettas of those that have been hurt over the years; or, (c) where a President has stolen and looted so much wealth from the national treasury of his country or/and has not only perpetuated but has also shielded corrupt practices of others while in power.

Other reasons why some dictators opt to remain in power are as follows: (d) where a President has been practicing blatant tribalism by favouring or appointing to most lucrative political posts people from his own tribe or tribal region, or where he has been supporting ethnic prejudices against a people that are now likely to win the elections; and, (e) where a President's sons, daughters or relatives have done so much damage to the nation through corrupt practices as well as through other crimes, and he fears that should the opposition or someone else win the elections then the necessary prosecutions will follow.

Also, a dictator may choose to stay put and not vacate office at the end of his constitutional term where: (f) his spouse, the First Lady (or even some of his sisters-in-law and brothers-in-law), has been bullying people around and behaving as though she is invincible to a point where it becomes public knowledge that she is the one who usually recommends and endorses most presidential appointments, and that, by parity of reasoning, she is the one behind most dismissals that are made by the President; (g) a President has been running the country as though it is his own small village or personal-to-holder farmhouse; (h) a President has made so many false promises to the people just to win an election and ascend to power, but then realizes that he will be held accountable for his lies after leaving office; (i) where a President has been grabbing other people's wives or girlfriends, and he is now fearing that he may face vendettas and retribution from those that he hurt, especially that there will be no State machinery to protect him; or, (j) where the law does not provide for some form of pension, gratuity or allowance to a former Head of State, and he begins to worry how he will survive financially after leaving office.

Because of all these fears, anxieties and uncertainties, many a dictator are faced with two possible choices: (i) to hung on in there and seek a third-term of office (or even more terms of office) in order to avoid being prosecuted (or rather 'persecuted', as they often claim) by their political foes; or (ii) to anoint a political stooge or protégé to take-over the Presidency so that the new guy feels indebted to his predecessor and will be expected not to throw his predecessor underneath the bus or in harm's way. But as experience has shown, especially in Southern Africa, the new guy may just turn around against his predecessor after tasting power and realizing that after all he can do whatever he wants, irrespective of the 'great' favour done to him by his predecessor. So, what to do now, as they would say in Russia?

Many a dictator realize that the safest and surest way to stay out of harm's way is to remain in power by seeking another term of office as President, notwithstanding the limitations of terms in the constitution. For these dictators, that is the only way to remain shielded from the law catching up with them, especially if there are examples in parallel jurisdictions where the immunity of a former Head of State has been lifted by parliament to have him face trial on charges of corruption.

But, Africa is not the only the place where folks do not want to leave the Presidency when their time is up. We see this in many other parts of the world too. The interesting thing about Africa, though, is the common tendency for some Heads of State to try to emulate the concept of traditional chieftaincy when serving as Head of State. They behave as though they are chiefs running a village with subjects, and thus can choose their own successors, forgetting that the office of president does not come by through inheritance but through elections. Also, it is not always true, as some of these folks would want us to believe, that they choose to stay on in power because 'It is the people themselves who want me' or because 'there is no one to take over after I leave office'.

In the US, it was merely by tradition from the times of President George Washington that a US President served not more than two terms until the four terms served by President Franklin D. Roosevelt (FDR). Indeed, prior to the enactment of the twenty-second Amendment of the US Constitution, there was no written law that required a US President to serve for a maximum of not more than two terms. The twenty-second Amendment of the US Constitution now sets a term limit for an individual to serve as US President. The US Congress passed the amendment on March 21, 1947, and it was ratified by the requisite number of states on February 27, 1951.

The relevant provisions of this amendment read as follows:

"*Section 1.* No person shall be elected to the office of the President more than twice, and no person who has held the office of President, or acted as President, for more than two years of a term to which some other person was elected President shall be elected to the office of the President more than once. But this article shall not apply to any person holding the office of President when this article was proposed by the Congress, and shall not prevent any person who may be holding the office of President, or acting as President, during the term within which this article becomes operative from holding the office of President or acting as President during the remainder of such term... *Section 2.* This article shall be inoperative unless it shall have been ratified as an amendment to the Constitution by the legislatures of three-fourths of the several States within seven years from the date of its submission to the States by the Congress."

The implications of Section 1 of this US Constitutional amendment are that it does not matter whether or not an individual took a 'cooling-off' period after serving for two-terms as the US President. That individual is still not eligible to go for another term. This prohibition extends to a Vice-President who has acted as US President for more than two years (that is, in the absence of the actual President) and then goes on to win an election as US President, serving thereafter a term as the incumbent President.

By contrast, an English translation of Article 81(3) of the Russian Constitution provides as follows: "One person may not hold the position of Russian president for more than two terms in a row." Here, the last three words, namely, "...in a row", entail that an individual can serve as Russian President for two terms and then take some 'cooling-off' time before returning for another term of office as President or even more terms. In essence, this Russian constitutional provision permits an individual to serve for three or more consecutive presidential terms of office. So, there is no need to amend the Russian Constitution to allow an individual to serve for a third-term. Article 81(3) implicitly allows for that as long as one takes some 'cooling-off' time before going at it again.

In Zambia, Section 35(2) of the 1996 Constitution of the Republic of Zambia provides that: "35(2) Notwithstanding anything to the contrary contained in this Constitution or any other Law, no person who has twice been elected as President shall be eligible for re-election to that office." Like in the case of the US, in Zambia, there is no such thing as a cooling-off period after an individual has served as President for two terms. Once the two terms are over, that is it. Be that as it may, both in the US and in Zambia, an individual can serve as President for one term only, and then take some 'cooling-off' time before returning for another one term as President. Indeed, the Zambian and US Constitutions do not bar such a thing.

CHAPTER 59

CONSTITUTIONAL LEGITIMACY AND THE GROWING OF CONSTITUTIONS IN CONTEMPORARY COMMONWEALTH AFRICA

Why are the constitutions of many developing countries, such as countries in much of contemporary Commonwealth Africa, failing the people? Why are we constantly changing constitutions? Is it that we often get it wrong in the drafting or development of a constitution? Why is it that, despite cries for constitutional autochthony, we often end up with a constitution that fails to withstand the test of time? Some of the laity might scream: "The constitution is illegal!!!" Others would say, "We were not consulted properly and fully, and so we do not recognize this sham constitution."

There are many reasons that help to explain the failings and trappings of constitutions in much of contemporary Commonwealth Africa. Mindful that every country will have a different set of variables that are country-specific, there are, however, some parallel comparisons among most of these countries. It is to the latter view that we lend our reasoning.

A notable argument why many constitutions in contemporary Commonwealth Africa have failed is that they simply lack legitimacy. Now, we need to understand that *legitimacy* and *legality* are two different things, just as the term *illegality* is different from *unlawfulness*. Whereas an act that is done outside or beyond the ambit of the legal framework may not necessarily be unlawful, it can be considered illegal if it has been executed outside the law. For example, an *ultra vires* act may not necessarily be unlawful or criminal, but it will be illegal. By contrast, an unlawful act often tends to offend the law in a criminal sense. Likewise, a legally binding constitution can still fail the test of legitimacy in spite of being born out of legal and lawful circumstances.

To understand the implications of legitimacy here, we have to go beyond the black letter law. We have to bring on board other relevant aspects of the social sciences such as political science. Black letter law alone is not enough. It has its limitations, unless we embrace jurisprudence and legal philosophy as the underbelly of the law. Indeed, only a good understanding of the philosophical foundations of a constitution can help us to understand why many constitutions are often rejected by the same people they are intended to serve.

A notable way in which a constitution can gain legitimacy is through a widely accepted ideology. Propaganda, when articulated nicely and convincingly, can win you legitimacy. As they say, the same lie when repeated all too often ends up as the truth. So, the effective and strategic use of ideology can help to legitimize a constitution. Also, the role that ideology can play in winning over legitimacy is not confined to propaganda only. Once you get stakeholder buy-in through appropriate consultations, you know you have won over the other stakeholders. And that is why many constitutional law reformers talk of consultations and mass participation in decision-making processes leading to the development of a constitution. In essence, they are looking for a common ideology as a pedigree for the legitimacy of the constitution.

A second but somewhat contentious approach to entrenching constitutional legitimacy is through the use of force. We have seen this happen in situations of military coups, for example. The regime that comes to power through such radical means will often suspend the constitution of the country and introduce immediately some military orders and directives. For all intents and purposes, if the new military regime is in control of the country, then those military orders and directives become the new constitution. The said orders and directives may even gain legitimacy as long as the military regime is in control. Here, the old constitution is superseded and will no longer be enforceable as long as the military orders and directives are in force. Professor Hans Kelsen has expounded on this positivist theory of jurisprudence, although not to the extent of the issue of constitutional legitimacy that I am now introducing.

Against this background, how should we go about in drafting or preparing a new constitution for the Republic of Zambia? Whereas some may be preoccupied with seeking such means as a referendum to reflect the best wishes of the majority of the people, others would be inclined to think a constitutional review commission is the best way forward, especially if a referendum might prove too costly. Whichever way, this does not tell us much on why our constitutions often fail. Many constitutional lawyers will be busy sifting through the various legal provisions of the constitution or other legislative documents to find permissible legal means to usher in a new constitution. But they will not find anything in those statutory and constitutional provisions on how a constitution can withstand the test of time. Neither will they find anything there that will tell them why many constitutions fail. You have to be a committed, erudite and ardent reader of constitutional developments worldwide in order to grasp these issues. And you must read beyond the law, stretching further into other closely related disciplines.

Many countries have toyed around with the concepts of prime ministerial versus presidential systems of government in their constitutions. In Zambia, like the US, we have a presidential system of government. The president is the head of state. By contrast, in the UK, they have a prime ministerial system of government. In many prime ministerial systems of government, such as was Zimbabwe upon attaining political independence, the prime minister is the head of state. In these States, if ever there is such a position as president, then the president is a titular or nominal head.

What has been happening in much of contemporary Commonwealth Africa is that there has been a tendency to grow our constitutions like a Christmas tree. Our constitutions have been suffering from the Christmas tree effect. Now, what do I mean by this? We tend to grow convoluted constitutions on which we hang everything. It is like the case of a Christmas tree on which all cards and small presents are placed. And we tend to borrow from different constitutional models and traditions, combining, for example, aspects of presidential and prime ministerial systems of government. Sometimes we want a very powerful Supreme Court. At other times, we want a powerful and supreme parliament.

In some States that have strong traditions of parliamentary supremacy or parliamentary sovereignty, for example, the State has maintained a bicameral system for the legislature. But this does not exclude possibilities of a bicameral system of parliament in a presidential system of government. For example, both the UK and the US have two legislative chambers, namely, the House of Lord and the House of Commons for the UK and then the Senate and the House of Representatives for the US.

Thus, it matters not that the State is a federal or unitary State.

Now, in Zambia, we have a presidential system of government under a unitary State, with a unicameral system of the legislature. Indeed, we only have one house of parliament. Therefore, the checks and balances that our parliament performs on the functions of other arms of the State must be seen to be as effective as those checks and balances performed by a system that hosts a bicameral or tricameral system of parliament. Mindful that Zambia does not follow a system of parliamentary supremacy or parliamentary sovereignty, the excesses of the executive arm of the State are to be limited not only through the constitution and the doctrine of constitutionalism, but also through a strong and effective parliament, accompanied by an independent and active judiciary. In this sense, judicial activism does not become an affront to the role of the legislature in developing law.

But for all the above to work, we should move away from the idea of a Christmas tree constitution. Some issues are better dealt with or captured in other statutes, but not in the constitution. We cannot have everything under the sun loaded into the constitution. Besides, it is not merely a question of whether we should have a referendum or not for a constitution to be born. Rather, the issue is why do our constitutions often fail whether or not we go through a referendum or a constitutional review commission? And what can we learn from our past mistakes to avoid repeating the same mistakes?

Granted that the legitimacy of the constitution can be eroded where the executive arm of the State manipulates the selection of the constitutional review commissioners or where it doctors the findings and recommendations of such a commission to suit its own political interests, the people may also not have much confidence in the caliber of people that are charged with drafting or debating the constitution. Sometimes, it is the lack of transparency in the whole constitutional development process that erodes constitutional legitimacy. But, where the citizenry has faith in the checks and balances that parliament can offer, there tends to be greater prospects for attaining constitutional legitimacy. The same is true where a judiciary embraces judicial activism appropriately to safeguard the rights of the people. But if, say, parliament is weak or is controlled by one majority party, then the last man standing remains an active and independent judiciary. Even so, the judiciary cannot re-write the constitution. The net result is that the people will have little faith in the constitution, and then that will erode the legitimacy of the constitution.

\- *Kenneth K. Mwenda*

CHAPTER 60

THE CONSTITUTIONALITY OF DECLARING ZAMBIA A CHRISTIAN NATION

While it may not be international best practice to spell out in the Republican Constitution the predominant religious aspirations of a large faction of the population, it is not unconstitutional to provide for this as long as other people's freedom of conscience and worship are also protected and upheld. Time and again, we hear commentators and pundits in Zambia agitate for a home-grown Constitution. But what does this entail?

In political science, the doctrine of 'constitutional autochthony' is synonymous with developing a 'native' or 'indigenous' Constitution. It denotes national efforts at developing a Constitution that is reflective of the main native or indigenous values of the people. Perhaps, it is through such attempts that the Zambian parliament ended up spelling out in the Preamble of the 1996 Republican Constitution the predominant religious aspirations of the country.

But then, one would ask: is Christianity an indigenous religion in Zambia, or is it enough, for purposes of satisfying the test of autochthony, that Christianity is the most widely practiced religion in Zambia?

By law, as provided under Zambia's Republican Constitution of 1996, Zambia is not a monolithic religious society. That Constitution recognizes the right of individuals to practice different religions, if they so wish. We must, therefore, look beyond the Preamble of the Constitution, which traditionally is confined to some general aspirations of the people, and focus instead on the inviolability of the constitutionally guaranteed freedoms in the Bill of Rights. Against this background, to spell out the dominant religious value system in the Constitution's Preamble is not tantamount to discriminating against other religions. It is simply a statement regarding the dominant religious values, as represented by those entrusted with enacting laws.

While the Constitutions of many English common law jurisdictions do not have a Preamble provision that states that a particular country has officially declared itself a Christian nation, the declaration of Zambia as a Christian nation should not be seen as a source of concern. I opine that the whole hullaballoo from the critics is somewhat an exaggeration. As far as I can tell, there is no major shenanigan behind the declaration of Zambia as a Christian nation. I write here not as a religious fanatic or Christian fundamentalist. By contrast, I am concerned primarily with the constitutionality of declaring Zambia as a Christian nation.

Mindful that such a declaration could have political and ideological implications, I argue here that, at law, strictly speaking, it does not raise any threats or fears. But I must admit that international best practice, especially in the English common law world, does not favour making explicit religious preferences in the Republican Constitution. Indeed, if I were the legislative draftsman, I would not have included such a provision, although I remain indifferent now given that the provision is already in the Preamble of the Constitution. Even in secular schools and workplaces, matters of religion can be very sensitive. It is often wise to keep them out of the workplace or learning environment, unless they are part of the work-programme or curriculum. Some folks just do not want to hear anything to do with religion and they easily get worked up when they hear anything to do with religion. Others believe that their religion is the best, and that only they know God best.

Now that we have the declaration of Zambia as a Christian nation in the Preamble of Zambia's 1996 Constitution, we cannot be talking in hypotheticals. We need to address what this declaration means constitutionally. As a general rule, the declaration of Zambia as a Christian nation does not offend the Constitution or any law of the land and it does not infringe upon any freedoms enshrined in the Bill of Rights. It is just an aspiration.

- *Kenneth K. Mwenda*

In the US, a recent article in the online version of The Christian Post, dated Saturday, July 2, 2011, reads in part, "They want to live in the land of the free and the home of the brave, but they will not sing about it." The article then continues: "A Mennonite pastor from Waynesboro, Va., is catching the media's attention this week by reviving his religion's belief to ban the 'Star Spangled Banner' from athletic events – or anywhere else for that matter. Mark Schloneger, pastor of Springdale Mennonite Church, wrote a letter this week voicing his objections to America's national anthem and to explain why a college in Indiana has banned the song. Mennonites firmly believe the lyrics in the Star Spangled Banner violate their pacifist ideals. They firmly believe that an individual's allegiance should be to Christ rather than country". In Zambia, this issue has been fully settled by the famous case of *Feliya Kachasu v. The Attorney General* [1967] ZR 145. We will not go into details of this case. Suffice it to say it is no good constitutional law argument to argue that singing the national anthem contravenes one's freedom of conscience under the Republican Constitution.

When you look at a US Dollar bill, for example, you will find the following words printed at the back: "In God We Trust". These words appear on the money. And the US Dollar is a well-regarded monetary currency worldwide. So, as you embrace that precious US Dollar in your wallet or pocket, know ye that the underlying norm there is that "In God, You Must Trust"! Now, could it be argued that by declaring this religious dictate on its national currency the US has violated its Federal

Constitution? Let us assume that Zambia were to make such a declaration on the Zambian Kwacha. Would that offend our Zambian Republican Constitution? In any event, who would have the *locus standi* to claim that he or she has been injured or has suffered a detriment as a result of the declaration? And what constitutionally guaranteed freedom would have been impaired or prejudiced by the said declaration?

I have read the 1996 Constitution of the Republic of Zambia, as amended by Act No. 18 of 1996. The fifth paragraph of the Preamble, when read together with the first paragraph, provides as follows: "WE, THE PEOPLE OF ZAMBIA by our representatives, assembled in our Parliament, having solemnly resolved to maintain Zambia as a Sovereign Democratic Republic; DECLARE the Republic a Christian nation while upholding the right of every person to enjoy that person's freedom of conscience or religion." This provision of the Preamble does not prohibit or bar other religions in Zambia. It actually allows for the practice of other religions, too. Article 11(b) of Part III of the said 1996 Constitution sets forth the following provision: "It is recognised and declared that every person in Zambia has been and shall continue to be entitled to the fundamental rights and freedoms of the individual, that is to say, the right, whatever his race, place of origin, political opinions, colour, creed, sex or marital status, but subject to the limitations contained in this Part, to each and all of the following, namely: ...(b) freedom of conscience, expression, assembly, movement and association." This constitutional provision is buttressed by Article 19(1) which provides that: "Except with his own consent, no person shall be hindered in the enjoyment of his freedom of conscience, and for the purposes of this Article the said freedom includes freedom of thought and religion, freedom to change his religion or belief, and freedom, either alone or in community with others, and both in public and in private, to manifest and propagate his religion or belief in worship, teaching, practice and observance."

Recently, I read on the website of Lusaka Times an article titled, 'The Declaration of Zambia as a Christian Nation' (dated Friday, January 22, 2010) by **Elias Munshya wa Munshya. In that article, responding to Professor Henry Kyambalesa's submission in an earlier** Lusaka Times article **on the declaration of Zambia as a Christian nation, Munshya wa Munshya avers that,** "Kyambalesa's assertion that the Declaration was an imposition of religion on the Zambian society is not quite right", and that "Zambians have always been a religious people." **Munshya wa Munshya continues:** "Secondly, Kyambalesa alleges that the Declaration is unconstitutional and as such is likely to lead to religious intolerance. In asserting this he quotes Dr. Seshamani. But Dr. Seshamani himself supports the declaration and asserts that, Hinduism has no problem with the Declaration since Hinduism is polytheistic. The Islamic Council of Zambia has, while being cautious, as well supported the

Declaration."

Munshya wa Munshya posits further, "Zambia's constitution as it stands now does guarantee freedom of conscience for all. The Declaration that we are a Christian nation does not automatically lead to intolerance at all. All religions and a citizen's entitlement to practice that religion are guaranteed to all. In fact, the courts of law have on a number of occasions asserted this important constitutional principle. In the cases of the Universal Church of the Kingdom of God (UCKG), Zambia's High Court and even the Supreme Court have protected this church from closure. So far there have been no religious riots in Zambia. When Zambians rioted against the UCKG or against the Hindu Temples in Livingstone, it was not because of religion per se, but it was due to false rumors that had circulated that these institutions were participating in ritual killings—a very sensitive matter for witchcraft conscious Zambians."

Closely related to the foregoing, Zaccheus Mwanza, writing in the Post newspaper of Zambia, in a short article titled 'Declaration of Zambia as a Christian Nation', dated Monday, March 21, 2011, observes that: "A lot of people have questioned the credibility of the declaration of Zambia as a Christian nation. As a serious Christian and a theologian, I have doubts on whether the declaration of Zambia as a

Christian nation was done in good faith. A Christian nation must be governed by Christian principles and virtues. I strongly believe that this declaration was just an ideology as opposed to divine conviction."

It would be interesting to ask ourselves why it is that in Zambia, like in many other English speaking countries, we often use the Bible when swearing an oath, say, before a court of law. Likewise, when a couple is getting married or when there is a funeral, the Bible is the most visible and pronounced religious book. Why is this so? Could this just be accidental or a simple coincidence? Admittedly, while there could be some procedures to dispense with the requirement to use the Bible, allowing a deponent to use his or her own religious book, the starting point for many is the Bible. Let us take a more reasoned look.

The Republic of Zambia has not changed its official name to the "Christian Republic of Zambia". And there are no known plans to do so. By contrast, it is not uncommon for other States outside the Commonwealth to change their names to reflect certain religious values. For example, Wikipedia postulates that the term *Islamic Republic* "...is the name given to several states in the Muslim world including the Islamic Republics of Pakistan, Iran, Afghanistan, and Mauritania. Pakistan adopted the title under the Constitution of 1956. Mauritania adopted it on 28 November 1958. Iran adopted it after the 1979 Iranian Revolution that overthrew the Pahlavi dynasty. Afghanistan adopted it after the 2001 overthrow of the Taliban. Despite the similar name the countries differ greatly in their governments and laws." According to Wikipedia, "The term *Islamic republic* has come to mean several different things, some contradictory to others. To those Muslim religious leaders in the Middle East and Africa who advocate it, an Islamic Republic is a state under a particular theocratic form of government. They see it as a compromise between a purely Islamic Caliphate, and secular nationalism and republicanism. In their conception of the Islamic republic, the penal code of the state is required to be compatible with some laws of Sharia, and the state may not be a monarchy as many Middle Eastern states are presently. In other cases, it is merely a symbol of cultural identity, as was the case when Pakistan adopted the title. In fact many argue that an Islamic Republic strikes a middle path between a completely secular and a theocratic (and/or Orthodox Islamic) system of government."

One would be inclined to argue that the declaration of Zambia as a Christian nation is nowhere close to the concept of an Islamic Republic, as noted above. The Zambian penal code, for example, is not expected or required to have laws that are compatible with the Bible. Although some degree of morality maybe injected into the law when enacting or interpreting certain laws, there remains a marked distinction between the natural law school of jurisprudence and the positivist approach to the law. And so, the Christian Bible does not form part of the penal code of Zambia. Neither is Christianity taken by many as the only acceptable way of life. Many people go to church but not everyone is a committed or devout Christian.

Thus, the declaration of Zambia as a Christian nation is not an affront to democracy or the rule of law. Other religions can also thrive in Zambia. Besides, there are no religious persecutions in Zambia. Everyone has a constitutional right to enjoy his or her constitutionally guaranteed freedom of conscience and worship. That said, it is healthy to hold such debates, and Christians should be encouraged to criticize their own religious and belief systems without fearing that they will be punished in Heaven. It is through such self-criticism and introspection that many Christians can grow in their faith towards objectivity. Indeed, nobody has the monopoly of knowledge. So, we must continue to ask questions. And democracy should allow people the freedom to worship under any religion, or to switch religious allegiances without any fear or threats. The Zambian Constitution of 1996 allows for all this, but adds only that the large faction of the Zambian people, through their parliamentary representatives, aspire towards Christian values. To use a metaphor here, the Bembas say, "A-koni kekala umuti ka temenwe..." (*i.e.* a bird perches on a branch of its choice, and you cannot force it to sit on another branch). Akin to this, to tell a friend that you do not drink beer does not mean you are stopping him from drinking beer. You are merely expressing your own preference which may not even be binding on him. He is free to drink, if he feels like. What is impolite, by contrast, is to ask him not to drink any beer just because you do not drink or just because you feel that you are holier than thou and can thus assume the role of a merchant of morals.

CHAPTER 61

THE RETURN OF THE ERA OF MILITARY COUPS IN AFRICA

In legal theory and jurisprudence, it is fondly pronounced: "*Constitutions est tutissila cussis: sub clypes constitutions nemo decipitur* – the constitution is the safest helmet; under the shield of the constitution no one is deceived." And just when we thought that the African continent was now done with the era of military coups we are greeted with a déjà vu in Mali and Guinea-Bissau. It was only a few months ago when the military in Mali took-over political power through the unconstitutional means of a coup d'état. Now the same has occurred in Guinea-Bissau. While West Africa remains the major culprit for entertaining military coups in Africa, there have also been similar experiences in Egypt, Democratic Republic of Congo (DRC), Libya, Uganda, Ethiopia, Chad, and Central African Republic (CAR).

Some of the reasons advanced by pundits on why military coups occur in the developing world include the following: (a) the increase in public access to arms as well as to knowledge and skills in the use or handling of arms; (b) the rise of asymmetric forces and failed states; (c) the influence of international forces and bureaucracies; and (d) continuing political and socio-economic challenges of globalization.

In a 1985 paper titled, "Military Coups in Africa: The African 'Neo-Colonialism' that is Self-Inflicted", Major Wangome of the Kenyan Army observes that: "With the advent of independence in the late 50's and early 60's euphoria and new hopes swept through Africa as nation after nation attained self-government. There were new dreams and expectations as the colonial masters packed their bags and handed over the instruments of power to the indigenous peoples. To most Africans this was the end of a long freedom struggle in which so many had suffered."

Major Wangome continues: "It was the end of slavery, human degradation and exploitation. However, these dreams were soon shattered as government after government fell victim to the coup d'etat across the continent. The new military rulers accused the civilian government of everything from corruption and incompetence to mismanagement of the national economy. However, experience in Africa has shown that the military are no better than civilians when it comes to running governments. Rather than solve African contemporary political and socio-economic problems, military coups d'etat in Africa have tended to drive the continent into even further suffering and turmoil."

Issaka Souare, in his 2011 essay titled, "The Coup d'État in Mauritania: Why the Military Still Intervenes in African Politics," argues that the story in the rest of the continent and the West Africa sub-region in particular is not much different, for since independence in or around the 1960s, the military has supplanted civilian governments in nearly half of Africa's states. According to Souare, "The frequency of coups d'état in the region reached the point where in Benin, for instance, in just one decade (1963 – 73), there were six successful coups! This averages to about one coup in every twenty months. Nigeria, Ghana and Burkina Faso are not very far behind on this table. Of the 16 countries in West Africa, only the Archipelagos of Cap Verde and Senegal have been spared the whips of men on horseback."

Souare contends further that: "Throughout the continent, there have been striking similarities between military coups... They all claimed that the old regime was despotic, authoritarian and corrupt... They all promise to honour the country's international obligations and respect human rights. There are other similarities. Most of the coups that are described as bloodless have taken place while the head of state is away (e.g. Ghana's Kwame Nkrumah in February 1966; Nigeria's Yakubu Gowon in July 1975; Seychelles' James Mancham in June 1977; and CAR's Jean-Bedel Bokassa in September 1979; etc.), and are usually the handiwork of people either currently or formerly close to the deposed regime."

- *Kenneth K. Mwenda*

A number of theories in political science have been advanced over the years to explain the occurrence of military coups in developing countries. These theories evolved mainly in the late 1960s and early to mid-1970s when military coups in Africa, Asia and Latin America were commonplace. According to Souare, "The first of these theories is attributed to authors such as Samuel Finer, Bienen, Andreski, Le Vine, and, to a lesser extent, Janowitz. According to this theory, military coups happen because of what they describe as 'social and political environments' in the countries affected. The theory is that Third World countries, in general, and African ones in particular, being of low or minimal political culture, are particularly susceptible to military intervention. Bienen argues that the military is able to intervene 'because it does retain legitimacy untainted by civilian failures'..."

Closely related to the theory noted above is the Contagion Thesis. Souare argues that this theory contends that the occurrence of a coup in one country, due to the social and political environment, stimulates more coups in other countries, especially neighbouring ones. In other words, as Souare observes, while one country might be immune from military intervention, its military officers might be tempted to intervene if they can refer to a previous successful attempt in a neighbouring country. Souare posits further that the second main theory of military coups focuses on the internal structure of the military itself; that is, its hierarchical organisation and its distinctive patterns of recruitment and training, control and alleged discipline.

The third main theory, Souare contends, can be divided it into two distinctive but related theories. According to Souare, "The common feature between the two is their assertion that the occurrence of military coups d'état cannot be predicted in the Third World in general and in Africa in particular. The difference between the two schools is that one argues for the 'idiosyncratic nature' of coups and the other one defends a 'multi-causal' approach to explaining the causes of military interventions."

But what does the law have to say about all this? Does the law support or give any blessings to military coups? Mindful that the law does not offer blessings to unconstitutional means of ascending to power, we can proceed now to a more reasoned look at the legality of a legal order introduced by a military regime that has just come to power through a coup d'état.

In the famous case of *Madzimbamuto v Lardner-Burke* (1978) 3 WLR 1229, Daniel Madzimbamuto, a resident of Southern Rhodesia, was detained by an order made by the Minister of Justice in Southern Rhodesia in 1965 under the Emergency Powers Regulations 1965. These Emergency Powers Regulations had been made by the Officer Administering the Government in Rhodesia who had been appointed under a Constitution of Southern Rhodesia enacted by the Parliament of Southern Rhodesia after Mr. Ian Smith's Government in Southern Rhodesia had declared, unilaterally, that the country which was previously a colony of the United Kingdom was now independent. The British Government did not accept that Southern Rhodesia was independent and took steps to regain control of the country, principally by passing legislation to declare that the 1965 Constitution and all actions taken under it were void and of no effect and by imposing economic sanctions on the country. The Privy Council held, reversing the decision of the High Court of Southern Rhodesia, that the 1965 Constitution was not valid since it had not been made by lawful means and Mr. Smith's Government was not in fully effective control of Southern Rhodesia.

Closely related to the *Madzimbamuto* case, in the Ghanaian case of *Edward Sallah v. Attorney-General,* (Ghanaian Court of Appeal (sitting as Supreme Court), 20 April 1970) ([1970] 2 G&G 493)), the Supreme Court of Ghana, after the constitution of 1969 came into effect, was called upon to determine the legal implications of the military coup d'etat on the pre-existing legal system in Ghana. The court held that the suspension of the constitution of 1960 by a military coup had no effect of destroying the pre-existing legal order. This ruling, like the *Madzimbamuto* case, has generated a lot of debate. An illustrate bibliography on the debate includes the following: Ofori, *Kelsen, The Grundnorm and the 1979 Constitution – A Rejoinder* 16 UGLJ 169; Tsikata and Tsikata, *Sallah v. AG, Kelsen and Other in the Court of Appeal* [1970] 7 UGLJ 142; *Re Akoto* [1961] 2 G&G 160; and, *Shalabi v. AG* [1972] 1 GLR 259 at 267-268.

While some pundits have criticized Prof. Hans Kelsen's Pure Theory of Law as being somewhat vague and not too helpful in interpreting the legality or constitutionality of the legal order introduced by the military after it takes over political power, Kelsen expounded his Pure Theory of Law, as a theory of positive law, postulating that the constitution of a State rests on a grundnorm that gives validity successively to other laws of the land placed hierarchically below that constitution. Although Kelsen's theory has been criticized for failing to distinguish between coups and revolutions, the said theory has been interpreted broadly by some courts that once the constitution is supplanted or replaced by an intervening legal order of, say, a military regime that comes to power through a coup, then the military regime's legal order will rest on the grundnorm and become effectively the new constitution as long as the military regime is in effective control.

In the Ugandan case of *Uganda v. Commissioner of Prisons, ex parte Matovu* (1966) E.A.514, the Prime Minister of Uganda issued a statement on February 22, 1966 declaring that, in the interests of national stability, public security and tranquility, he had taken over all powers of the Government of Uganda. He was completely successful, and the High Court had to consider the legal effect. In a spirited judgment, Sir Udo Udoma C.J. ruled: "...we hold, that the series of events, which took place in Uganda from February 22 to April, 1966, when the 1962 Constitution was abolished in the National Assembly and the 1966 Constitution adopted in its place as a result of which the then Prime Minister was installed as Executive President with power to appoint a Vice-President could only appropriately be described in law as a revolution. These changes had occurred not in accordance with the principle of legitimacy. But deliberately contrary to it. There were no pretentions on the part of the Prime Minister to follow the procedure prescribed in the 1962 Constitution in particular for the removal of the President and the Vice-President from office. Power was seized by force from both the President and the Vice- President on the grounds mentioned in the early part of this judgment."

Sir Udo Udoma C.J. continued: "...our deliberate and considered view is that the 1966 Constitution is a legally valid constitution and the supreme law of Uganda; and that the 1962 constitution having been abolished as a result of a victorious revolution in law no longer exists nor does it now from part of the Laws of Uganda, it having been deprived of its de facto and de jure validity."

Similarly, in the Pakistan case of *State v. Dosso* (1958) 1 PLD 533, when General Ayub Khan took over political power in 1958 through a military coup, he decided also to abrogate the Constitution of 1956. And when the implications of the military coup were challenged before the courts of law, the majority of the Supreme Court of Pakistan, relying on Hans Kelsen's theory, upheld the validity of the legal order introduced by General Ayub Khan's military coup.

CHAPTER

62

BOOK REVIEW OF "CHISANGA PUTA-CHEKWE, *GETTING ZAMBIA TO WORK*, (LONDON: ADONIS & ABBEY PUBLISHERS LTD, 2011)"

Written by one of Zambia's most distinguished and accomplished professionals, the book, "Getting Zambia to Work", is cast in 212 pages. This book came out in the last half of 2011 and was published by Adonis & Abbey Publishers Ltd in London, United Kingdom. It is set out in ten brilliant chapters that will bring the reader to quick speed on political-economic developments in Zambia over the last three to four decades.

Getting Zambia to Work is a must-read for all those interested in the future of Zambia and Africa. The book's author, Mr. Chisanga Puta-Chekwe, is an eminent lawyer and political-economist who has worked in international banking in London, United Kingdom, before moving to and settling in Toronto, Canada. A Rhodes Scholar and Oxford graduate, Mr. Puta-Chekwe has held several senior corporate executive positions in Canada and is currently the Deputy Minister for Citizenship and Immigration as well as Women's Issues in Ontario, Canada.

A well-written and researched intellectual contribution, *Getting Zambia to Work* is simply a masterpiece. The book is a highly resourceful text; encyclopedic in richness and depth. It examines most of the great milestones in the political-economic history of Zambia, starting with the Mulungushi and Matero economic reforms, through Zambianisation and into the political realm of the Kaunda, Chiluba and Mwanawasa eras. The arguments in the book on Zambia's constitutional reforms are also quite illuminating. This is an excellent book whose lifespan cannot be confined to the bookshelf. The author draws on his rich interdisciplinary background as a seasoned lawyer and a learned technocrat in the fields of political science, philosophy and economics.

The book begins by examining how a young and politically independent Zambia with a visibly healthy and buoyant economy at political independence regressed into economic malaise. As the author observes, Zambia's fall from grace was closely tied to the entrenchment of political dictatorship in the country. The author, having been arrested and detained in Zambia on political grounds for allegedly agitating against a One-Party State System, has first-hand experience of the political dispensations of Zambia's previous One-Party State System. He provides some valuable insights on the One-Party State, although taking great care not to derail into personal vendettas against those that persecuted him politically at the time. The decorum displayed by the author on such an emotionally sensitive topic is simply enviable and edifying.

The second chapter of the book examines what the author calls a 'Southward Bound Economy'. In this chapter, Zambia's post-independence economic policies are examined critically. The author examines also issues such as the nationalization of the Zambian copper mines and the Zambianisation of the national economy, contrasting that with Leninist-Marxist ideology in some parts of contemporary Africa. The analysis in the chapter then proceeds to look at the introduction of multi-party politics in Zambia. The economic reforms that came with the introduction of multi-party politics and the prevailing dictates of the international political economy are also examined.

In the third chapter, the author turns to examine the failure of governance in Zambia. Among the notable issues examined are the increasing levels of corruption and the glaring absence of [many] principled political leaders in the country. Closely related that, the author identifies the abuse of human rights in Zambia, especially during the One-Party State, and the general lack of political will by successive Zambian Governments to fight corruption as stumbling blocks to good governance. The author also questions the wisdom of the MMD Government in establishing the Task Force on Combating Corruption when the country had sufficient, albeit underfunded, institutions to fight corruption. The dismal performance of the Task Force and the colossal sums of money spent by the Zambian Government on paying legal fees to many 'average-performing' lawyers on the Task Force team are also highlighted.

In the fourth chapter, the author decries the emergence of a culture of neglect in Zambia where patriotism has long ceased to be a guiding philosophy in the lives of many. The author notes that neither is the law taken seriously by many who engage in economic crimes and corrupt activities. The fifth chapter advocates for the need to change this retrogressive culture. The chapter argues for the importance of inculcating a sense of civility and self-esteem in the citizenry as well as in those serving in politics.

The sixth chapter brings on board the idea of governing with equity. Here, the author examines the various constitutional reforms that have taken place in Zambia over the years, contending that 'Zambia has never been governed on the basis of a constitution created by the people of the country for the benefit of all citizens.' It is a tough judgment call, but the author is courageous and candid enough to make the bold assertion. He also examines the issue of citizenship in Zambia as well as the prospects for dual nationality, an independent legislature and an effective executive.

In the seventh chapter, author comes out swinging against those that subscribe to or practice tribalism.

He implores strongly that Zambia is a nation and not a tribe. In so doing, the author also asks whether it is possible for Zambia to have its own indigenous national language. This is a question, though, that is not free from polemics. It is a moot issue that has confronted many Afro-centric social scientists in the past.

In the eighth chapter, the author looks at the issue of international aid to Zambia, exploring links between aid and corruption as well as between aid and national self-esteem. He concludes with a proposal for Zambia to consider a new engagement with the international community, as opposed to traditional foreign aid cravings. The ninth chapter is devoted to the value that should be placed on education and the critical role that education plays in developing society whilst the tenth chapter focusses on the road ahead for building a people's economy. Such an economy, the author observes, should address the development of sound infrastructure, the devolution and decentralization of executive powers, the improvement of social services as well as the effective enforcement of laws and the promotion of a suitable environment for economic growth.

In this book, Mr. Chisanga Puta-Chekwe has given the reader a gem. He should be commended for an insightful and illuminating book. The reader will not be disappointed. The author has scored a first.

- *Kenneth K. Mwenda*

CHAPTER 63

BOOK REVIEW OF "MUNYONZWE HAMALENGWA, *THE POLITICS OF JUDICIAL DIVERSITY AND TRANSFORMATION*, (TORONTO: AFRICA IN CANADA PRESS, 2012)"

The author of the book, 'Politics of Judicial Diversity and Transformation', Mr. Munyonzwe Hamalengwa is a distinguished Zambian lawyer who has been practicing law in Ontario, Canada, for over twenty years. Mr. Hamalengwa has appeared before the Canadian courts of law, including the Supreme Court of Canada, in many high profile court cases. And he was won several of these cases, including a prominent case that involved the Extradition Treaty between Canada and India. Mr. Hamalengwa has not only practiced law defending several victims of human rights abuses and violations, but has also tasted the bitter end of the law under Zambia's One-Party State system.

As Mr. Hamalengwa observes on his personal

website, "The teenage stubborn years that followed, full of teen rivalry and rebellion were replaced by years of youthful idealism at the University of Zambia in Lusaka. In 1976 Munyonzwe was detained with other student leaders in solitary confinement following demonstrations against the Zambian government's handling of issues related to Angola's Independence and issues of freedom of speech and expression. Six months later he was released and threatened with banishment to the countryside. He then fled to neighboring Tanzania and from there came to Canada in 1977."

In this book, *Politics of Judicial Diversity and Transformation*, the author examines topical themes and issues relating to judicial choices within the context of judicial diversity in multicultural and multiracial societies. In the Western world, whilst many intellectuals and professionals, including some prominent politicians, would rather avoid discussing the elephant in the room (that is, racism), the author takes on the challenge with such finesse and diplomacy, but without diluting the potency of the message. But his book is not about racism as such. The author examines also gender prejudices at the bar and the bench.

Today, more so than yesterday, it is a truism that to be open about issues of racial prejudice and bias, especially as a minority in the western world, that can cost you an election or your job. Many folks would rather pretend that cultural issues, whether in politics or in an organization, are seemingly colourless. And so, they would rather leave the elephant in the room undisturbed so as to walk away safely. Disturbing the elephant in the room can cost you a career or ruin your business prospects, especially where the main cultural paradigm places a subtle unspoken and unwritten 'gag' on matters of racial discrimination or racial oppression. Only the outcasts are expected to talk about such issues because they have been written-off anyway. But, the author refuses to succumb to such mediocrity. He rises to the challenge and grabs the elephant in the room by the neck. Whilst many others would rather talk about such less politically controversial issues as gay and lesbian rights, partly as way of diverting public attention away from the more pressing economic issues that often entangled with race relations, the author does not shy away from the main controversy. And he must be commended for that bravery.

The author argues that judicial diversity can both negatively and positively impact on some of the greatest divides in the experience of equality. He points out that these divides include race and gender. To buttress his view, the author posits that 'every person ought to know that the decisions of the courts do not find themselves on paper in a pre-fabricated fashion. They are woven by sitting judges who incorporate their prejudices, biases, training, experiences and cultural milieu' (p 29).

In tackling the issue of judicial diversity to demonstrate who is likely to be deported from Canada, and why, the author examines the issue of racial profiling, arguing that much of the literature on Canadian immigration law focuses on who is allowed into Canada and not who is to be deported from Canada. And a thoughtful read of the book shows that Chapter 7, for example, is devoted to a criticism of racial profiling jurisprudence in Canada. Then, Chapter 8 deals with how the judiciary has been responding to racial profiling. The author is not shy or timid to opine that there is a certain conspiracy of silence in Canada's criminal, civil and immigration courts and tribunals, and that such silence only provides fertile ground for racial profiling and discrimination against minorities.

This book, it could be argued, provides lessons of experience that are not only unique to Canada, but much of the western world when it comes to the administration of criminal justice. And, in Chapter 19, the author turns to examine the concept of judicial diversity and judicial independence in the colonial and post-colonial world. It is at this point that he brings the discussion in the book to the Zambian context. He argues, for example, that: "At independence there were generally no or very few indigenous lawyers who could be appointed to the judiciary. In Zambia, for example, the first Zambian Lawyer to be appointed to the High Court was appointed in 1970, six years after independence. This prompted Professor Nwabueze to state 'the intellectual quality of the Bench in Commonwealth Africa has been rather poor. This has resulted in an intellectual inability to appreciate some of the issues presented for decision; the judgements are thus often devoid of insight and of intellectual stimulation.'.." (p.416).

To put matters in context, an observation that merits mention her is how, we, as a country, together with many other developing countries, can learn from the experiences of countries such as the US and Ghana that have been able to appoint to the bench as some of their High Court judges and Supreme Court judges some of their leading intellectual luminaries. There need not be a disconnect between those in academia and those practicing the law. Both can sit at the Bench if they qualify. We need not shun some of our brightest and best intellectual luminaries at the expense of promoting mediocrity. Now, some superficial cynic out there may be quick to interject and ask: can you give us an example where you have seen a prominent intellectual luminary transition to the Bench as a judge? Need we be surprised that President Obama recently filled a position on the Bench of the Federal Supreme Court of the United States of America with a Harvard Law School professor?

Obama, himself a former part-time Law Professor at the University of Chicago Law School, did not confine his search to fill that vacancy on the Bench of the US Supreme Court to the famous law firms of Washington DC, Los Angeles, New York or Chicago. He instead went back to Harvard Law School. In Ghana, Professor Kludze, Ghana's first and only Higher Doctorate in Law (LLD earned from the University of London in the early 2000s), was appointed straight from the University of Rutgers in the US as a Judge of the Supreme Court of Ghana, together with the now deceased Professor Modibo

Ocran from Akron University School of Law in the US. Zambia can learn something from these experiences, especially when it comes to appointments at the Supreme Court-level where a greater degree of weight points more to matters of substantive law than procedural law.

In this book, *Politics of Judicial Diversity and Transformation*, the author examines, inter alia, the issue of judicial immunity and its implications. Without a doubt, he has succeeded at providing an insightful and erudite jurisprudential treatise on how judges function as well as on their rule-making. The author has done some extensive review of the relevant literature on the topic, including a review of some postgraduate degree dissertations written and submitted to the University of Zambia Law School. It cannot be disputed that this is a remarkable piece of scholarship by someone who has been there; someone who has seen it, and someone who has done it. The author also cites some valuable examples from the judicial system of the then apartheid South Africa to demonstrate how there can be miscarriage of justice in certain situations where there is little regard for judicial diversity and inclusion. He weighs on this issue in light of the modest efforts at promoting judicial diversity in Canada. The author laments at the shortcomings of the Canadian efforts, providing additionally some extensive evidence to support his claims and arguments.

In this 589 pages book, Mr. Munyonzwe Hamalengwa has provided the readership with an excellent piece of legal scholarship that will benefit not only the judges and the legal practitioners, but also several university law professors, law students, as well as many other interested readers from the social sciences. It must be added that one of the greatest contributions of this book is its weighty and valuable use of international and comparative law materials. The author is definitely in command of the literature, and he has been able to traverse and articulate issues intelligently across jurisdictions as diverse as the US, the UK, India, China and South Africa. He should be commended for such an excellent and erudite piece of scholarship, especially that it is coming from someone who is not engaged as a full-time academic, but one who is inundated with the many daily chores of day-to-day law practice. It is, indeed, a challenge to many practicing lawyers in Zambia and elsewhere that law is not just about going to court and making money, but that all lawyers must be seen to immerse themselves and indulge in intellectual leadership too so as to ensure a better development of the judicial system and the legal process.

- *Kenneth K. Mwenda*

CHAPTER 64

UNDERSTANDING THE ECONOMIC ANALYSIS OF LAW

Law, as a social science, is closely related to many cognate disciplines in the social and natural sciences. And law does not operate in a vacuum. Its relevance must relate to the overall values of society. As such, the competing approaches of Black Letter Law and Law-in-Context are a natural reflection of this view. The efficacy and content of any law is often influenced by, *inter alia*, the normative fabric of society. Law, therefore, cannot stand outside society or alien itself from the people. It must relate to and embrace the ideals, normative values and ethos of the very society it regulates.

But why should lawyers be bothered with getting schooled in the economic analysis of law? Is it not enough that lawyers have a good law degree and are successful in their law practice? In short, what additional value would insights into economic thinking bring to lawyers? While this article may sound like EC101 for some economic students at university, it may not be so for many lawyers. Lawyers have much to learn from the article.

Economics, it is said, is the science of rational choices in a world of limited resources. And the term 'resources' here does not relate only to money but can be of any type. The field of economics deals with the use of scarce resources to maximize utility value. Alternative uses are expected to lead to the satisfaction of an individual. So, economics is often pre-occupied with the allocation of scarce resources among an array of infinite choices. And in contract law, for example, the law is the vehicle through which such constrained allocations are made. Lawyers should therefore have some insights into economic thinking.

In a contract, the parties to a contract can choose which remedies to have or whether to include covenants for judicial or out-of-court settlement of disputes. So, in drafting contracts, lawyers can use the economic analysis of law to get helpful insights into and a greater understanding of how to allocate scarce resources among an array of infinite choices as well as how to allocate risk between or among the contracting parties. From an economic point of view, the terms 'risk' and 'cost' mean two different things. Generally, a risk is understood as the potential cost that is likely to be incurred by a party whereas a cost is the risk that has already matured or transformed into a loss. That said, in practice, there is a thin line between the two, especially when one refers to what is apparent or explicit; in this case, a risk is more of an apparent outcome whereas a cost is more explicit.

Exercising choices in the formulation of contractual terms will always have some cost to it. For example, for X to do something, he may have to forgo the luxury of not doing the opposite. The cost of doing something must be seen as giving up the opportunity of doing something else. Economists call this the 'opportunity cost'. And determining costs is so much affected by assumptions (*e.g.* the value of the cost is as perceived by the individual who forgoes the opportunity).

Likewise, in taking a decision, the benefit is determined individually by the decision-maker. In making a rational choice among alternatives, it is expected reasonably that the benefit will be greater than the cost. Therefore, it is reasonable to assume that we are all rational beings with adequate and reliable information on which we base our choices, and that such decisions will usually be predicated on a cost-benefit analysis. Economists are concerned mainly with who bears the cost as well as the cost over time (spill-offs). By contrast, lawyers look at the immediate impact of the costs. For example, how do we calculate the costs of losing one's left finger? The issue of assessing *future* losses is something that many lawyers struggle with since they are not usually trained or schooled in quantitative methods of assessing *future costs*. But lawyers can learn from economists.

In contrast to lawyers, economists often differentiate between private and social costs. As lawyers, we can learn from economists by understanding that we should first look at both one's own risk as a cost, and the risk to others as the cost of maintaining something and so forth. So, risk is an important element of the cost. A lot of tort law, for example, can be seen as forcing someone to pay for the costs affecting other people (*e.g.* people are injured as a result of X's dangerous driving. If negligence is proved, X will be asked to pay for the costs. Where negligence is not proved, the cost will remain external and need not be internalized by X).

In general, there are different types of costs. And so, when drafting or interpreting contracts, or when presiding over claims of liability in tort law, lawyers and judges must have a good economic understanding of risk allocation and costs. For example, social costs usually affect society or the general public. Social costs are the aggregated of private and external costs. In the law of torts, the law is trying to make the culpable party internalize the external costs so that he or she can deal with the consequences of his or her deeds. Here, the costs will be internalized when the culpable party is found liable and he or she compensates the injured or aggrieved party. Lawyers need to understand that this is what happens from an economic point of view when someone is said to be liable.

Indeed, economic analysis of law is very useful for lawyers, including judges, when analyzing, for example, the quantification of damages in the law of tort. In cases of the tort of nuisance, the judges may ask themselves whether or not to order an injunction to stop a factory from polluting the neighbourhood or to ask the factory to compensate the affected members of the public. In doing so, the judges are faced with the task of making a choice against the backdrop of scarce resources to address an array of infinite choices. The injunction may force the factory to stop operating and to shut down, and thus leading to massive unemployment of the workforce. There would be a heavy social cost resulting from the unemployment. On the other hand, the judges may decide not to order an injunction but rather to ask the factory owners to buy and install pollution filters to stop the pollution, whilst also ordering the factory to compensate the people affected by the past and existing pollution.

From an economic perspective, the question for the judges to consider is, which of the two alternatives, an injunction or the factory installing pollution filters and compensating the affected community of persons, would lead to a Pareto efficient outcome? Since we have an idea of the risks associated with the pollution, what is the cost to the factory of internalizing such risks? If, say, the factory makes a profit of US$20,000 a day, and buying and installing the filters will cost only US$5,000, would it be beneficial to shut down the factory through an injunction or to ask the factory to buy and install the filters? Arguably, the decision here could depend on the nature and extent of the pollution as well as on the cost to the affected community.

Be that as it may, if the factory is shut down, what are the risks for it to internalize the social costs pertaining to compensation of affected community as well as meeting redundancies packages for all its workers (*i.e.* assuming that the shut-down of the factory is over an extended period of time such that many workers will have to be laid-off permanently)? From the factory's point of view, what legal advice would be best from its lawyer? Would it be more efficient for the factory to go on and fight in court the injunction application/petition presented by the plaintiffs (*i.e.* the affected community) or would it be best for the factory to quickly buy and install pollution filters and then seek some out-of-court settlement with the said plaintiffs?

As noted above, in drafting contracts, lawyers can use economic analysis of law to be able to get a greater understanding of how to allocate scarce resources among an array of infinite choices as well as how to allocate risk between and among contracting parties. Economics teaches us that lawyers need to understand the concept of efficiency as it applies to economic analysis of law. For example, production efficiency will be key when X wants to produce 1000 bags of cement. He will try to look around for the most efficient way of doing so. He will possibly look at the cheapest inputs, the quickest time and specialized labour and so forth. By contrast, when it comes to allocative efficiency, the focuss is mainly on society as a whole, as opposed to an individual. If, say, the government wants to build a road across an occupied piece of land, it may ask some land occupants and owners to assign off by contract the land that they occupy. The assumption here is that when the land owners agree to assign off part of their land for the purposes of the government building the road, then they have made contracts to their benefit. A notable criticism of this view is that the idea that people are their own judges is in theory good, but it can have costs externally on other people not consulted.

For lack of space in this paper, lawyers are encouraged to read and understand economic concepts such as Pareto efficiency and Hicks-Kaldor efficiency in order to give fuller thought to the economic implications of certain legal rights and duties in private law and public law. Also, it is important to understand and appreciate some shortcomings of some of these concepts. For example, the Hicks-Kaldor efficiency theory postulates that if, hypothetically, the costs of the losers are not higher than the aggregate gain then there is an efficient outcome. Here, the average gain should be higher than the aggregate loss. However, the Hicks-Kaldor efficiency theory can work well if the gains can compensate the losses and still retain some gain. The concept is thus weak on the distributive aspect. And lawyers often worry about the distribution of the cake (*i.e.* justice), as opposed to merely maximizing the cake (*i.e.* efficiency and gains). Indeed, the law is concerned mainly with equity and not only maximizing the gains. The key assumption of Pareto optimality is that none of the parties to the contract should be better off than the other (*i.e.* the plaintiff and the defendant both feel that gains have been maximized). So, economists can teach lawyers on dealing with the law as an incentive provider, or dealing with the law as a risk-creator.

Closely related to the foregoing, the quantification of damages in matters involving, say, nominal damages, aggravated damages or punitive damages goes beyond mere principles of compensation in contract law or tort law. For example, where there is a breach of contract, the lawyer for the complainant should look not only at the expenses and the opportunity cost incurred, but also on expectant losses, including the consumer surplus forgone, had it not been for the breach of contract.

Economics teaches lawyers that sometimes it may be efficient for a party to breach a contract and then enter into a more lucrative contract if the second contract can give the breaching party some substantial gain that would enable him to compensate the other party under the first contract without leaving the said breaching party worse off than he was. The theory of efficient breach here assumes that the cost of abandoning the first contract and then switching to a new contract, or, rather the 'switch costs' of the breach, are zero. For example, where the total costs incurred under the first contract, including transaction costs and taxation costs, when subtracted from the expected profits would leave the breaching party with a net profit of US$5,000 only, and the alternative contract would produce a net profit of US$40,000, it would be more efficient for the breaching party to abandon or breach the first contract. The idea here is that the breaching party can use the net profit of US$40,000 from the second contract to compensate the aggrieved party under the first contract whilst maintaining some gains above what he would have made under the said first contract.

Lawyers need to appreciate also the underpinnings of economic reasoning when it comes to matters relating, say, to the Coase theorem. This theorem postulates that if property rights are well-defined and transaction costs (including costs of negotiating) are zero or negligible, then the most efficient or Pareto optimal economic activity will occur regardless of who initially owns the property rights. According to the Coase theorem, negotiation and market transactions will ensure optimal allocation of property.

Admittedly, the Coase theorem, like many other economic theories, has its shortcomings. It assumes, for example, that the parties are both rational in their negotiations and that there are no transaction costs, taxation costs or information costs. But life teaches us that individuals can at times be driven by their own idiosyncratic values which make them want to get the lion's share. Besides, in the real world, there will be transactions costs when negotiating. And information is not usually freely available to the parties. That said, lawyers still need to understand the scope and usefulness of the Coase theorem, especially when dealing with out-of-court settlements and transactions.

It cannot be overemphasized that the training of lawyers in Zambia today should take into account the various linkages between law and other cognate disciplines of the social and natural sciences. The old way of confining oneself to a single discipline is long gone. For example, many lawyers today manage corporations. If they do not have good management skills honed through, say, an MBA or other management qualification, how do they expect to navigate through managerial and executive leadership tasks? Even the idea of running a law firm requires managerial skills. Not many law firms in developing countries hire professional managers to run the firm whilst the lawyers concentrate on tasks associated with the legal profession. It is the lawyers themselves that dub as managers as well. And so, a law degree alone today is not enough. The world is fast changing and has become a global village. There is an increasing interchange and interaction between law and other disciplines. It need not be surprising, for example, to find a medical doctor who switches to law so that he or she can specialize in medical malpractice cases. Likewise, it need not be surprising to find a biochemist who switches to studying law and thereafter practicing law so that he or she can concentrate on litigating intellectual property law cases focussing mainly on industrial designs and patents in the bio-chemical industry. These are the emerging trends in the global practice of law today.

CHAPTER 65

THE CASE FOR A LEGAL FRAMEWORK FOR CROSS-BORDER INSOLVENCY

In my book, *K.K. Mwenda, 'Contemporary Issues in Zambian and English Company Law: A Comparative Study', (Amherst, NY: Teneo Press, 2011)*, I have examined pertinent issues in Zambian company law arising from the enactment of the Zambian Companies Act 1994. The book focuses on some of the issues that are not fully addressed or settled by Zambian jurisprudence and/or the Companies Act 1994. These issues include the legal status of the *ultra vires* doctrine in company law, the liability of company directors for wrongful or fraudulent trading, the concept of issuing shares of *par value* as well as that of issuing shares of no-par value, including the concepts of share watering, allotment of shares at a discount, and financial assistance in the acquisition of a company's shares.

As a corollary, I have argued in the said book that the issue of cross-border insolvency should have been covered by the Zambian Companies Act 1994 or, at least, through the enactment of a closely related statute. We have seen, for example, how some multinational companies as well as some group conglomerates have been faced with insolvency of one kind or another. We do not have to go far than to look at the example of the now defunct Meridien Bank and its group companies located abroad. The question is: how does a Zambian liquidator or insolvency practitioner ensure that Zambian creditors can reach the assets of a financially distressed multinational company or group conglomerate whose assets are located outside the Zambian jurisdiction? Would it be enough to rely solely on civil procedure for the registration and enforcement of a Zambian judgment in a foreign country? What if that foreign country does not allow for reciprocity for the registration and enforcement of Zambian judgments? What to do, as they would say in Russia?

As a general rule, where separate legal entities with cross-shareholding structures in a group of companies are perpetrating a fraud or engaging in co-mingled activities, the corporate veil of these companies can be pierced to make them liable for debts incurred by one of the companies. Taking an example of Meridien Bank and its group companies that were located abroad, if the Zambia-based companies were seen to be engaging in fraudulent or co-mingled activities with the foreign-based companies, then a liquidator in Zambia could go after some of the assets of those companies that were based abroad even though the latter companies, unlike the Zambia-based companies, were still solvent. But such precepts of the common law need to be strengthened through the codification of a law that deals with cross-border insolvency. Indeed, it is now time for the Zambian Government to consider introducing legislation or a robust regulatory framework for cross-border insolvency. Not much thought was accorded to this issue when enacting the Zambian Companies Act 1994. The said Companies Act does not have statutory provisions on cross-border insolvency. Yet, we do not have to go far to find a model law on cross-border insolvency.

The United Nations Commission on International Trade Law (UNCITRAL) in Vienna, Austria, adopted on May 30, 1997, a model law designed to assist countries to equip their insolvency laws with a modern, harmonized and fair framework to address more effectively instances of cross-border insolvency (see: Mwenda, 2011: 145-149). Those instances include cases where the insolvent debtor has assets in more than one country or where some of the creditors of the debtor are not from the country where the insolvency proceeding is taking place.

The UNCITRAL model law respects the differences among national procedural laws and does not attempt a substantive unification of insolvency law (see: Mwenda, 2011: 145-149). By contrast, it offers solutions that help in several significant ways, including: foreign assistance for an insolvency proceeding taking place in the enacting State; foreign representative's access to courts of the enacting State; recognition of foreign proceedings;

cross-border cooperation; and coordination of concurrent proceedings (see: Mwenda, 2011: 145-149). To that end, a country can, in adopting the model law, enjoin or adapt the said model law to its own country-specific conditions.

Professor Roy Goode argues (*see: R.M. Goode, 'Principles of Corporate Insolvency Law,' (second edition), (London: Sweet and Maxwell, **1997**), p. **495***), however, that countries differ in their approach to addressing problems of cross-boder insolvency. According to Goode, "Two opposing pairs of principles are of particular siginificance. They relate respectively to jurisdiction over a company and jurisdiction over assets... The principle of unity ascribes exclusive jurisdiction over winding-up to the courts of the state of the company's incorporation, to which all other courts defer. If strictly applied such a principle would route winding-up to a single forum and avoid the problems of cocurrent liquidations, but would also expose local creditors in other states to risk of loss of the assets within their jurisdiction. The principle of unity is a theoretical model, not a reality, for in no jurisdiction are courts willing to give up all control over local assets where there are local creditors." (see: Goode: **1997**: **495**)

Goode argues further that the principle that is adopted almost everywhere is that of *plurality*, which admits of concurrent proceedings in different jurisdictions (Goode: **1997**: **495**). According to Goode, in most States the plurality arises through adoption of the principle of *territoriality*, and that some States, however, recognise the concept of a main liquidation in one jurisdiction and one or more ancillary liquidations in other jurisdictions which are confined to local assets and, in some countries, to local creditors (Goode: 1997: 495). Referring to the principle of *territoriality* and that of *universality* in cross-border insolvency, Goode observes: "Under the principle of universality, to which English law subscribes, a winding-up proceeding covers not only the company's local assets but assets situated anywhere in the world, though it is recognised that the ability of the liquidator to have resort to those assets is dependent on local law and recognition by local courts. However, the majority of jurisdictions adopt the principle of territoriality, by which the winding-up process is confined to assets (and sometimes to creditors) within the jurisdiction. The principle of universality would, of course, be a necessary concomitant of the principle of unity, but can also apply in jurisdictions (of which England is one) which recognise plurality of jurisdiction. This creates potential conflict where there are concurrent liquidation proceedings in two different jurisdictions and both rights over the debtor company's assets on a world-wide basis reclaimed in both jurisdictions." (Goode: 1997: 496)

Closely related to the concepts of *unity* and *universality* is that of *non-discrimination against foreign creditors*. Indeed, 'if all the company's assets, in whatever part of the world, are to be subsumed within a single liquidation, then claims of foreign creditors must be admitted on the same basis as those of local creditors.' (Goode: 1997: 496-7). This principle was ably articulated in an opinion on US bankruptcy law for the assistance of the English court in *Felixstowe Dock and Railway co. v. US Lines Inc*_[1989] QB 360 by Judge Howard C. Buschman of the US District Court for the Southern District of New York (see: Goode: 1997: 497). Judge Buschman observed: "The intended scope of bankruptcy and reorganisation jurisdiction extends beyond the border of the United States... The nature of the jurisdiction is in rem. The res, the estate of the debtor created by the commencement of a bankruptcy or reorganisation case, is viewed as a single entity to be dealt with in a single proceeding. The broad scope of bankruptcy jurisdiction under United States law is intended to permit similarly situated creditors, regardless of where they are located, to be treated equally in a bankruptcy or reorganisation case. Discrimination of the basis of citizenship is not permitted. All creditors are given the opportunity to file claims against the state and their recovery is not limited to the assets in their own country." (See *Felixstowe Dock and Railway co. v. US Lines Inc* [1989] Q.B. 360. An extract from the opinion is set out in the judgment of Hirst J. at 368).

According to Goode, the position is the same under English insolvency law (Goode: 1997: 497). Likewise, the position is no different under Zambia's insolvency law. The jurisdiction of the Zambian courts in insolvency proceedings is governed generally by the Zambian Companies Act 1994 and by the English common law rules pertaining to conflict of laws. In the case of banks and financial institutions, Zambia's Banking and Financial Services Act 1994 provides an additional legal regime for determining the jurisdiction of the Zambian courts.

Generally, it is a widely accepted principle that the law of the place where the liquidation is opened (*lex fori concursus*) governs all matters relating to the winding-up, whether substantive or procedural, including the assets comprising the estate, the proof and ranking of claims, the admissibility of set-off and the avoidance of preferences and other transactions (cf. There is, however, some uncertainty regarding the relationship between *lex fori concursus* and the law governing the creation of security interests and other real rights in assets in the possession of the debtor company). However, the efficacy of these general principles of law can be strengthened further if the Zambian Government were to enact a piece of legislation to deal with cross-border insolvency. One may be tempted to ask: where has this been done before in parallel or closely related jurisdictions, say, in Southern and Eastern Africa? You just have to look southwards towards South Africa. And we have a lot of South African multinational firms in Zambia today. So, what to do now?

CHAPTER 66

FIGHTING CORRUPTION THROUGH INTERNATIONAL LAW

It is now more than twenty (20) years since I studied public international law as a Rhodes Scholar at Oxford under the very able guidance of the legendary intellectual luminary, the late Professor Sir Ian Brownlie. Yes, I was Brownlie's student. And that experience brought a whole new perspective to my understanding of public international law. In my latest book, "K.K. Mwenda, *Public International Law and the Regulation of Diplomatic Immunity in the Fight against Corruption*, (Pretoria: Pretoria University Law Press, 2011)", I have examined critically the legal and policy aspects of preventing and combating corruption from a public international law perspective. The book also debunks the superficial argument that Africa should not receive foreign aid.

As noted in the Preface of the book, my thanks go out to, *inter alia*, many of my former law students at many leading universities where I have taught in

Europe, North America and Africa for their questioning minds on certain intellectual issues that form the core of this book. Some of my former law students have gone on to become prominent Supreme Court and High Court judges. Others are now distinguished political figures (*e.g.* Cabinet Minister) in their native countries, not forgetting, of course, those that are working in public international organizations as well as those that are heading the legal departments of such organizations. There is also a faction that comprises notable legal practitioners as well as a faction comprising emerging legal authorities in academia, including heads of academic departments and law practice institutes. And many other young lawyers have gone through the teaching hands of my former law students at different universities. Through my intellectual leadership, it is my prayer that I have not failed my country and people. I am pleased to share my latest book whose electronic copy is available for free download at the following website: <<http://www.pulp.up.ac.za/cat_2011_07.html>>

Public International Law and the Regulation of Diplomatic Immunity in the Fight against Corruption is a sequel to my previous scholarly work on anti-corruption initiatives and efforts (see also: K.K. Mwenda, *Legal Aspects of Combating Corruption: the Case of Zambia*, (Amherst, NY: Cambria Press, 2007); K.K. Mwenda, *Combating Financial Crime: Legal, Regulatory and Institutional Frameworks*, (Lewiston, NY: The Edwin Mellen Press, 2006); K.K. Mwenda, *Anti-Money Laundering Law and Practice: Lessons from Zambia*, (Lusaka: University of

Zambia Press, 2005); and K.K. Mwenda, "Can 'corruption' and 'good governance' be defined in legal terms?" *Rutgers University Journal of Global Change and Governance*, (Vol. 2, No. 1, Fall 2008)).

Hardcopies of *Public International Law and the Regulation of Diplomatic Immunity in the Fight against Corruption* can be purchased directly from the publisher by completing and submitting a book order form available on the above-referenced website. It should be noted that the said publication, now my twenty-second (22nd) book, does not profess to provide an exhaustive treatment of all legal instruments relating to public international law in the fight against corruption. Neither does the book delve into historical aspects of the fight against corruption under public international law. The extensive body of the literature reviewed during the preparation of this book shows that there are far too many strands on the role of public international law in the prevention and fight against corruption. Also, many treaties have now been signed and ratified on the prevention and fight against corruption, and these include, *inter alia*, the United Nations Convention against Corruption 2003, the United Nations Declaration against Corruption and Bribery in International Commercial Transactions 1996, the United Nations International Code of Conduct for Public Officials 1996, the Convention against Transnational Organized Crime 2000 (*i.e.* the Palermo Convention), the OECD Convention on Combating Bribery of Foreign Public Officials in International Business Transactions 1997, the Convention of the European Union on the fight against Corruption involving Officials of the

European Communities or Officials of Member States 1995, the Convention of the European Union on the Protection of its Financial Interests (1995) (including the two Protocols thereto (1996 and 1997)), the Council of Europe's Twenty Guiding Principles for the Fight against Corruption 1997, the Council of Europe's Criminal Law Convention against Corruption 2002, the Council of Europe's Civil Law Convention against Corruption 2003, the Inter-American Convention against Corruption 1997, and the African Union Convention on Preventing and Combating Corruption 2003.

However, none of the treaties cited above is the central focus of this, my latest, book. By contrast, through the prism of public international law, the book identifies and sustains a thesis relating mainly to immunities and privileges of diplomatic agents of sovereign States. A thesis is maintained that while the fight against corruption internationally does not necessarily entail that such established norms of international law as diplomatic immunity should be watered down as a way of preventing corrupt diplomats from abusing their immunities and privileges, or as a way of gagging outspoken and controversially vocal diplomats who query recipient-States of donor funds on the abuse or misuse of these funds, both customary international law and conventional international law do provide for some safeguards to prevent a corrupt or outspoken diplomat from abusing his or her immunities and privileges. In essence, the book posits that diplomatic immunity should not be abused by diplomatic agents who perpetuate or engage in corrupt practices, and that diplomatic immunity should only shield those diplomatic agents who inquire from the receiving State, genuinely and for *bona fide* reasons, how donor funds have been utilized by the receiving State, but not those that enthusiastically or spiritedly intermeddle in the internal affairs or security of the receiving State. And a discussion of what constitutes the 'internal affairs' of a receiving State is provided in Chapter 3 of the book.

The book also draws distinctions between the diplomatic immunity enjoyed by a diplomatic agent of a sovereign State and the type of immunity enjoyed by some public international organizations. An argument is made that, in the case of the latter, except for a few senior staff and those representing political constituencies of member States, most regular staff and employees of public international organizations do not enjoy diplomatic immunity. Against this background, if, say, a senior officer of a public international organization sits on the board of a private corporation or commercial bank, he or she should observe the internal laws of the host country so as to avoid committing any crime or omitting any obligations. That said, the individual can be removed from the board for misfeasance or other corporate governance related issues. And if that individual does not enjoy any immunity from the originating public international organization, then he or she cannot claim any immunities or privileges.

In this latest book, *Public International Law and the Regulation of Diplomatic Immunity in the Fight against Corruption*, I have argued that it would be ill-advised for the recipient-State of donor funds to try to gag the donor-State by invoking the principle of sovereign equality of states each time the donor-State wants to find out how the donor funds have been utilized. The principle of sovereign equality of states should not be abused. It should only be invoked in *good faith*, but not to try to thwart legitimate efforts at promoting good governance, accountability and transparency.

That said, the fact that a donor-State has provided donor funds to a recipient-State does not provide the donor-State with a legal basis to insult or unfairly criticize the recipient-State. The provision of donor funds alone does not constitute a blanket license to criticize almost everything that the recipient-State is doing in the spheres of politics and economic development. If anything, a consolation that the donor-State has is in limiting its criticism to the recipient-State's prudent management of the donor funds. If it is a question of donor funds having been provided to the recipient-State for budget support, then let the donor-State that has provided that support focus primarily on the sector and purpose for which the support has been rendered. Indeed, there must be a link between the donor's intervention and the funds in question. Otherwise, it would be irresponsible for a donor-State that has not even given much money to the recipient-State to be making noise as if that donor is such a great messiah. As noted above, the there has to be a correlation between the noise being made by the donors and the funds that they have each provided.

And where the funds provided by a donor have been properly utilized by the recipient-State, there is no basis for that donor to be making noise. It is only where the donor funds have been misappropriated or misused that a donor can complain. Even so, the complaint must relate directly to the misuse or abuse of donor funds.

It is important to observe that the provision of donor funds alone should not be seen as a blanket license for the donors to criticize recipient-States for almost everything that they do. If there has to be any criticism, it should be limited to the misappropriation or misuse of the donor funds. Chapter 1 of the book sets the discussion in context, outlining the methodology for the study. Chapter 2 provides a conceptual framework for understanding the term 'corruption'. And conceptual issues relating to legal definitions of 'corruption' and 'good governance' are examined. Chapter 2 also identifies the relationship between corruption and good governance. It argues that the term 'good governance' is simply a restatement of such existing concepts as constitutionalism, rule of law, accountability, transparency and the doctrine of separation of powers. And a view is advanced that while corruption can be defined in legal terms, a legal definition of good governance remains elusive. A further argument is made that while it is feasible to identify closely related definitions of 'corruption', as evidenced, say, in international treaties and various pieces of legislation of different countries, including decisions of domestic courts, there remains a marked absence of statutory, treaty or judicial definitions of 'good governance'. For example, although the African Charter on Democracy, Elections and Governance 2007 has the word 'governance' in its title, Article 1 of that treaty on definitions of terms makes no provision for a definition of 'governance'. Yet, the said treaty has a lot to do with 'governance'. Essentially, this treaty only sets forth prescriptive aspirations for State parties to the treaty on matters of democracy, elections and governance, leaving it up to the States themselves to enact legislation to domesticate these aspirations. So, as noted above, there remains a marked absence of statutory, treaty or judicial definitions of 'good governance'. And Chapter 2 in this book posits that it is even doubtful that 'good governance', as a term, is justiciable.

In Chapter 3, we examine the concept of diplomatic immunity in international law where there is evidence of corrupt practice by a diplomatic agent of a State. Such instances occur, for example, where a diplomat is found in possession of such illegal substance as marijuana or cocaine, or where he or she is engaging in criminal conduct relating, say, to drug trafficking, money laundering or smuggling of prohibited pornographic material. Chapter 3 argues that whereas a diplomat may enjoy, generally, diplomatic immunity in the State to which he or she is accredited, thus shielding him or her from criminal prosecution in that jurisdiction, the diplomat will have limited jurisdictional immunity in a third State to which he or she has not been accredited. And if the diplomat is arrested in that third State for an offence under the laws of that

State, he or she may not be allowed to invoke diplomatic immunity by the third State since such immunity, it is argued, should apply only when the diplomat is passing through the territorial zone of the said State with innocent passage analogous to that postulated under Article 19(2) of the United Nations Convention on the Law of the Sea 1982. The said treaty provision, codifying customary international law, postulates that innocent passage must not be prejudicial to the peace, good order and security of the coastal State. By parity of reasoning, the same analogy should be extended to the case of diplomats passing through a third State. Their passage must not be prejudicial to the peace, good order and security of the third State. However, if the criminal conduct of a diplomat occurs in the accrediting or receiving State, then the receiving State can issue a diplomatic démarche to the State that is represented by the erring diplomat, protesting the criminal conduct of the diplomat. Also, in extreme but rare cases, the accrediting or receiving State can declare the diplomat *persona non grata*. But the declaration of a diplomat *persona non grata* does not in itself entail that the diplomat can now be prosecuted by the receiving State. In cases of universal jurisdiction, for example, the receiving State can arrest a culpable diplomat and have him or her extradited to the sending State or to any impartial third State to stand trial. The sending State, on the hand, can recall a diplomat to stand trial in its courts of law even though the diplomat enjoys diplomatic immunity in the receiving State. And the sending State can also waive the immunity of its diplomat to allow the receiving State to prosecute him or her.

Chapter 4 then examines the right of foreign diplomats accredited to a recipient-State of donor funds to demand that the recipient-State accounts for the misuse or abuse of donor funds received from the diplomat's State. An argument is made that where a diplomat from a donor-State queries a recipient-State on the latter State's misuse or abuse of donor funds that does not amount to 'interfering in the internal affairs' of the recipient-State. The law on diplomatic immunity is examined, and the discussion is informed by both international conventional law and international customary law, as well as by judicial decisions of international courts and the writings of most highly qualified and eminent publicists in international law. Chapter 4 argues further that right of a diplomat from the donor-State to inquire from the recipient-State on the latter State's misuse or abuse of donor funds cannot be the basis of declaring the diplomat *persona non grata.* The concept of *good faith* when a State is asserting its rights international law is discussed, and an argument is made against the State's capricious and unrestrained application of its right to declare a foreign diplomat *persona non grata.* A related argument in the said chapter is that, in the absence of binding legal covenants to empower the donor-State to supervise and oversee the administration of donor funds, the concept of a non-charitable purpose trust could be imported, and that through paragraph (c) of Article 38(1) of the Statute of the International Court of Justice, regarding 'general principles of law recognized by civilized nations', this concept could prove a useful source of law.

Chapter 5 concludes the study, integrating the main arguments and providing some policy recommendations. It is expected that this book will stand as an indelible and erudite contribution to the fight against corruption.

\- *Kenneth K. Mwenda*

CHAPTER 67

LEGAL ASPECTS OF ODIOUS DEBTS

What do we mean when we say 'odious debts'? Writing in the *American Economic Review*, Volume 96, Issue No. 1, (2006), Jayachandran and Kremer postulate that the legal doctrine of *odious debt* holds that debt should not be transferable to successor regimes if: (a) it was incurred without the consent of the people; and, (b) was not for their benefit (see also: Alexander N. Sack, 1927; Ernst Feilchenfeld, 1931). But how can we tell if a debt was incurred without the consent of the people and if it was not for their benefit? Is there an objective yardstick? Jayachandran and Kremer maintain that the underlying principle against odious debts is that just as an individual does not have to repay money that someone fraudulently borrowed in her name, and a corporation is not liable for contracts that its chief executive officer entered into without authority to bind the firm, a country should not be responsible for debt that was incurred without the people's consent and was not used for their benefit. In essence, the term odious debt refers to debt obligations of a State incurred by a previous regime or government for purposes that were not in the best interests of the State. Such purposes could include carrying out wars of aggression or for personal aggrandizement by the head of State.

There is a lingering minority view among some commentators and non-governmental organizations (NGOs) that odious debts should not be enforceable at law. However, no customary international law, conventional international law or general principle of law supports this view. Rather, the doctrine of freedom of contract and that of sanctity of contract, in the absence of any vitiating factor, take precedence. And this is in line with the Coase theorem in economic analysis of law. So, the commonest State practice has been for a successor State or government to try to restructure the large sovereign debt incurred by the predecessor State or government on the basis that that debt was odious. From a moral and political standpoint, odious debts are considered personal debts of the regime or government that incurred them and not debts of the successor State or government. In this sense, the concept is seen as analogous to the invalidity of contracts signed under coercion. It has been argued by those against the enforcement odious debts that the doctrine of odious debts was given more prominence in a 1927 treatise written by Alexander Nahum Sack, a Russian émigré legal theorist. Sack's treatise was based on 19th Century precedents, including Mexico's repudiation of debts incurred by Emperor Maximilian's regime, and the denial by the

United States of Cuban liability for debts incurred by the Spanish colonial regime.

According to Sacks: "When a despotic regime contracts a debt, not for the needs or in the interests of the state, but rather to strengthen itself, to suppress a popular insurrection, etc, this debt is odious for the people of the entire state. This debt does not bind the nation; it is a debt of the regime, a personal debt contracted by the ruler, and consequently it falls with the demise of the regime. The reason why these odious debts cannot attach to the territory of the state is that they do not fulfil one of the conditions determining the lawfulness of State debts, namely that State debts must be incurred, and the proceeds used, for the needs and in the interests of the State. Odious debts, contracted and utilised for purposes which, to the lenders' knowledge, are contrary to the needs and the interests of the nation, are not binding on the nation – when it succeeds in overthrowing the government that contracted them – unless the debt is within the limits of real advantages that these debts might have afforded. The lenders have committed a hostile act against the people, they cannot expect a nation which has freed itself of a despotic regime to assume these odious debts, which are the personal debts of the ruler."

Generally, debts are considered 'odious' when they are contracted without the consent of the people and not spent in their interests and when the creditor is aware of this. But how can we tell that the creditor is or was aware or had knowledge that the borrower obtained the loan without the consent of the borrower's people and that the loan would be used for purposes other than the interests of these people? In many cases, States have taken on the odious debt of former dictatorships as a result of political pressure or fear of being penalized by creditors in the future. There are, however, some emerging precedents for odious debt being repudiated, such as Mexico (1867), Cuba (1898) and Poland (1919). But, can States such as Iraq and Congo DRC, for example, choose to repudiate debt obligations entered into by their previous regimes under Saddam Hussein or Mobutu Sesseko, respectively, if creditors refuse any form of arbitration? Should creditors be required to demonstrate that these debts are not odious? Who has the burden of proof? And are there any lessons of experience to share on how some States have dealt with the issue of odious debts?

Let us take the 1867 example of Mexico's repudiation of Austrian debts (see Jubilee Iraq-Odious Debts: Online, Spring 2010). Between 1863 and 1867, the Habsburg Emperor Maximilian contracted debts at onerous rates of interest to maintain his sovereignty over Mexico and suppress an uprising there. In 1883, sixteen (16) years after the fall of Maximilian, the Mexican government under President Juarez repudiated the entirety of the alleged debt against them. J.N.Pomeroy, an international legal scholar of the time, mentions that "...a large part of those debts has been created to maintain that usurper in his place against the legitimate authority and all of them were most scandalously usurious."

Closely related to the Mexican experience is the 1898 US repudiation of Cuban debt after the Spanish-American war (see: Jubilee Iraq-Odious Debts: Online, Spring 2010). The Cuban loans negotiation at the Paris Conference of 1898 that followed the Spanish-American War is generally regarded as the first direct application of a doctrine of odious debts. The Cuban debts consisted of various loans issued by the Spanish Government after 1880 and secured on the revenue from the island. The Spanish asserted a principle of international law: that state obligations belong to a land and its people, not to a regime. The Americans replied that the debt was 'imposed upon the people of Cuba without their consent and by force of arms, was one of the principal wrongs for the termination of which the struggles for Cuban independence were undertaken.'

Furthermore, the Americans added, much of the borrowing was designed to crush attempts by the Cuban population to revolt against Spanish domination, and so was expended in a manner contrary to Cuba's interest. According to Jubilee Iraq-Odious Debts (Online, Spring 2010), "From no point of view can the debts above described be considered as local debts of Cuba or debts incurred for the benefit of Cuba. In no sense are they obligations properly chargeable to that island. They are debts created by the government of Spain, for its own purposes and through its own agents, in whose creation Cuba had no voice, from the moral point of view, the proposal to impose them upon Cuba is equally untenable. 'As such, the Americans argued, these debts could not be considered Cuban debts, nor could they be binding on a successor state. As for the lenders, the Americans replied that 'the creditors, from the beginning, took the chances of the investment'."

In the case of the Boer War in South Africa, Jubilee Iraq-Odious Debts (Online, Spring 2010) observes, for example, that the Boer Republic borrowed money in order to try to repel the British in South Africa. After the end of the Boer War, the Supreme Court of the Transvaal declared that the debts had devolved upon Britain as the new sovereign. However, Britain refused all legal responsibility, denying that the Boer Republic could validly issue debt.

In 1919, the coming into force of the Treaty of Versailles repudiated some Polish debts. The German government (and its Prussian predecessor) operated a fund to enable ethnic Germans to buy estates in Poland in order to colonize the country. Since few Poles were prepared to sell, the government enacted a compulsory purchase law in 1908 and issued bonds to finance the purchases. At Versailles, as noted by Jubilee Iraq-Odious Debts (Online, Spring 2010), the Reparation Commission refused to charge these bonds to the newly liberated state of Poland as a just reversal of "...one of the greatest wrongs of which history has record."

Then, in 1923, there was the arbitration of a Costa Rican dictator's debt to Great Britain. After the fall of Federico Tinoco, dictator from 1917-19, the new Costa Rican government passed the Law of Nullities to repudiate debts lent to Tinoco by the Royal Bank of Canada. Great Britain challenged this and Chief Justice Taft of the U.S. Supreme Court arbitrated between the countries. Justice Taft ruled that the loans did not constitute transactions of an ordinary nature and were 'full of irregularities,' were made at a time when the popularity of the Tinoco Government had disappeared, and when the political and military movement aiming at the overthrow of that Government was gaining strength. The $200,000 in loans were made by the bank to Federico Tinoco himself 'for expenses of representation of the Chief of the State in his approaching trip abroad,' and as 'four years salary and expenses' for his brother whom Tinoco had appointed ambassador to Italy. Justice Taft noted: "The Royal Bank...must make out its case of actual furnishing of money to the government for its legitimate use. It has not done so. The bank knew that this money was to be used by the retiring president, Federico Tinoco, for his personal support after he had taken refuge in a foreign country. It could not hold his own government for the money paid to him for this purpose."

Turning to the present day former Yugoslavia, it can be seen that the International Conference on Former Yugoslavia (Working Group on Succession Issues) has been inundated with issues relating to the apportioning of debts and assets among the successor States. Initially, there were some modest indications that these successor States would not be required to assume any of the debts contracted by the former Federal government for the purpose of waging war against the said States. However, in a 2007 article titled, "Renegotiating the Concept of Odious Debt" (*70 Law & Contemp. Probs. 7),* Tai-Heng Chen observes that, "Repudiation risks depriving the successor government of foreign capital that is often needed after a traumatic succession. Further, investors may increase the cost of lending or refuse to extend fresh credit until old debts are paid. The successions of the Socialist Federal Republic of Yugoslavia (SFRY), Czechoslovakia, the Soviet Union, and Iraq have all shown that some form of repayment is often necessary to secure fresh loans that the successor entity requires."

But what are some of the critical issues to consider in international law when examining the concept of odious debts? Notable among the questions are the following. Are odious debts illegal or simply unenforceable under international law? What about the issue of debt relief? Is there an obligation for creditor nations and institutions to provide debt relief to indebted nations on the grounds that the debt incurred is or was odious? The 1983 Vienna Convention on Succession of States in Respect of State Property, Archives and Debts stipulates (Article 38) that by default 'no State debt of the predecessor State shall pass to the newly independent State.' However, the Vienna Convention has not yet received enough signatures to enter into force and may never do so. Interestingly, the original draft of this treaty contained a direct reference to odious debts. But what about the argument that the enforcement of odious debts would only breed unjust enrichment in favour of creditor States and institutions?

Jubilee Iraq-Odious Debts contends some somewhat controversially that unjust enrichment is a generally recognised principle of law. An argument is made that unjust enrichment would occur when a country repays odious debt because the creditor is unjustly enriched through payment from the people of the debtor state who received no correlative benefit for the debt payments that are now being made. A second argument advanced against the enforcement of odious debts is that when a creditor contracts an odious debt with a dictator, and enforces repayment later, it commits an abuse of rights against the population. This 'abuse of rights' argument holds that the exercise of apparently lawful rights can be unlawful when to do so would allow the rights holder to intentionally harm another, or when such an action is excessively harmful, unjust, or unreasonable. Indeed, in the case of Haiti, for example, José De Côrdoba reports in the Wall Street Journal (Online: January 2, 2004) that 'more than two decades after rebellious former slaves vanquished troops from Napoleon's army here in 1803, France's King Charles X made the fledgling republic of Haiti an offer it couldn't refuse. In 1825, as the king's warships cruised just over the horizon from the Haitian capital, a French emissary demanded 150 million gold francs in exchange for recognizing the new republic. The implicit alternative was invasion and re-enslavement. It was a huge sum, about five times Haiti's annual export revenue. Haiti's then-president reluctantly agreed, taking on a crushing debt. Today, as Haiti celebrates the 200th anniversary of its independence amid growing political unrest and a collapsing economy, one of its few glimmers of hope is that long-ago deal. Haiti wants its money back – with interest." Perhaps, we should now be asking: is there a link between odious debts and vulture funds?

CHAPTER 68

LEGAL ASPECTS OF VULTURE FUNDS

What do we mean by 'vulture funds'? In a nutshell, vulture funds are companies that buy up the debt of poor nations cheaply when it is about to be written off. They then sue for the full value of the debt plus interest. For an insightful analysis of the concept of vulture funds, please see: H. Rosenberg, *The Vulture Investors* (New York, NY: John Wiley & Sons, 2000). There have been a number of court cases in the US, UK, France and other countries where vulture funds have sought to enforce the debt obligations of some impoverished and financially distressed debtor countries. These cases include: *Allied Bank Int'l v. Banco Credito Agricola de Cartago*, 566 F. Supp. 1440 (SDNY,'83) aff'd, 757 F. 2d 516 (2nd Cir. '85); *Lordsvale Finance v. Bank of Zambia*, 1996 Q.B. 752; *Elliott Associates LP v. Banco de la Nacion and the Republic of Peru*, 194 F. 3d 363 (2nd Cir. 1999); *Donegal International Ltd. v. Republic of Zambia & Another* [2007] EWHC 197 (Comm.); *FG Hemisphere Assoc. v. Democratic Republic of Congo & China*

Railway Group (HK App. Ct. Feb. 10, 2010); *FH Hemisphere Associated v. Rep. of Congo*, 455 F.3d 575 (5th Circ. 2006); and *Af-Cap Inc. v. Rep. of Congo*, 462 F.3d 417 (5th Circ. 2006). In pursuing their creditor enforcement rights, vulture funds have often relied on such international legal instruments as the Hague Convention on Recognition and Enforcement of Foreign Judgments in Civil and Commercial Matters. This treaty was concluded on February 1, 1971, and it entered into force on August 20, 1979.

In an article titled 'Vulture Funds: Ugly Name for an Ugly Reality' (Online: Feb. 9, 2010), Rocco Puopolo, Executive Director of Africa Faith & Justice Network observes that: "Vulture funds, often called 'Distressed Debt Funds' are predatory hedge funds that siphon off newly freed resources from poor-country debt cancellation efforts. They do this by buying up a poor country's debt in default for pennies on the dollar and then engaging courts in U.S., Britain and beyond to sue for the full amount of the debt plus exorbitant interest rates and court fees. Instead of this newly freed up money in a poor country going to poverty alleviation projects like building schools and treating HIV/AIDS, it goes into the bank accounts of these greedy vultures."

Though somewhat exaggerated, Puopolo's criticism of vulture funds above provides some helpful context to the way vulture funds sometimes operate. But put more objectively, part of the reason why vulture funds are quite unpopular is that they make large profits, sometimes five (5) times the amount at which they bought the actual debt. Vulture funds also seek to recover not only the principal, but also interest on the said principal as well as associated costs. The strategy of many vulture funds is to closely follow debt reduction negotiations with distressed countries, hold out from participating in those negotiations and then demand full payment from the debtor when they have a sense that money is available through the debt reduction negotiations.

Contractually though, under the doctrine of freedom of contract, is it not legally permissible for a creditor to assign his or her right of pursuit in a debt to a third party? For example, under concept of novation, there can be replacement of an obligation to perform with a new obligation or the replacement of a party to an agreement with a new party. And in an assignment, in contrast to novation, the obligee (person receiving the benefit of the bargain) can get creditor preference by virtue of earlier *notice.* That said, under novation, there has to be consent of all parties to the original agreement – that is, the obligee must consent to the replacement of the original obligor with the new obligor. So, why then should there be an issue when vulture funds pursue their contractually earned rights to enforce a debt owed by a financially distressed country? A plausible argument here is that such contractual rights, albeit being earned under the veil of freedom and sanctity of contract, are somewhat offensive to public policy in that they provide unconscionable bargaining power to the vulture fund. But then, what is public policy? Should the law concern itself with moral choices or should it focus solely on what the letter of the law says?

- *Kenneth K. Mwenda*

Over the years, concerns have been expressed that vulture funds are wiping out the benefits which international debt relief was supposed to bring to poor countries. There are instances, for example, where a vulture fund will also buy securities in distressed investments, such as high-yield bonds in or near default, or equities that are in or near bankruptcy. Even highly leveraged firms may be targeted by vulture funds if there is a chance that the owners will not be able to make all required debt payments. Some cautious and prudent creditors have bargained with debtor countries to include negative pledge clauses in their loan agreements, hoping to avoid the problem of vulture funds taking creditor preference and swooping all the major assets of the debtor country. What would happen, for example, where a floating charge-holder created and registered his security first, and the floating charge is also accompanied by a negative pledge clause, and then subsequently a fixed charge-holder created and registered his fixed charge but then sold it later to a vulture fund? Can the floating charge-holder claim priority over the fixed charge-holder or can the floating charge-holder invoke the negative pledge clause in order to stop the vulture fund from helping itself to the encumbered assets of the debtor country? It is trite law that a negative pledge clause in support of a floating charge cannot block the enforcement of a fixed charge even though the latter security was created and registered later. So, the vulture fund will succeed at racing to the top in spite of the negative pledge clause and the competing floating charge.

Be that as it may, the effective use of collective action clauses (in bond contracts, primarily) can help to prevent vulture funds from holding out during debt restructuring negotiations, and thereafter turning back to reap the benefits of the restructuring. In a 2002 article titled, "Sovereign Bond Restructuring: Collective Action Clauses and Official Crisis Intervention," (Online, Bank of England publications) Kletzer observes: "Collective action clauses allow bondholder trustees (for example, a bondholder assembly) to modify the repayment terms of bonds subject the approval of a qualified majority of bondholders (typically, those holding a supermajority of the outstanding debt). By contrast, the unanimous consent of all bondholders is required to revise the terms of repayment (amounts and timing) of a bond issue. This allows an opportunity for 'vulture funds' to seek a privately favorable outcome by holding a bond restructuring hostage. The Treasury response weighs in favor of the adoption of collective action clauses. Several authors have discussed the implications of collective action clauses and capacity of strategic behavior by small bond funds to gain under unanimous consent rules."

Generally, the goal of a vulture fund is to seek high returns at bargain prices. Some people have looked down upon hedge funds that operate like vulture funds, which have preyed on the cheap debt of struggling companies and forced these companies to pay it back, plus interest. The name 'vulture fund' is thus a metaphor comparing these investors to vultures patiently circling, waiting to help themselves to the remains of a rapidly weakening entity, or, in the case of sovereign debt, debtor country. Some market practitioners prefer to refer to vulture funds as distressed debt or special situations funds.

In 2006, Zambia was forced to pay a vulture fund $15 million, constituting over sixty percent (60%) of Zambia's debt cancellation savings that year (see: *Donegal International Ltd. v. Republic of Zambia & Another* [2007] EWHC 197 (Comm.). But, how did this happen? In 1979, the Romanian Government lent Zambia $15 million to buy Romanian tractors. Zambia was unable to keep up the payments, and in 1999 Romania and Zambia negotiated to liquidate the debt for $3m. But before the deal could be finalized, Donegal International, which is part owned by US-based Debt Advisory International stepped in and bought the debt from Romania for $3.3m. Thereafter, Donegal International sued Zambia, in the British courts, for $55 million, eventually winning $15 million in 2007, despite the judge expressing deep concern about the dishonesty involved in the case. Debt Advisory International founder Michael Sheehan was confronted by the BBC's Newsnight programme before the court ruling, but said only: *"No comment. I'm in litigation. It's not my debt."* (see: BBC Online, 'Zambia loses vulture fund case': Feb. 15, 2007).

In 2002, Gordon Brown told the United Nations that vulture funds were perverse and immoral: "We particularly condemn the perversity where vulture funds purchase debt at a reduced price and make a profit from suing the debtor country to recover the full amount owed – a morally outrageous outcome." (see: BBC Online, 'Zambia loses vulture fund case': Feb. 15, 2007).

Jubilee Debt campaigner, Caroline Pearce, said that vulture funds 'made a mockery' of the work done by governments to write off the debts of the poorest – a key theme of 2005's Live8 concert. "Profiteering doesn't get any more cynical than this," Ms Pearce said. "Zambia has been planning to spend the money released from debt cancellation on much-needed nurses, teachers and infrastructure." This is what debt cancellation is intended for, not to line the pockets of businessmen based in rich countries." (see: BBC Online, 'Zambia loses vulture fund case': Feb. 15, 2007).

Similar to Zambia's case, Congo DRC (formerly Zaire) began receiving debt relief from the World Bank and IMF as part of the Highly Indebted Poor Country (HIPC) Initiative in 2003 and continued to work to meet the conditions for full cancellation (see Jubilee USA Online, 'Vulture Funds Swoop in on Congo'; Sept. 16, 2009). A lawsuit was brought against Congo DRC by FG Hemisphere, a known vulture fund, threatening to swoop in to profit off of this critical debt relief at the expense of the impoverished people of the Congo DRC (see: *FG Hemisphere Assoc. v. Democratic Republic of Congo & China Railway Group* (HK App. Ct. Feb. 10, 2010); *FH Hemisphere Associated v. Rep. of Congo*, 455 F.3d 575 (5th Circ. 2006); and *Af-Cap Inc. v. Rep. of Congo*, 462 F.3d 417 (5th Circ. 2006).).

- *Kenneth K. Mwenda*

In 1980, the then Zairean President, Mobutu, obtained a $30 million loan from the Sarajevo-based company, ENERGOINVEST, to supposedly construct a hydroelectric facility and an electric power line. The debt remained in default for more than 20 years. After the Congo DRC qualified for debt relief, FG Hemisphere bought ENERGOINVEST's claim for an undisclosed amount. FG Hemisphere pursued the claim in the Washington, DC court system, suing the Congo DRC for $105 million — more than three times the original price of the debt. As partial payment, FG Hemisphere tried to seize the Congo DRC's embassy properties in DC. The Washington DC courts rejected this claim, but ordered the Congo DRC to document all of its assets outside the country. The Congo DRC failed to locate all of the documents, arguing that the court's demands were overly broad and burdensome, and now faces the threat of fines of an additional $4 million per year (see: Jubilee USA Online, 'Vulture Funds Swoop in on Congo', Fall 2009 Newsletter).

So, what are some of the critical issues to reflect on regarding the legal aspects of vulture funds? Perhaps, we need to ask ourselves, is there a legal basis for striking down contractual agreements entered into by vulture funds to pursue the entire full debt (plus interest) owed by a highly indebted poor country? And do financial claims made by vulture funds take precedence over multi-lateral debt relief initiatives? Also, should a developing country apply the savings it makes from a multi-lateral debt relief initiative to servicing the debt owed to a vulture fund? Can't these saving finance social services to improve the lives of the local population after debt relief? Or, should we just focus on meeting the demands of vulture funds? What about the doctrines freedom of contract and sanctity of contract, including those of sufficiency of consideration, as well as the principle of *pacta sunt servanda* in international law? What legal wrong is there in the deals struck by vulture funds? Or, is this just a moral argument devoid of any legal basis?

Around the world, people have been protesting vulture funds' role in preying on the world's poorest. In May 2008, Belgium passed a law and a non-binding resolution aimed at safeguarding the country's development cooperation and debt relief initiatives from the actions of vulture funds. In 2010, the UK also enacted a law to protect poor countries against vulture funds profiteering off of debt relief resources. The UK law, the Debt Relief (Developing Countries) Act 2010, bans vulture funds from pursuing in the UK courts the world's poorest countries for debts.

Until recently, section 9 of the UK Debt Relief (Developing Countries) Act 2010 provided for a short duration of the statute: "(1) This Act expires at the end of the period of one year beginning with commencement; but this is subject to subsections (2) and (3). (2) The Treasury may by order provide that this Act (instead of expiring at the time it would otherwise expire) expires at the end of the period of one year from that time. (3) The Treasury may by order provide that this Act has permanent effect. (4)

An order under this section is to be made by statutory instrument. (5) An order under this section may be made only if a draft of the statutory instrument containing it has been laid before, and approved by a resolution of, each House of Parliament."

In the US House of Representatives, the Stop VULTURE Funds Act (HR 2932) failed to attract much support for enactment into law when it was presented. Had it passed into law, the Stop VULTURE Funds Act (HR 2932) would have placed a limit on the profits that a vulture fund could make, reducing the incentive to sue. But, then, the Stop VULTURE Funds Act (HR 2932) remains a pipedream, especially that some of these vulture funds are known to be effective financiers of some election campaigns. And many politically astute legislators know full well that you do not bite the finger that feeds you.

CHAPTER 69

STRENGTHENING CENTRAL BANK INDEPENDENCE IN ZAMBIA

This article is based on aspects of Chapter 3 of my book on banking regulation in Zambia. The book, published last year (2010) by Pretoria University Law Press (PULP) in Pretoria, South Africa, is titled: *K.K. Mwenda, 'Legal Aspects of Banking Regulation: Common Law Perspectives from Zambia,' (Pretoria: Pretoria University Law Press, 2010).* I am planning to launch this book officially in Lusaka, Zambia, sometime soon. It is certainly the first and only scholarly book on banking regulation in Zambia. And although the interpretations and conclusions expressed in this article are entirely mine, and that they do not represent the views of any institution, person or body to which I am affiliated, it is pleasing to note that the book referenced above is written by a Zambian expert and authority on banking regulation. For those who care to read, free electronic copies of the book can be downloaded from the following website: http://www.pulp.up.ac.za/cat_2010_07.html

---

- *Kenneth K. Mwenda*

Now, the concept of independent regulation, as argued in one of my previous books (*K.K. Mwenda, 'Legal Aspects of Financial Services Regulation and the Concept of a Unified Regulator,' (Washington DC: The World Bank, 2006))*, whose free electronic copy is also available Online, has come to be associated more with the service sector than with the goods sector (see: Mwenda: 2006, 81-91). Examining the idea of central bank independence, Nobel Laureate, Professor Joseph Stiglitz, puts it succinctly (see: Mwenda: 2010, 81-91): "An independent central bank focused exclusively on price stability has become a central part of the mantra of 'economic reform'. Like so many other policy maxims, it has been repeated often enough that it has come to be believed. But bold assertions, even from central bankers, are no substitute for research and analysis."

Although section 3 of the Bank of Zambia Act 1996 provides that the Bank of Zambia is a body corporate, with perpetual succession and a seal, capable of being sued and suing in its corporate name, and with power to do all such things as a corporate body may by law do or perform, SADC Bankers.org (*i.e.* the Committee of Central Bank Governors in SADC) observes that the Bank of Zambia, as a central bank, is not independent (see: Mwenda: 2010, 81-91). Please understand here that the aspect of independence that we are talking about does not concern itself exclusively and narrowly with controlling inflation or price stability, but rather with the broader aspects of political interference in the decision-making processes of the central bank.

And although the Bank of Zambia has prepared draft legislation which, at the time of publication of this article (November 2011), is before the Ministry of Finance for scrutiny and further analysis, it will be interesting to see how the issue of central bank independence will be tackled when the draft law is finally presented before parliament.

As argued below, to a large extent, the Bank of Zambia operates under the influence of the Executive arm of the State. Yet, Core Principle 1 of the *Basle Core Principles for Effective Banking Supervision* requires that every banking regulator, such as the Bank of Zambia, should enjoy 'operational independence, transparent processes, sound governance and adequate resources, and be accountable for the discharge of its duties.' We are, however, mindful that the issue of compromised independence of the Bank of Zambia is a moot one that may not be readily acceptable to some interested parties.

That said, there is little evidence to suggest that the Bank of Zambia is an independent regulator. In fact, in its Financial Sector Development Plan (2004-2009), the Bank of Zambia admits that: "The major challenge facing the central bank and other regulatory authorities is the need to achieve adequate operational autonomy. In the case of the central bank, this autonomy would be enhanced through a robust institutional and legally binding mechanism of securing the tenure of office for the central bank Governor... Under the current legal framework, the operational independence of the regulatory authorities is not fully assured. In this regard, the enactment of new legislation for the BoZ..., which is presently pending, must be expedited."

Strengthening our view that the central bank enjoys limited and constrained autonomy, a media report published some years back provides as follows (see: *Times of Zambia* Newspaper of Monday, September 20, 2004, '*Fundanga calls for delinkage of BOZ chief's tenure of office*'): "BANK of Zambia (BoZ) Governor Caleb Fundanga says the tenure of office of the bank governor should not run concurrently with the term of office of a particular government to enhance professionalism and remove patronage. Dr. Fundanga also says the Republican President should continue appointing the Central Bank governor who should only take office after ratification by Parliament. This is contained in Dr. Fundanga's written submissions to the Constitution Review Commission (CRC) made available in Lusaka yesterday. Dr. Fundanga submitted that the removal of a governor from office should be by a tribunal constituted by the Chief Justice. He said currently, there was no mechanism for removing a non-performing governor and submitted that it should be clarified in the reviewed laws. The governor's term of office could be curtailed involuntarily only for dereliction of duty, misconduct in office or physical or mental incapacity."

Admittedly, the then Bank of Zambia Governor's submissions here stand on firm ground. However, when it comes to adopting such recommendations, the drafters of the Republican Constitution should be mindful that the Constitution may not be the best document in which to repose the powers to appoint and dismiss a central bank governor and his or her deputies. We contend that matters of this nature are best dealt with through an amendment to the Bank of Zambia Act 1996.

Further arguments advanced by the then Governor of the Bank of Zambia included the following: "In order to ensure accountability, the governor should pursue objectives set by government and the law should specify how the governor would be accountable. Dr. Fundanga said the appointment of deputy governors at the Central Bank should be done by the board and not the President as was the case now. He said the current arrangement of appointing board members by the minister should continue because a system of appointing directors by a management consulting team was not appropriate. And the Bank of Zambia has submitted that the capitalisation of the bank be increased to not less than K50 billion from the current K10 billion. 'We believe that adequate capitalisation of the bank is a pre-requisite for meaningful independence of the bank as it guarantees financial autonomy,'..." (see: *Times of Zambia* Newspaper, *Ibid.*)

At present, the overarching managerial powers of the Bank of Zambia, under the Bank of Zambia Act 1996, are vested in the Board of the Bank of Zambia. The Board is responsible for policy formulation and general administration of the Bank of Zambia (see, for example, Section 4 of the Bank of the Zambia Act

1996). In addition, the Minister of the Finance can convey or delegate to the Governor of the Bank of Zambia such general powers of particular Government policies as would affect the conduct of the affairs of the Bank of Zambia, and the Bank of Zambia will have to implement and give effect to such policies. But in the absence of effective checks and balances on the use of such discretionary powers by the Minister, there is a high likelihood that the said powers can be abused for political ends by the State, especially where the country is faced with presidential and general elections. Indeed, such abuses can, in turn, compromise the independence of the central bank. Elsewhere, I do show, for example, that in nearly every major financial crisis of the past decade—from East Asia to Russia, Turkey, and Latin America—political interference in financial sector regulation made a bad situation worse (see: Mwenda: 2006, 29-35).

Under the Bank of Zambia Act 1996, the Republican President is vested with legal authority to appoint, subject to ratification by Parliament – a '*person with recognized professional qualifications and experience in financial and economic matters to be Governor of the Bank*' – the Governor of the Bank of Zambia for a renewable contract period of five years (see: Bank of Zambia Act 1996, sec. 10(1),(2)). Here, parliamentary ratification provides effective checks and balances on the President so that he or she acts reasonably and does not abuse his or her discretionary powers of determining the appropriate qualifications of a candidate for the position of the Bank of Zambia Governor.

The Governor of the Bank of Zambia can, however, be relieved of his duties by the President whenever he (the President) deems it fit (see: Bank of Zambia Act 1996, sec. 10(7)). This unfettered political power of the President to remove the central bank Governor, whenever he (the President) deems it fit, compromises the political independence of the Bank of Zambia. Unlike the case of appointing the Governor, there are no checks and balances to control the President's discretionary powers here.

Compounding this weight of political bias, it would be difficult for a politically appointed Governor to act entirely apolitical and out of purely professional considerations, without worrying about what the Republican President is thinking. Indeed, how can we stop the President or the Minister of Finance from 'phoning' the central bank Governor, say, at midnight? It is even worse if the political directives coming through such phone-calls are predicated on uninformed and misguided views, such as was the case at some point in Uganda during the late Idi Amin's reign.

Although a number of years have gone by since the Amin days, such developments cannot be dismissed easily as things of the past. In Africa, like everywhere else, history has a tendency of repeating itself. It has been reported of Amin (see: Mwenda: 2010, 86-87): "For those who were around during Idi Amin's regime (1971-79) this may not sound strange: The burying a Chief Justice and a Bank of Uganda Governor in one grave. At Luzira prisons near Murchison Bay, there lie the remains of the two great Ugandan men, Joseph Mubiru and Benedict Kiwanuka, who are believed to have been murdered by then President of Uganda Idi Amin Dada... The woes that led to Kiwanuka's death started after he presided over a case involving an English man, one Stuart who was found in possession of printed materials, which condemned the government of Amin over human rights violations. All the judges feared to handle the case and as Chief Justice, Bendict Kiwanuka decided to take it on."

"'My father decided to handle the case and he released the white man after the trial,' says Kagimu who has been MP for Bukomansimbi in Masaka district. Kagimu is convinced that the release of Stuart was the main cause of Kiwanuka's death. 'On that evening of the ruling, Amin called my father on the phone and said, '*You said I have no powers to arrest the white man,*' reminisces Kagimu. Kiwanuka pleaded with Amin saying the government had powers to arrest but the man was bailed out and would always report to the Court. Amin banged the phone on the table and hang up on Kiwanuka" (see: Mwenda: 2010, 86-87). And regarding the demise of Uganda's central bank Governor during Amin's reign, little is known about Mubiru's death, but Kagimu says 'he was killed after he refused to print more money as President Amin had ordered. His death forced many Bank of Uganda workers to flee into exile.' (see: Mwenda: 2010, 86-87).

Against this background, it is no academic exercise that we are raising the issue of the importance of central bank independence. Admittedly, such independence should come with the accountability of the central bank within the confines and limits of the law. But, then, for Zambia, can the central bank Governor decline, for example, to carry out political directives of the Executive arm of the State, especially that such directives would be coming from the authority that put him or her in office, and that that authority has the unfettered discretionary power to fire the central bank Governor?

As a recommendation to improve the legal and regulatory framework in Zambia, the Bank of Zambia Act 1996 should repose in the legislature the powers to appoint and dismiss the Governor of the Bank of Zambia, spelling out clearly the grounds upon which a central bank governor can be appointed or relieved of his or her duties. The President and the Minister of Finance should only be allowed to nominate individuals that Parliament can then consider for appointment as Governor of the Bank of Zambia. Such an approach would build into the legal and institutional framework an element of political independence of the Bank of Zambia.

Further, as a matter of best practice in corporate governance, it is difficult to understand why the Governor of the Bank of Zambia is the Chairman of the Board of that very institution. Section 10(3) of the Bank of Zambia Act 1996 clearly spells out that the Governor of the Bank of Zambia is the chief executive officer of the central bank, and that he is responsible to the Board for the execution of the policy and management of the central bank. Yet, section 13(1)(a) of that same statute presents a paradox by stating that the Governor of the Bank of Zambia 'shall be the Chairman of the Board.' How can the chief executive officer of an organization be made accountable to a Board of which he is the Chairman? Shouldn't there be a distinction between managerial powers, on the one hand, and the role and functions of a non-executive Board, on the other?

CHAPTER 70

CHAMPION THEORY

There is no dispute that the Constitution is the supreme law of the land. That position is not in contest here. We fully respect and subscribe to this jurisprudential view. By contrast, the champion theory, though cognizant of existing laws in the country and respecting the promotion of compliance with the laws, seeks to understand what else is there beyond but not above the electoral laws. The champion theory looks, *inter alia*, into the political discourse and culture. In essence, the champion theory is not about bending rules or abrogating laws. It is about adhering to the law whilst thinking through other scenarios that could affect the choices that the electorate makes.

Both in the art of diplomacy and in heated political contests, we must understand the different vantage points enjoyed by a champion. But who is a 'champion', or what do we mean by the term 'champion'? In boxing, for example, a champion is the one holding the belt. The champion often has a greater say on when he will fight or who he will fight. Contenders do not force a fight on the champion when he is still warming up, unless the fight is sanctioned by the boxing board in accordance with the existing laws and regulations. Otherwise, the champion can keep the contenders waiting with much anxiety, while guarding secretly information on when he will announce the day of the fight. That is OK as long as in doing so the champion is acting within the discretionary powers afforded to him by the law or regulations. It is all part of the champion theory. This theory has been observed repeatedly and systematically in many different walks of life. And it tends to follow a similar scientific path and discourse.

Very often, we choose to shut our eyes to the truth. We are either too busy, ignoring useful analogies from our daily lives as they relate to certain political developments, or we are fixated so much on legalistic interpretations of politics. But law is only a means and not an end. So, we cannot divorce the human variable from the law. There are some critics who argue that we should not be too academic when analyzing life. But I tend to disagree with such views. There is nothing as practical as a good theory. All good theory is based on sound practice that has been repeatedly tested and systematically observed. Many pre-Socratic philosophers, for example, debated the relevance of empiricism when pitted against sound reason. The mind was seen to be more critical in answering questions about human existence than the material conditions supporting human existence. Others argued that inductive logic denied us of the opportunity to know the truth, and that we should strive towards deductive logic instead, proceeding in our arguments from the general to the specific. But there were also some who argued that we can draw some helpful inferences from inductive logic about certain phenomena in life. And the debate went on.

The theory of a champion, as demonstrated through some instructive African proverbs below, helps us to understand that, although a champion can be defeated, it happens rarely and mainly where the champion has been knocked out or where he loses on a unanimous decision. A champion hardly loses on a split-points decision. That, we must understand, whether we are lawyers or politicians. Here, it is reality that we are talking, as opposed to idealism. There is a difference between political science and politics. The latter is what we are talking about and it is characterized mainly by conflict. Where there is consensus, as opposed to conflict, politics withers away and gives room to policy. So, how then do political parties manage conflict when dealing with the politics associated with winning an election? Should they rely solely on promoting ideology through such means as the use of propaganda or should they resort to the use of force in order to entrench themselves? We know that political legitimacy is often won through the use of ideology or the use of force.

But, understand this: whenever there is a split-points decision, the presumption is that a champion will retain his or her belt. Now, this is not a partisan view. We all have at one time or another seen a boxing match. The same logic applies here. This is, indeed, the wisdom imbedded in the champion theory. You can only defeat a reigning champion by either knocking him out (such as where there is overwhelming national consensus agitating for the change of government as was the case in Zambia during the 1991 elections) or through a unanimous decision (such as would be the case where the opposition is strong and not fragmented). It is common knowledge that a fragmented opposition, even though showing some isolated pockets of strengthen, often leads to a split-points decision in favour of the champion. As noted above, a reigning champion hardly loses on a split-points decision, notwithstanding the provisions of the Constitution and the electoral laws. This is just common sense and remains an unwritten tradition in many parts of the world today.

And if the match ends in a split points-decision, do not be surprised that the champion walks away with the belt. We have seen this happen in boxing and many other sports, notwithstanding that elections are governed by different laws from boxing. It is even hard, though not impossible, to beat a reigning champion where the champion is fighting at home, or where he or she has some home-ground advantage. It becomes an uphill battle. It is like playing an away soccer game and hoping to win through penalties when the home team has so much home-ground advantage. Here, the state machinery is the home team's advantage. And in many cases, the local media focuses on televising the practice matches and preparatory games of the home team when they are warming up for the tournament. Understandably, the champion gets more media coverage, especially if we follow the rule that 'he who pays the piper calls the tune', unless the opponent is a really famous and crowd-pulling opponent who can mint in some cash for the media.

In Zambia, for example, while the then ruling party, the Movement for Multiparty Democracy (MMD), had been in power for twenty (20) years after winning an election against the United National Independence Party (UNIP) in October 1991, it suffered a humiliating defeat at the hands of the Patriotic Front (PF) in September 2011. Unlike the 1991 election which was mainly about fighting a dictatorship and introducing democracy in Zambia, the 2011 elections were underscored by an element of class struggle to improve the livelihoods of the suffering masses and to remove from political power the increasingly wealthy political elites. The PF had initially struck an alliance with other opposition political parties to fight the ruling party, MMD, but the alliance collapsed mainly due to the selfishness and greediness of the leadership in both camps. Riding on the economic frustrations of many Zambians, the PF marshaled a populist campaign to outwit the MMD, and succeeded at scooping the Republican Presidency by a wide electoral margin. And so it came to pass; the champion, the MMD, had been knocked out! It would appear that the MMD had become too complacent, thinking it would be in power forever. As we all know, complacency is a recipe for disaster. That aside, the Zambian people had just gotten fed up with the MMD after not realizing some improvement in their living standards. The irony, however, is that the PF has in its ranks many recycled politicians who were previously part of the MMD but only left the MMD after falling out of favour with the leadership of that party (MMD). The question is: could this be the same old wine in a different bottle?

Coming back to the reason why in many countries the State media often gives the ruling party greater coverage during campaigns for elections, generally, the State media, in contrast to much of the private media, is not adequately insulated from political interference. In many parts of the developing world, the distinction between interests of the ruling party and those of the government is often blurred, especially in political set-ups where the ruling party occupies most of the seats in the executive and legislative wings of the State. The ruling party becomes the government, and the government is the ruling party. In such situations, state institutions like the State media respond accordingly. While some critics may be quick to argue that the State media is funded by public funds accruing from such public sources as taxes, it is also a truism that the public generally is represented by the political representatives chosen through the ballot into public office – that is, the ruling party itself! So, *what to do now*, as they would say in Russia?

Closely related to the foregoing, in many parliamentary elections the prodigal son/daughter argument is often welcomed by many rural-based voters, especially if the prodigal's return is supported by the traditional African chief's endorsement. Again, such developments are addressed in the champion theory. But we are mindful also that there could be some reasons why some prodigal sons and daughters are shunned, especially where such individuals associate with unpleasant company. The discourse of the champion theory is very much awake to such realities.

We should understand that the theory of a champion draws inspiration from many sources, including insights from African old-age wisdom, political savvy dispensations, book smartness and shrewdness imbedded in street smartness. In Swahili, for example, to warn you against some sly and deceitful people, they say, Machoni Rafiki moyoni mnafiki (Friendly in the eye, hypocrite in the heart). Other instructive Swahili proverbs include Usisafirie Nyota ya mwenzio (Don't set sail using somebody else's star), Mutumai cha ndugu hufa masikini (He who relies on relatives dies poor), Mchezea wembe humkata mwenyewe (He who plays with a razor is bound to cut himself), Usinione nasinzia uyasemayo nayasikia (You see me dozing but I hear whatever you say) and Nazi mbovu haribu ya nzima (One bad coconut renders good ones bad).

Our forefathers developed various proverbs in an attempt to concretize clairvoyantly some of the experiences that they encountered so as to help posterity understand human existence better. It is such experiences that inform the champion theory. To put the discussion in context, let me flesh out a few proverbs from some African countries. I understand that in one Kenyan tribe, for example, they contend that, "when a man is stung by a bee, he does not set off to destroy all beehives." In Ethiopia, it is argued, "the man who marries a beautiful woman, and the farmer who grows corn by the roadside have the same problem." And in Nigeria it is postulated, "a short man is not a boy", and that "no matter how hot your anger is, it cannot cook yams." Interestingly, the Nigerians, I am told, also hold that "the frown on the face of the goat will not stop it from being taken to the market", and that "the same sun that melts the wax, hardens the clay." Such is the beauty of African wisdom.

On the one hand, the Ghanaians, I understand, maintain that, "it requires a lot of carefulness to kill the fly that perches on the scrotum", and that "an old lady feels uneasy when dry bones are mentioned in a proverb." Here, it does not require much thought to understand how useful these proverbs are. You certainly will be making a big mistake to smack that fly dead. On the other hand, the Ugandans, I am told, have a famous saying that "if you don't know where you're going, any road will take you there." It makes sense that should you get lost, it is alright since in the first place you did not know where you were going. In Cameroon, they maintain that "there's no virgin in a maternity ward", whereas in Guinea they will counsel you wisely that "a child can play with its mother's breasts, but not its father's testicles." And in Seychelles, so it is argued, they pontificate thoughtfully that, "if the throat can grant passage to a knife, the anus should wonder how to expel it." All these African proverbs help to inform the theory of a champion.

In Zambia, the wonderful and lovely men and women who originated from the Kola Empire have some equally compelling proverbs that sit well with the theory of a champion. I will examine some of these proverbs below while providing a political twist and slant to the English translation. The men and women from the Kola Empire aver, for example, that ABAPUSHI TABATEMWANA (rent-seeking opportunists in political parties tend to hate each other very much because they are all seeking political fortune), AKABWELELO KA LALYA (baby-come-back to the political party that you once left can be quite dangerous), AKAFUPA UTEMENWE EKA KUSHA UMUCHENE (the political position that you want so badly will cause you so much misery and grief if you lose the elections or if you are not adopted), AKAKUNYELELE TAKALABWA (certainly, you will never forget the person that beat you in the elections), AKONI KEKALA UMUTI KATEMENWE (for this non-partisan writer, you cannot force him to join a particular political party or to be partisan), and AMANO YAFUMINE MWIFWESA YAYA MUCHULU (the young ones, too, can think intelligently and responsibly).

Other closely related wise threads from the Kola people include AMENSHI BALINGA NO BUNGA (please do not be too ambitious politically for nothing), UMWANA ASHENDA ATASHA NYINA UKUNAYA (the experience of having been to different places in life, or 'exposure' as it is often called, brings forth new and valuable perspectives to life), BAMUKOLWE NGA BAFULA TABUCA BWANGU (where you have too many political parties and too many party presidents, the electorate will have sleepless nights due to the lies being peddled by the politicians), ICHIKWANKA BACHIMWENA KU MAMPALANYA (he who will be there to cast that critical vote when you need it most tends to have or share similar values and attributes as you), IMISU YA MWANAKASHI TAICILUKA LUPUTA (you must be man enough to win elections in Africa), IMITI IKULA E MPANGA (please give a chance to the young people to rule as well), IMITI IPALAMINE TAIBULA KU SHENKANA (colleagues in a political party will sometimes differ as they fight for political posts) and KAPOSA MABWE NINKASHI AKWETE (the one insulting other politicians is doing so to protect his or her political fortunes).

In concluding, we note the champion theory lays bare the thinking behind such proverbs as MAYO MPAPA NAINE NKAKUPAPA (this relates to one who cries that 'please give me a political post and I will ensure that you are safe and will not be prosecuted for corruption when you leave office'), MUKOLWE PA KUKULA EPO AFUNA IPINDO (many young and overzealous politicians tend to make poor political judgments before they mature as politicians), NGOLELYA NO MUKANKALA BULA UMWELE UBIKE PAMUKOSHI (if you are competing against a financially sound candidate in an election, you have to be very shrewd in order to win), PAKWAKANA UBUNGA TAPABA NSONI (let us just share and allocate ourselves political positions without feeling shy about it), PANSAKA TAPABULA CHIWELEWELE (in politics, there will always be some loser and jerk), SUNGO MUKOSHI UBULUNGU TABWAYAFYA (be patient, son, and wait for your turn so that you can get the presidency after you have been groomed well politically), UBUKULU BWA NKOKO MASAKO (the strength of a political party lies in the numbers of its committed membership), UBUNGA BALINGANYA NAMENSHI (there is no need to contest elections when you do not have enough political clout and muscle), UKUPOKA ICHINSENDA KU NKOKO KUNAKILILA (patience pays, if you really want the presidency so badly), UKUTAMFYA LUNSHI PAMAFI KUNYA PABILI (to really win elections convincingly, you must take both the presidency and most parliamentary seats so that the other parties remain dazed), ULULUMBI LWA MULANDA KUKAKATA (stubbornness and shrewdness can at times make a poor chap sound clever), UMULILO UCINGILE ABAKULU TAOCA (you may have to resort to old-age superstition, if need be, to secure your political fortunes), UMWANA WA NGWENA AKULILA KWI TETE (the really smart political opportunists know that you never insult your political party and leader, not even the opposition, even if your party has not given you a political post) and UWINGILA MU MUSHITU TOMFWA NSWASWA (please, be weary of those sly politicians who switch political parties now and again for their own political fortunes).

CHAPTER 71

WHEN POLITICS BECOMES A CAREER

Politics in many parts of the world is a lucrative business. Even some clerics tend to tinker with it once in a while, pretending to be speaking for the voiceless. Others go to the extent of leaving the pulpit for full-time political careers. But, wait a minute. What is a 'career'? The American Heritage Dictionary defines a career as 'a chosen pursuit; a profession or occupation.' So, if a career is a profession or occupation, is *politics* a profession or occupation? If it is not, why are some folks so obsessed with getting into political power such that they can do anything to get there?

Time and again, we hear of different politicians switching political parties the moment that they are dropped from a cabinet post or the moment that they lose elections in the party where they belonged initially. This type of political prostitution and cheap opportunism has now become the *modus operandi* of some politicians in Zambia. Uncouth and unprincipled as political prostitution may seem, some of these political prostitutes are people who have been to school. But, one wonders what has become of them! Matters of the stomach have a strange way of affecting the way some people think. Imagine supporting such a politician with all your enthusiasm only to learn later that he or she has jumped ship to the opposition. How would you feel?

To put issues in context, imagine for one moment if Charles Musonda or Kalusha Bwalya were to take off their Zambia National Soccer Team jerseys back in the days to join a foreign national team in the few instances when Zambia failed to beat an opposing side. But Charlie and Kalu, like all our great sportsmen and sportswomen, remained professional and never switched allegiance throughout their playing careers. In the military, the consequences are severe if you defect to the opposition. Our politicians need to learn from the military on the consequences of mutiny, for example. Some of these politicians can be insulting the opposition today, and the next day they will be in bed with the same political party that they were insulting yesterday. What kind of people are these who behave like they have no morals or sense of shame?

We need to re-think the way we conduct our politics. There are not many role models in politics today. We must build and nurture our political role models. I have met many Heads of State in my professional life, including several Cabinet Ministers, from different continents. I have also taught some university students that have gone on to become

Cabinet Ministers in their home countries as well as some former Heads of State and former Cabinet Ministers, including leading judges. We must find that talent of young leaders that can drive Africa to posterity. Even at independence, the Kenneth Kaundas, the Kwame Nkhrumahs, the Jomo Kenyattas, the Julius Nyereres and many others were all middle-aged young leaders. In fact, a good number of them had just returned from their studies abroad to provide political leadership to their people and countries. While there could have been other much older men within Africa at the time, it was the middle-aged that were given the chance to lead, especially that these middle-aged had some levels of intellectual sophistication to discern quickly the colonial master's mentality. One would be inclined to think that the old men of those days were not as selfish as the current lot that does not want to retire.

And many of our African politicians today, whether middle-aged or old, have a propensity to fake it. But they are not alone in such pretentions. Even in lands afar you will find fakes from such remote places as Alaska trying to fake it against a well-respected and well-accomplished leader. These types of politicians lack originality and authenticity, and are often rent-seekers in different political agendas. Some are very well-educated, yet are willing to throw principle to the wind just to secure something for their stomachs. Others just want fame, but they are not enlightened or principled. Yet, they are willing to put up spirited fights just to secure their political fortunes.

- *Kenneth K. Mwenda*

When much of the politics are marred with ideologically bankrupt persuasions, including suspicions of superstition and sorcery, it is difficult for many young people to commit. They are afraid for their lives because some people have taken politics as a source of their livelihood. Such career politicians will contest elections for as long as they live and no matter how many times they keep losing. They will never give up. For them, it is tenacity without hope. It is a sad state of affairs. I have always been a great admirer of noble men like President Nelson Mandela who just gave it up on a silver plate and moved on to other things after having been in prison for so long. I also like young enlightened leaders, such as President Obama, who are bringing fresh air and great ideas to international politics, notwithstanding some misguided criticisms from the far right. Obama has shown that you do not have to be too old to be a politician. And you do not need all the long political experience some politicians will tell you that you need before you can run for presidency. In Africa, for example, we have seen former disc jockeys (DJs) become Heads of State. Even former police constables want to be Heads of State. It seems the race is open to all. There are no qualifications required to be a Head of State, other than being a national of the country and meeting a certain age-limit. That's how simple it is to stand for presidency. And if we continue on the path we are on, very soon even hoodlums and rogues will be forming political parties to try and chance the presidency. After all, the Republican Constitution provides for the right for any individual to express his or her views through a political party or platform as well as to choose whichever party or person to associate with. Indeed, as we are so often told, that is what democracy is all about. You can chance it if you really want it bad. But remember also that, to whom much is given, much is demanded. Leadership is not just about chancing it or exploiting opportunistic tendencies. It demands more than that. If we continue allowing and celebrating mediocrity, permitting even hustlers to ascend to the helm of power, then it is hard to understand where we are headed to. I ask again – when will the generation of independence politicians retire from active politics, and why do they keep holding on?

As a fable would show, Uncle Mukandambolo, a maternal uncle to young Chileshe, was visiting Chileshe's family in Lusaka. Uncle Mukandambolo came from one of the villages in rural Zambia, but appeared content with life in Lusaka. And he made no mention of when he would return to the village. Chileshe's father, Bob, being a brother-in-law to Mukandambolo, found it culturally constraining to ask Mukandambolo when he would return to the village. In the meantime, young Chileshe was displaced from his bedroom by Uncle Mukandambolo's arrival and he was now spending nights on the couch in the living room. Fed up with all this mess, young Chileshe mustered some courage to ask Uncle Mukandambolo when he would be going back where he came from. Uncle Mukandambolo felt so offended. As an elderly African man engrossed deeply in matters of African cultural values, Uncle Mukandambolo began to suspect that Chileshe's parents must have told Chileshe to ask him when he would be leaving. In the evenings of that same day, Uncle Mukandambolo boycotted dinner, claiming that he was not feeling well. For young Chileshe, it was a relief given that Uncle Mukandambolo had such an appetite that he could collapse a mountain of nsima in a few seconds. And Uncle Mukandambolo had the habbit of aiming for big portions of food at the dinner table, drowning all the soup with his ing'nkondwa style of nsima lumps. The next day, as young Chileshe and his parents were watching television in the company of Uncle Mukandambolo, an advert for the sale of mealie meal appeared on the television screen. Upon seeing the advert, young Chileshe retorted innocently: "Aaahhh, the price of mealie-meal has gone up again, mummy!" That innocent remark offended Uncle Mukandambolo even further. Uncle Mukandambolo could not take it anymore. He was by now convinced that young Chileshe was being coached by his parents to make all the insinuating utterances. So, Uncle Mukandambolo decided to leave for the village immediately and right in the middle of the night, claiming that he had had enough of insults from Chileshe's parents. But, Bob and his wife were shocked. They had no idea what had ticked-off Uncle Mukandambolo.

As the fable shows, if only some of our politicians can tell us why they never retire from politics or when they will ever leave politics, we would not be asking too many questions. The tired argument that a country needs old people that have a lot of political experience to run it, and that the presidency is not meant for the young ones that are seeking job-on-training type of experience, is a lame excuse. In the fable presented above, the young boy, Chileshe, was asking innocent questions like any young kid would. At no time was Chileshe acting under the directions of his parents. However, if young Chileshe had an iota of an idea on how his questions or utterances would be perceived by Uncle Mukandambolo, he would not have asked those questions or made those utterances. But, then, Uncle Mukandambolo, too, should have indicated to the family when he would be going back to the village. His dishonesty in keeping quiet led to the misunderstandings.

Today's young people are growing up in a more inquisitive and questioning culture. And cultural differences and generational disparities between the older generation and the younger can only lead to more misunderstandings, especially if the old people want to continue with politics even when they know that their prime time is long gone. Closely related to this, it would be too risky for any well-meaning citizen to be regurgitating dogmatically the cajoleries being peddled by some of our politicians. Theirs is a quest to secure their political fortunes. And the danger with entertaining too many falsehoods and cajoleries from politicians is that, as the great Vladimir Lenin once said, "A lie told often enough becomes the truth." Eventually you begin to perceive the lie to be the truth in the same way that an ugly-looking and tired old man will eventually seem alright in the eyes of a young pretty lady if all she is looking for in him is finance, or just as a not-so-pleasant looking female bartender will eventually begin to look pretty in the eyes of a lustful drunken man.

Indeed, not everyone will question lies or falsehoods. In fact, many people will believe a falsehood, depending on how shrewdly that falsehood is peddled. Often times, a deliberate and purposeful combination of fiction and fact, or half-lies and half-truths, can easily win the hearts of many, especially those that are only familiar with a portion or fraction of the fact. But we must be mindful that coffee is still coffee whether it has in it some milk or not. Likewise, a lie is a lie whether or not it has some degree of truth in it. To put issues into perspective, in much of the Western world, when it comes to matters of race and people with African ancestral heritage, you are considered black whether or not one of your parents is Caucasian. There is no middle ground, or anything like, "No, me, I am not black. I am coloured. In fact, I am from Thornpark". You are black, period. The milk in the coffee will not give the coffee a different name. Even those black sisters that specialize in using skin-toning and lighting creams have never succeeded at toning some hidden parts of their bodies. It just tells you who you are and that you just have to be comfortable with yourself and the way God has made you. You don't have to fake it in order to make it. And you don't need a blonde wig or a fake foreign accent.

The other day I was looking at parallel developments in some countries. The current presidents of Ghana and Nigeria are both very solid intellectuals. Even their immediate predecessors are equally solid intellectuals. And matters are beginning to take shape in both countries. It is not surprising that President Obama flew to Ghana on his last trip to Africa. He must have known that he would have an enlightening conversation with his counterpart there. These are not small issues that you can just dismiss as rhetorical. Perception is very important in politics.

If you look at the American presidency, for example, looking closely at the credentials and professional backgrounds of the respective chief office-bearers, you will notice that lawyers have done a good job. Presidents John Adams, Thomas Jefferson, James Madison, James Monroe, John Quincy Adams, Martin Van Buren, John Tyler, James Knox Polk, Franklin Pierce, Woodrow Wilson, Franklin Delano Roosevelt, Bill Clinton and many others, including Barack Hussein Obama, Jr., are all lawyers. They were, and are, not strangers to matters of constitutional law and the limitations of government excesses. Some of them, including President Clinton and President Obama, have served previously as constitutional law professors.

Closely related to that, President John Atta Mills in Ghana is a former Law Professor at the University of Ghana. But I am not saying that law is the only profession that speaks well to the position of Head of State. No, that is far from my argument. I am also not arguing that we only need people with degrees to run a country. No, that is not my argument. Even people without formal education can make a good president as long as they have the right character and the leadership vision, and they are also disciplined and principled quick learners who are able to understand systemically how government and politics relate and function. But you do not have to be too old to succeed at this kind of work. And you do not need to have been in government before. Even newcomers can make it. Although it is said that the best school is at the feet of the elders, it is also known that it is the young people that are moving technology worldwide today.

Niccolo Machiavelli, the Italian philosopher observed astutely: *"You must know there are two methods of fighting, the one by law, the other by force; the first method is of men, the second of beasts; but because the first is frequently not sufficient, one must have recourse to the second. Therefore it is necessary for a prince to understand how to use the methods of the beast and the man... A prince...ought to choose the fox and the lion; because the lion cannot defend himself against traps and the fox cannot defend himself against wolves. Therefore, it is necessary to be a fox to discover the traps and a lion to terrify the wolves. Those who rely simply on the lion do not understand this."* Interestingly, Machiavelli believed that Italy could not be united unless its leader was deceptive and ruthless. We have seen many Machiavellians in African politics. Some rely on charisma and populism to deceive the masses. But we must ask ourselves? To what do all these machinations point? One thing, and one thing only – an insatiable appetite for power! And power corrupts while absolute power corrupts absolutely.

It is alleged that shortly after the political upheavals of 2011 leading to the ouster of autocratic regimes in Tunisia and Egypt, respectively, the people of one other African country under the rule of a long-standing dictator mustered some courage to ask their President also to step down. The people decided to approach a close aide and confidant of the President, asking him to deliver the message to the President. As the seas of people gathered outside the Presidential palace, demanding that the President steps down, the Presidential aide and confidant entered the Presidential Office to deliver the message. He found the President in a calm and relaxed mood, sipping a glass of champagne. Trying to find the right words, with perfected etiquette and euphemism, the Presidential aide and confidant stammered, "Your Excellency, if I may, the people have come to say goodbye." Unperturbed, the President calmly cleared his throat, looked outside the window, and said, "Oh, I see... And where are they going?"

We have to move away from such stone-age politics. We are now in the digital and hi-tech era. And it would be unwise to think that a politician will give you a job when you campaign for him vigorously, knowing full well that he has promised the same thing to many others who are campaigning for him. Besides, as one would say in Bemba, 'Ubwingi bwa bipa fye pa kwa-kana umunani, lelo te ku-milimo...'. An African fable could explain this better. When faced with a famine, a group of villagers may decide to get together and go fishing so as to feed the village. The selfless effort of getting together comes naturally since they all face the same predicament – hunger! But as soon as they have caught enough fish, problems then ensue. The greedy one among them will want to get the lion's share, pocketing also the consumer surplus and the surplus value of everyone. And this is exactly what happens in politics, especially if politicians do not want to retire. They will promise different sympathizers various political posts, claiming that 'pa kwa-kana ubunga ta-paba nsoni' (i.e. we should not feel shy when sharing mealie-meal or, rather, when sharing political posts amongst ourselves), yet it will be folly to expect politicians to honour their promises even though you could have spent nights with them fishing for political votes. Besides, it is a wrong concept to support someone politically with the expectation that he or she should give you a post when he or she wins the elections. You must either have the political and ideological conviction, without necessarily expecting any corrupt favours in return, or remain apolitical. To the latter, I belong, but don't uku-beba!

CHAPTER 72

SHOULD UNSUBSTANTIATED CLAIMS OF OLD-AGE WISDOM BE A CRITERION FOR ELIGIBITY TO THE PRESIDENCY?

Can an individual the age of a traditional grandfather in an African setting make a good President? How alert will he be when faced with topical issues confronting modern and contemporary society today? What about elders that thrive in trading profanity publicly against each other so as to scandalize one another, can they make good leaders? You have heard allegations and accusations of who has been smoking marijuana or who still smokes? If, indeed, true, can an individual that smokes marijuana make a good President given that much of sub-Sahara African weather is quite hot and sunny? If you have smoked marijuana before, or if you know of someone who has smoked pot before, then you will understand easily the correlation between sunny hot weather and the effects of having smoked marijuana. You may have to keep such a leader under air condition facilities for the most part in order to cool him off. So, what type of leader does Zambia need? Organizational psychologists have spent great amounts of ink on understanding the concept of leadership. Political philosophers, too, have added their ink to the debate. However, some observers wonder the relevance of some petty accusations and counter- accusation amongst some of our political leaders. Accusations keep flying around on who has a big flat nose with sleepy-looking eyes or who has reddish 'serpent like' eyes with unpleasant facial looks. Others question whether a leader should be handsome or ugly, worrying mainly about the sight of the Presidential portrait in their governmental and business offices. Closely related to that, the troubling question keeps popping up on whether a leader should be one who is already financially comfortable, although he does not smile, not even to the media. Others wonder how such financially sound folks ended up making money without much borrowing or engaging in what is known as 'gearing' or 'leverage' in corporate finance. Maybe there is a new dimension to capital structuring that Modigilliani and Miller forgot to include in their theory. There have also been accusations and counter-accusations of infidelity amongst some politicians, others too quick to even point to leaders with notorious polygamist tendencies. Some have been accused of fathering children outside wedlock or grabbing other men's wives. Yet, there is also a section of critics that keep accusing other political figures of marrying young spouses. Then, there are those that wonder if a leader should be a short man or a religious prophet.

Some have argued superstitiously that we should also be looking at the context in which political leadership is exercised. Such pundits argue that, in the context of Africa, a smart leader should also possess some supernatural magical powers, such as disappearing in broad daylight behind a shrub or home-made computer, even if it means doing so in spite of holding a PhD from a top leading whiteman's university. This, they argue, can shield him or her from the mysterious arsenals of his adversaries.

However, as a student of leadership, I have paid close attention to a number of these theories as well as to those emanating in the field of leadership. And an abundance of literature exists in management sciences on theories such as Trait Theory, Behavioral and Style Theories, Situational and Contingency Theories, Functional Theories, Transactional and Transformational Theories, Environmental Theories, Neo-emergent Theory as well as the Leadership and Emotions Theory. But none of these theories help to explain to us the meaning of "wisdom", which item many argue is the most important qualification for one to become a Republican President in a country such as ours. Be that as it may, the anatomy and epistemology of wisdom, like that of witchcraft, remain a mystery to many, professed mainly by those who feel that it can advance their political cause. But wait a minute before you rise up in your chair. Let us take a more reasoned look.

I have been a student of leadership for many years

now. Some argue that we cannot transplant leadership models from the corporate world into the political domain. Others confuse the concept of Executive Leadership with that of Management. But not every manager is a leader. And not every leader is a manager. While a corporate executive leader often inspires and motivates others through a shared vision as evidenced in the crafting, execution and implementation of effective and sound corporate and business strategies, a manager who lacks leadership skills will often be bogged down with tasks related to the accomplishment of an assignment, without taking into account the bigger picture. But, leadership is not all about accomplishing a task. It involves also navigating with tact in the milieu of people-skills. We sometimes hear of phrases such as Intellectual Leadership. What does this mean? Who is a leader? Boje (2000), in his discussion of Transformational Leadership, citing Burns (1978), observes that: "An intellectual leader is devoted to seeing ideas and values that transcend immediate practical needs and still change and transform their social milieu. 'The concept of intellectual *leadership* brings in the role of *conscious purpose* drawn from values' (Burns, 1978: 142). The intellectual leader is out of step with their own time, in conflict with the status quo. The intellectual leader is a person with a vision that can transform society by raising social consciousness."

In essence, leadership is about vision as well as motivation. In that light, politics should be about character as opposed to opportunity! The mere attainment of certain levels of higher schooling does not make one an intellectual leader. Neither does it make him a better candidate for political office. The accumulation of academic credentials alone does not confirm a person to the status of enlightenment. Intellectual leadership in any person, politician or otherwise, calls for much more than acquiring academic credentials or propounding controversial but unenlightened views. Intellectual leadership is often rooted in serious erudition, casting one into the age of enlightenment. It is that aspect of intellectual leadership that often distinguishes mere rote learning from intellectual stewardship. Rote learning, as many can attest to, often avoids the critical and analytical understanding of a subject, preferring memorization to the former attributes. Although there are people that have excelled in school through rote learning, that in itself does not equip them with the necessary tools for critical thinking. And it is at this point that I turn to ask the question: what is it about political leadership that cannot be learned or taught? Recently, I was interested in seeing how young Nigeria's new President is. Even his predecessor was not that old. And I could see a common thread of intellect and enlightenment between them; that is, a thread that I have also seen in Ghana's two recent Presidents as well as in the new young American President, Obama. Are we, as a nation, though peaceful, getting anywhere close to that, or do we still prefer the ages of darkness? The recent violence during the parliamentary by-elections in Eastern Province is characteristic of the politics of the Dark Age. Both the opposition and ruling party seem to have had a share in the mess.

Many a time, we hear arguments that you don't need a university degree to be a president of a country, and that all you need is wisdom. But it is also true that science is yet to define the meaning of "wisdom"! And quite true as well, a university degree alone is not all there is to acquiring leadership skills. There is much more to it than just a university degree. And some life experiences can equip someone who has no university degree with valuable "transferable skills" of leadership. Take for example, an inspiring individual who has served as a General in the Army. He or she will have mastered certain valuable lessons of leadership. For it is in the military that a part of the history of management finds its sanctuary. Likewise, certain leadership skills in the corporate world can be transplanted effectively to leadership in the political domain. We don't live in isolated worlds, but inter-connected and inter-related worlds. But that does not mean that anything can now pass for transferable skills. There has to be a meaningful and reasonable sense of erudition pertaining to one's life experiences. That said, it is not the aim of this paper to cause any trouble or problems. We are mindful, however, that the parameters of what we often call "wisdom" range from mere eccentric behavior of some political actors to erudite dispositions of others. Against this background, is there an objective and scientific means of capturing or determining "wisdom"? Or, should we simply leave this to guesswork? Although I have heard that a standard philosophical definition of "wisdom" postulates that it consists of making the best use of available knowledge, or that wisdom is the capacity to distinguish between authentic meaning and erroneous meaning, I would still be inclined to argue that the distillation of valuable lessons of experience and a collection of certain idiosyncratic values, including some anecdotal conjectures pointing to some form of higher moral and ethical ground, might help to explain what is meant by "wisdom". To argue that wisdom is not something you attain as much as it is something you grow into implies that wisdom comes with age. Yet, we know that not everyone gets wiser as they grow old. So, what is wisdom, or what kind of wisdom should a political leader possess? That is the question that we should be asking ourselves today.

CHAPTER 73

SHOULD THE PRESIDENT OF A COUNTRY BE SOMEONE WITH A UNIVERSITY EDUCATION?

That an individual's formal university education alone is not, and must not be, the sole criterion for determining the individual's leadership qualities is a settled view that requires no contest. But to argue that illiteracy or semi-literacy, even in situations where such illiteracy or semi-literacy is devoid of wisdom and decency, are credible values that can propel an individual to the helm of political leadership is a totally misguided view. If anything, the very constitutional argument imbedded in the Constitutions of many countries, stipulating that the Republican President should be at least of a certain age and should be a national of that particular country, does favour a certain kind of reverse discrimination against those individuals resident in a particular country that are below that constitutional age requirement and those that are not nationals of the said country, though having close ties to the country.

\- *Kenneth K. Mwenda*

Against this background, to contest the merits of a proposal that the Republican Constitution should provide that a Republican President should have at least a university degree or some professional certification equivalent to a university Bachelors degree is a conundrum that is not free from illogical difficulties. I am awake to the fact that some arguments have been advanced from certain quarters of society, postulating that championing such a proposal is tantamount to targeting a particular individual and thus discriminating against that individual. To some extent, this view could be true, especially where the proposal is hijacked by opportunistic politicization. Sometimes, a well-meaning developmental goal can be hijacked by those with a self-interest political agenda. But then, what does experience teach us?

In Zambia's political history, haven't there been cases where individuals with decent academic credentials, and sometimes even PhDs from reputable international universities, after forming a political party, could not field a presidential candidate from amongst themselves partly because the majority of the party leadership was below the constitutional age requirement to contest the Republican Presidency? But nobody ever cried foul that the Republican Constitution was discriminatory or should be amended to allow such young intellectuals to contest the Republican Presidency. Indeed, nobody complained that the age requirement in the Republican Constitution infringed the rights of these citizens.

It is therefore ironic that the issue of a university degree should appear so troublesome and burdensome to some. How different is this from the example of age restriction noted above? Even from a labour law or human resource management perspective, do we not see many companies spelling out specific job requirements for hiring, say, their chief executive officer or managing director? Can we then challenge the constitutionality of these job adverts for setting forth that the company is only looking for candidates who hold, inter alia, a university degree or a certain professional qualification that is equivalent to a university degree? Even in the public service, is it not acceptable practice that certain jobs require applicants to have attained a particular level education? By parity of reasoning, why all this fuss about the Republican Presidency? Are people defending their own personal interests or what? And is presidency not just a job like any other job? Yes, presidents come and go. We have seen them come and go. So, what's the big deal really? Even a priest must have some minimal levels of education no matter how well-anointed he or she is with the Holy Spirit! Yet, nobody cries foul that there is discrimination against the already anointed when we send them to seminaries for years of training, with almost no prospect for a lucrative salary after they graduate.

By contrast, it is perfectly conceivable that there would be discrimination if the hiring of employees was done along tribal or ethnic lines because such criteria have no direct bearing, first, on an individual's ability to perform effectively, and, secondly, on fostering meaningful competition to get the best candidate. It is in this vein that the use of educational levels as one of the basic requirements for an individual to aspire for public office should be embraced without hesitation. This approach will help us identify and attract the right people into politics and positions of leadership. Experience alone, without grounded theory, is dangerous. There are some people who claim, and proudly too, to have many years of practical experience in doing the same thing over and over again, forgetting that they may have been doing that same thing wrongly much of their life. Such human failings, predicated on robotic and dogmatic intuitions, are often a result of treating lightly, or paying insufficient attention to, valuable and useful theories or ideas in a relevant discipline. Indeed, practice devoid of enlightenment is a good recipe for failure, as much as the carrying out of unintelligent repetitive tasks does not make one a genius. There can be no substitute for erudition. Exceptions should only be permitted rarely, such as where an individual is of such unquestionable international stature, despite not having a formal university education. We have seen, for example, how Ghana has been heralded internationally as a success African story of good governance and economic growth. President Kufuor, an Oxford graduate, handed over the torch of leadership to Professor John A. Mills, a former Associate Professor of Law at the University of Ghana Law Faculty. It was a peaceful transition, albeit the tightly contested presidential elections. But we are not saying Ghana is completely free of what obtains in many developing countries. Ghana, like many West African countries, has experienced a troubled political past with routine military coups. But, in the modern age of technology, where a Republican President should be in a position to understand complex issues of globalization that are so often juxtaposed between norms of international trade and finance as well as those of law and economics, surely we cannot remain glued to the old ways of tired politicians of the past. A Republican President should not only have a reasonable understanding of quantitative analysis and logic, be he or she should also be computer literate so as to be able to send or receive email, including browsing the internet. Indeed, a number of countries are moving away from the old era of mediocre leadership that was evidenced through military dictatorships, corrupt and compromised political leaderships, and the often less visionary governing classes. But then, as we have argued above, education alone is not enough. What about those wise elders in many an African traditional society, who presided over complex disputes, resolving these disputes without resort to theories of modern education, how did they succeed? As a tool for effective leadership, education is only meaningfully functional if it is supported by qualities of high moral and ethical values. As noted above, education alone is not enough. So, then, how are we to determine an individual's levels of ethical and moral standing?

A well-informed electorate in a society that is not easily susceptible to corruption can point us to some quality leadership. But, where hunger and poverty are overwhelming and have disenfranchised much of the electorate, some voters tend to be compromised. We are then left to look at what the Republican Constitution says. As argued above, it is not discriminatory to enshrine in the Republican Constitution that a candidate for the Republican Presidency should have at least a university degree or some parallel professional qualification. That said, we need to exercise caution here. There are a lot of diploma mills out there that award fake degrees. Also, honorary degrees should never count as an earned degree. As a policy recommendation, the Supreme Court should be bestowed with powers to screen the eligibility of Presidential candidates in Zambia, consulting, where appropriate and necessary, any relevant institution in Zambia or abroad, such as the University of Zambia, the Copperbelt University, the Law Association of Zambia, the Zambia Institute of Certified Accountants, the Medical Association of Zambia, the Institute of Directors, the Office of the President, the Anti-Corruption Commission, the Anti-Drug Commission, the Bank of Zambia, the Securities and Exchange Commission, the Pensions and Insurance Authority, and any line ministry or regulatory body within Zambia or abroad, on the eligibility of the candidates. We have to move away from the culture of *politics of the stomach* which is currently endemic in Zambia. And the idea here is not to try and fix any particular individuals, but rather to fix those socio-economic problems that are rooted in mediocre leadership!

CHAPTER 74

THE PLIGHT OF AFRICAN INTELLECTUALS

In his famous treatise, "Black Skin, White Masks," Frantz Fanon decried the apologetics that often choose to rationalize the misconception of truth. Fanon posited, "Sometimes people hold a core belief that is very strong. When they are presented with evidence that works against that belief, the new evidence cannot be accepted. It would create a feeling that is extremely uncomfortable, called cognitive dissonance. And because it is so important to protect the core belief, they will rationalize, ignore and even deny anything that doesn't fit in with the core belief." Does this sound familiar? Such is the underlying premise traversed by many an African intellectual in the post-colonial African States. A good number of them, such as university professors, lecturers, medical doctors and engineers, left Africa as they felt neglected, frustrated, rejected and let down by the State. In this article, we focus not on practitioners as such, but on those African intellectuals that were in, or contributed to,

- *Kenneth K. Mwenda*

academia before or after going into self-imposed politico-economic exile in much better developed foreign countries.

Over the years, Africa has witnessed a sustained and increased hemorrhage of its intellectual power to the Western world. It's called "brain-drain". A cadre of learned individuals that are expected to be more rational and objective in their thinking, relying on intellect rather than emotional sentiments or feelings, has left Africa, leaving behind only a handful of equally outstanding intellectual leaders. Together, these are individuals that were expected to provide intellectual leadership for the contient, engaging professionally in advanced forms of mental labor. These are individuals that were expected to be creative problem-solvers and to promote human values of pursuing intellect and its closely related forms of complex knowledge. They are individuals that were supposed to examine complex aesthetic or philosophical matters, especially on an abstract and general level. We call such persons "intellectuals". These are individuals that were to be paid just for thinking – and to think critically, creatively and systematically! Some of our intellectuals may seem crazy, but that is because they are constantly in deep-thought over various types of critical matter. Theirs is to find a nexus between scientific theory and grounded practice.

A fable has often been told of an old maverick professor, or rather a schizophrenic or eccentric one, as some may say, who always wore the same old sweater and carried a heavily battered and ragged leather briefcase. He was once seen walking in town in broad daylight with a heavily lit kerosene lamp. It was daytime and many people wondered what was going on. They thought the professor was going berserk. So, someone mustered enough courage to ask the professor what was going on. The professor was very patient with the inquirer and answered thoughtfully: "I am looking for an honest man, but cannot find one..." Does this sound familiar? Indeed, honest men are hard to find today. The professor had a good point, although everyone misunderstood him and many were too quick to judge.

Over the years, several African intellectuals have left the continent because many felt neglected, rejected and unappreciated. Their stories, with a few exceptions, are similar. Although not everyone that left Africa found fortune or fame where they went, the frustrations of leaving Africa came with some pain and nostalgic sentiments of the yesteryears. The issues of limited State budgetary allocation to the higher education sector as well as uncompetitive emoluments has had serious implications. Even to this day, the salaries of many academics in Africa are not inspiring. Besides, there are hardly any funds to support academic research in many disciplines. As noted above, many of our African intellectuals felt neglected and slighted, as well as maligned and disrespected, especially when the post-colonial African State would accord audience to ideas of the so-called Western experts, ignoring the views of the indigenous local experts. Yet, some of these Western experts are not even as qualified as the local experts. And other foreign 'experts' are just plain mediocre, although African governments still listen to them.

In the time of détente, those African intellectuals that embraced too much radical ideology often found themselves at cross-roads with the State machinery of the post-colonial African State. Criticizing the State in many nations, developed or underdeveloped, can get you into harm's way. At that time, the world was quite polarized between NATO and the Warsaw Pact, with each claiming sympathizers from various corners of the world.

Within Africa, the debate between African socialism and socialist Africa continued. There was also the superficial body of the so-called non-aligned States. Some African Heads of State propagated what they viewed as African indigenous ideologies such as Humanism, Negritude, Ujamaa and Pan-Africanism, all which were Afro-centric inspired, but with some modest infusion of tenets of other ideologies. It was a time when the post-colonial State, especially in those countries that pursued State Capitalism, witnessed the growth and proliferation of several State-owned enterprises. Almost every African nation that had just attained political independence built or enhanced its own national university, including many other institutions of higher learning. Most of these academic institutions were well funded by the State until the economies of many post-colonial African States began to crumble. The African university then entered a critical phase of underfunding.

Even as some African intellectuals tried to offer solutions to post-colonial African States on Africa's economic ills, much of that advice was either ignored or shunned. And those African intellectuals that persisted, especially with their leftist ideas, became victims of State brutality or were black-listed by the State intelligence system. Robert Witanek (see: "The CIA on Campus," Online, 1989) observes that, at the time, the US Central Intelligence Agency (CIA) was also infiltrating many African universities by covertly sending to Africa some academics to teach at these universities. A number of these academics are said (see Witanek, above) to have been CIA operatives.

During this period, military dictatorships and One-Party States in Africa were beginning to mushroom. Many African intellectuals began to look elsewhere and far beyond the geographical limits of their home nations. They sought some decent space which could allow them to think independently and where they could find the right kind of incentives to carry out intellectual work properly. Some sought the professional respect and recognition that they thought had been denied of them by their home countries. As Frantz Fanon would say, "He who is reluctant to recognize me opposes me..."! And the post-colonial African State, in particular, was reluctant to recognize and value academic freedom. Overall, the post-colonial African State remained ambivalent, struggling to appease a growing governing class of emerging petty bourgeoisie domestically and a foreign ruling class at the international level.

- *Kenneth K. Mwenda*

Given all these contradictions, many African intellectuals had either to leave their native home countries or bury their heads in the sand. Others opted instead to join (or as they would argue later, were "co-opted" into) the State system of the post-colonial African State. Those that crossed the chasm of ideological divide to join the State system had to become mute or make frantic efforts to try to 'intellectualize' some skeptical ideas of the State so as to safeguard and protect their newly found fortune. As they would say in Kenya, the guys had to protect their Ugali (i.e. protecting their Nsima). Such has been the plight of many an African intellectual. He or she had to adapt and adjust quickly, changing colours like a chameleon so as to make ends meet, while also dusting off his or her bookshelf and confining to the archives most of the great works of such eminent intellectual luminaries as Amilcar Cabral, Samora Machel, Eduardo Mondlane, Kwame Nkhruma, Joe Slovo, Frantz Fanon, Walter Rodney, Samir Amin, Archie Mafeje, Abdul Rahman Mohamed Babu, Mahmood Mamdani, Yash Gahi, Dan Wadada Nabudere, Issa Shivji, Thandika Mkandawire, and many others. And the language of class struggle had to be abandoned and desecrated. Good governance and human rights became the new vocabulary of these new converts to capitalism and State oppression. They had now embraced liberal and conservative ideology, seeking out what is supposedly referred to as 'peace', as opposed to 'equal rights', while overlooking the deepening social class divisions around them. Any type of association with Marxist ideas, it was feared, would deny them a chance to take a bite at the national cake.

The African intellectual was by now compromised. But what if Marx was right in the first place? Prof. Terry Eagleton asks this question in his recently published book, *Why Marx Was Right*, published by Yale University Press in 2011. He argues, "What if all the most familiar objections to Marx's works are mistaken?" As a fable would show, in one African country, a staunch critic of the President was appointed as a Cabinet Minister. Suddenly, he stopped talking. People began to wonder why. A journalist asked him during a television interview as to why he had stopped talking. The newly appointed Cabinet Minister thought for a moment, trying to find the right words, and offered the following response: "In Africa, it is bad manners to talk while 'eating'..."

At the time of all these socio-economic and political contradictions, Marxist-Leninist leftist ideas were the mantra of the day for many an African intellectual. But like culture, ideological persuasions also change and evolve over time. Today, most of these African intellectuals have now shed off or literally abandoned their Marxist-Leninist ideals for a petty bourgeois life. But back in the days, the increasing financial neglect of the African universities by the post-colonial African State, as well as the deposition of excessive power in instruments of the State, left many African intellectuals disillusioned. As noted earlier, some decided to leave and have never gone back. They simply went into self-imposed economic exile. However, a good number stayed behind, continuing to wage the ideological battle from the ivory towers of the academe.

By the dawn of perestroika and the eventual demise of détente, and with the increasing nternationalization of capital through what is now called globalization, the African university was a different place altogether. It became a shadow of its old self. For example, the Ugandan newspaper, *New Vision* (Online version: Wednesday, 24th February, 2010), writing on the 2010 appointment of Prof. Mahmood Mamdani as the new head of Makerere University's Institute of Social Research (MISR), observed: "In 2007, he published a book, *Scholars in the Market Place*, that caused unease within the university's administration. The book criticised the commercialisation of university education in Uganda and the lack of academic research and publications by professors. He accused the university of duplicating courses for the sake of generating revenues from private students."

Critically underfunded, many African universities were now having less ideological debates and had been transformed ideologically into less intellectually stimulating habitats. Academic research and scholarship was declining. Closely related to this, hardly would you find any meaningful think-tank or policy institution to collaborate with academia. Also, the venue of many academic conferences and workshops was no longer the university campus but hotels and other luxury resorts. And a number of the conference attendees would be more interested in their per diems as opposed to making intellectual contributions. Besides, many intellectual giants had by that time left the African university, and a new crop of young academics was coming on board to join vicissitudes of a few old guards. In some instances, even the curriculum of some degree programmes was being revised to accommodate the effect of globalization. For example, many Marxist and leftist ideas were being watered down or dropped off altogether from the curriculum. And monetary incentives gained greater primacy over intellectualism in the university. Also, donor agencies became more visible with the financially lucrative consultancy contracts that they would offer to academicians. A new blood-line for the economically distressed intellectuals had been discovered.

Other African intellectuals tried to form political parties in order to have a chance at redressing the economic ills of the country. Some simply wanted to share the national cake that was being enjoyed by those in power. Yet, there was also a small fraction that joined some public international organizations. In the end, scholarship and intellectualism suffered at many African universities. A number of these universities could not even fill to full capacity most of the vacancies for academic jobs. There were, and continues to be, simply not sufficient numbers of qualified individuals to fill these jobs, notwithstanding the national budget cuts on higher education spending.

By contrast, some parts of the economy did gain from absorbing some African intellectuals who were afraid of committing class suicide – to use the words of Amilcar Cabral – by remaining with their colleagues in academia. Opportunism began to show in some African intellectuals. Some were appointed by the State to senior management positions in State-owned enterprises. These appointments continued into the era of privatization and free-market economy. And when most State-owned enterprises were being privatized or liquidated, many African intellectuals that had sought economic refuge in these institutions had to come out. They quickly reinvented themselves. Some went back to the university. Others became full-time "street" consultants, providing consultancy services in virtually anything and everything, whilst also peddling a bit as academicians on the side or selling some chickens to make ends meet. Some even ran taxi businesses or sold vegetables at their residential homes. A few others even went as far as setting up some private universities. Then there was also a crop of those that just left the country altogether for greener pastures elsewhere or took up political appointments of some sort. Such is the plight of African intellectuals today. In a short essay such as this one, we can only flesh out the salient features. This topic requires a longer monograph to examine most of the pertinent issues. But at least, we have charted a path regarding the trajectory covered thus far by the African intellectual. Things have fallen apart. And the African intellectual is no longer at ease. In many cases, the African intellectual has felt alienated from his profession, leaving him or her hopeless and desperate to seek out para-professional callings.

CHAPTER 75

RE-THINKING THE CASUALIZATION OF ACADEMIC LABOUR

That casualization of labour is often an affront to the concept of job security is a dictum that requires no contest. The ever increasing casualization of labour in Zambia has not spared our State and private universities. Essentially, the idea of casualizing labour is a cost saving strategy employed by many companies, making **work less secure and** changing the working practices so that workers are employed on a freelance and occasional basis instead of being offered full-time and long-term contracts.

Casualization of labour is not only found in developing countries. We are seeing this in the developed world too. Some of the commonest strategies for casaulization of labour include outsourcing. Instead of hiring employees in the domestic labour market, some companies would rather produce their goods in another country where the cost of labour is low. Other companies may ask a shoddy sub-contractor to do the work instead of hiring, say, some full-time and well-qualified permanent employees. Also, the use of temporary staff, with high turn-over rates, is another strategy used in the casualization of labour. Allowing high turn-over of staff can give the company an excuse not to increase salaries and other perks since most of the employees are constantly 'new' to the company and thus do not have much work experience within the company. But the question remains: should casualization of labour be extended to the academic community? Indeed, should we be having constantly 'new' academicians at our universities?

Some proponents of casualization of labour have argued, inter alia, that by forcing companies not to casualize labour, we can end up with a situation where these companies are forced to get rid of most of their workers and retain only a few since the cost of labour will inevitably go up when the companies begin to provide permanent jobs. This argument is premised on the ground that permanent jobs often require better pay and more perks as well as improved job security. It has been argued, for example, that permanent jobs will only help those few permanent employees while the rest will remain worse off given that the latter have no job security or may not even have a job. This school of thought, favouring casualization of labour, postulates that governments, especially those in the developing world, should consider thoughtfully whether they would like to see more job security or more jobs created. But I will defer such arguments to the labour economists.

Here, suffice it to say, what about those sectors of the economy, such as the universities, where academic staff are so specialized and cannot be replaced easily? Do we just treat the university community like any other sector of the economy when it comes to casualization of labour? It is my humble contention that the greatest challenge to socio-economic development today, as many pundits argue, lies not in the absence or lack of finance but in the widening knowledge gap between the North and the South. We must close this gap if Africa is to move forward in the new millennium. Put simply, you can have a lot of money from the donors and have access to financial markets, but as long as you do not know how to invest and utilize that money, you will be back begging at the doorsteps of the donors again. To that end, there is simply no compromise or substitute when it comes to matters of knowledge and erudition. We must build and retain capacity in our universities. Also, we must recognize that from the time that our two leading public universities were established, there have been significant institutional and structural reorganizations that have taken place. And these changes have, in part, affected the working conditions and traditional structures of faculty governance. It is therefore time now to bring to the fore new perspectives and analyses.

Mindful that Zambia now has a third public university and many private universities, it should be noted that the cost of educating an academic or academician is relatively higher than that of educating, say, an ordinary (or average) technocrat in the civil service or private sector. An academician, it must be stressed, is paid to think. He or she must think creatively, systematically, scientifically and innovatively. And the evidence of his or her thought-process must be reflected in scholarly publications. An academician must produce scholarship. And where the academician is a lecturer, he or she must also lecture, while the professor must profess. By contrast, not every civil servant or technocrat in the private or public sector need be, or should always be, creative, systematic, scientific or innovative in their thought-process. And they need not lecture or profess knowledge or even publish any scholarly work. Many a time, these technocrats and civil servants execute duties in accordance with operational manuals, boiler-plates, templates or other laid down procedures and rules at the workplace. I have personally done such work before. So it's nothing to be ashamed of or to get upset about. Many discretionary decisions in industry are considered a preserve of the managers or supervisors. But, such is not the case with academicians. In carrying out their duties, save for mundane administrative-related functions, academicians should enjoy the independence of mind. Remember, they are paid to think! And this independence of mind is what is known as "Academic Freedom." It is only found in academia and is at the heart of the academic profession.

Ideally, it does not matter that an academic is eccentric or a maverick. All that matters is that he or she is able to think and produce valuable knowledge. It comes with the territory of academic freedom. Admittedly, it should come as no surprise that, in some instances, some academicians can have big intellectual egos since academia is supposed to attract only the brightest. Again, it comes with the territory. For one to survive in academia, you must have a thick skin, academically speaking. But a technocrat in industry need not have such a thick skin. He or she can do instead with good networking skills. And he or she cannot afford to be eccentric or a maverick. The technocrat in industry must be a conformist, adhering fanatically to the cultural dictates of his or her employer.

Now, when we casualize academic labour, we de-motivate our academicians because they cannot plan their careers long-term and they will be deprived of their academic freedom. We must understand that the principle of academic freedom is at the fulcrum of their profession and is there to allow independent and objective thinking. Academicians need not worry about the consequences of what they say or write. But when you casualize academic labour, many academicians are forced to conform to the political dictates of the day in order to have their employment contracts renewed. And why retire academicians when they are just beginning to reach their prime of the early to mid-fifties? It really does not make sense. For many an academician, the early to mid-fifties are really the epic years of their career. It is at that time when they will have really mastered their areas of expertise. Now, for us to tell them to go home and rest when they are just beginning to warm up is a serious affront to the raison d'être of academic freedom. As a result, some of our academicians are being disenfranchised in voice to criticize objectively or to offer alternative solutions. They cannot even criticize the administrative systems and structures of their own academic communities, fearing the repercussions from university management on the prospects for renewing their employment contracts.

As a country, we need to revisit the policy of retiring academicians at an early age. They are not civil servants and we cannot be casualizing their labour. All over the world, universities are supposed to attract the brightest brains around. But if we continue casualising academic labour, we cannot expect to attract or retain the brightest brains around. Neither can we stop or reverse the brain-drain. By casualising academic labour, we will end up with sub-standard academicians who have not been able to make a mark in industry and are now seeking refuge in academia by filling in the vacancies created by brain-drain. We must ensure that the right type of incentives is provided to the academic community. But to avoid the moral hazard of some academicians not publishing scholarly work simply because they have been provided with permanent jobs, our Zambian universities should consider seriously the merits of a tenure-track system where our academicians must prove themselves in order to earn tenure. That way, everyone will be busy on their toes.

In concluding, I would like to add that we cannot leave everything to the Zambian Government. Major stakeholders in the Zambian national economy benefiting from graduates of our local universities should also step-up their social responsibility by responding to the challenges of promoting higher education in the country. For example, there should be no reason why some of these mining companies cannot fund a Professorial Chair, say, at the University of Zambia, in Mining Engineering or Metallurgy. Zambia should be an undisputable centre of academic excellence in the mining sector given our resource endowment in the copper mines. Look, the Bank of Zambia has already shown some great leadership in supporting financially a number of academic initiatives at the University of Zambia and the Copperbelt University. Why can't the Zambia Revenue Authority and many other profit-making institutions, including those in the private sector, do the same? We cannot leave everything to government. It's an old and archaic way of doing business. Many companies are benefitting from the casualization of labour being provided by graduates of these universities. So, there is a moral responsibility to give back to these universities. In many countries, major auditing firms and leading commercial banks are known to finance endowed professorships at universities, with the name of the sponsoring institution attached to the professorial position. Why can't we have the same thing in Zambia? Additionally, the Zambian Government should provide some fiscal incentives to initiatives that support our universities so that the public and private sector players can move in to provide assistance in strengthening the higher education sector.

- Kenneth K. Mwenda

CHAPTER 76

WHAT IF MARX WAS RIGHT?

We begin our inquiry by asking: what if Karl Marx was right? Prof. Terry Eagleton pursues this discourse by asking the same question in his recently published book, *Why Marx Was Right*, published by Yale University Press in spring 2011. He argues thoughtfully, "What if all the most familiar objections to Marx's works are mistaken?" Indeed, what would we say?

Mindful that Marxism encompasses Marxian economic theory as well as sociological theory and revolutionary ideas for social change, a central theme underlying the political and economic philosophy of Karl Marx and Friedrich Engels is the concept of class struggle as observed through the prism of historical and dialectical materialism. While dialectical materialism, as the philosophical exposition of Marxist methodological thought, brings together Hegel's dialectics and Ludwig Andreas Feuerbach's materialism, historical materialism, as espoused by Karl Marx, provides a methodological approach to the study of society, economics and history. In the Marxian sense, the workers' cause, expressed through class struggle, continues to play a central role in the understanding of society's development through different historical epochs.

It has been reported that a leading Marxist scholar in the United Kingdom, now deceased, Prof. Ralph Miliband, had in the summer of 1940 visited Karl Marx's grave in Highgate Cemetary in London. There, young Ralph Miliband, as he then was, swore an oath to the workers' cause (Accessed Online: July 7, 2011 (Lipman-Miliband Trust website)). Thereafter, Prof. Miliband never failed the workers in his intellectual discourses. Writing for PBS Newshour, Mosettig (Published Online: September 27, 2010) observes that, when Prof. Ralph Miliband died, he was buried in London's Highgate Cemetary, close by the grave of Karl Marx.

Now, what if both Marx and Miliband were right about the workers' cause? Can we simply dismiss Marx and Miliband on the pretext that their views are outdated and not suited to the current political economic dispensation? Indeed, what if all those African Marxists who gave their lives for the liberation of Africa were right not only in as far as fighting colonialism is or was concerned, but also in dealing with the current developments in a globalised world? Paul D'Amato begins the first chapter of his book, *The Meaning of Marxism* (2006: 6), with a sound warning: "Every so often – usually after a period of economic instability and crisis that has given way to stabilization and growth – some talking head comes along and declares that Marxism is dead and capitalism is the final form of human fulfillment. ...The most common theme is that socialism has failed to make inroads, especially in the United States, due to the prosperity and social mobility that even the lowliest members of society can experience." Whereas it is not disputed that capitalism can produce some isolated anecdotes of such social mobility (*i.e.* specifics only as opposed to the general), D'Amato is on firm ground in his criticism of the proponents of capitalism. Indeed, if we pursued some deductive reasoning here, as opposed to inductive reasoning, we might just ask: what about the majority out there, will they also be able to move upwards on the echelons of social mobility?

Amilcar Cabral postulated in his address, *The Weapon of Theory*, delivered to the first Tri-continental Conference of the Peoples of Asia, Africa and Latin America, in Havana, Cuba, in January 1966 that: "Our refusal, based as it is on concrete knowledge of the socio-economic reality of our countries and on the analysis of the process of development of the phenomenon 'class',... leads us to conclude that if class struggle is the motive force of history, it is so only in a specific historical period. This means that *before* the class struggle — and necessarily *after* it, since in this world there is no before without an after — one or several factors was and will be the motive force of history. It is not difficult to see that this factor in the history of each human group is the *mode of production* — the level of productive forces and the pattern of ownership —

characteristic of that group. Furthermore,...classes themselves, class struggle and their subsequent definition, are the result of the development of the productive forces in conjunction with the pattern of ownership of the means of production. It therefore seems correct to conclude that the level of productive forces, the essential determining element in the content and form of class struggle, is the true and permanent motive force of history."

I have just finished reading Prof. Eagleton's book, *Why Marx Was Right*. Through this book, Prof. Eagleton has delivered a provocative piece of scholarship. The book is a timely study in the aftermath of the recent global economic meltdown. Are there any lessons to learn from Marxism in understanding some of today's political-economic crises? Already, there are several reviews of Prof. Eagleton's book all over the internet and on various academic forums. While many reviews carry a positive message, there are also a few that are expectedly cynical. Understandably, Marxist ideas have never sat well with much of right wing thinking.

While the concept of the proletariat, as it existed during the time when Marx was writing, may have evolved over time, with the traditional worker in the manufacturing industry or factories becoming increasingly marginalized yet vital, and today's skilled employee in the financial and capital markets, including in the information technology industry, take on more visible roles, capitalism has not succeeded at transforming itself. The euphoria with which the concepts of market economy and privatisation were met by many developing countries has now left a bitter taste in the mouths of many. In an article in the *Commonwealth Magazine* titled, "Was Marx Right? It's Not Too Late To Ask" (Published Online: April 8, 2011), Prof. Eagleton observes that: "From the mid-1970s onwards, the Western system underwent some vital changes. There was a shift from traditional industrial manufacture to a 'postindustrial' culture of consumerism, communications, information technology, and the service industry. Small-scale, decentralized, versatile, nonhierarchical enterprises were the order of the day. Markets were deregulated, and the working-class movement was subjected to savage legal and political assault. Traditional class allegiances were weakened, while local, gender, and ethnic identities grew more insistent."

The changes that Prof. Eagleton refers to above only serve to confirm that the capitalist simply succeeded in being craftier by reforming the relations of production under the same capitalist mode of production. This reformation has now brought about such subtle developments as outsourcing and casualisation of labour. Even with these subtleties, the worker remains alienated from: (a) *the work that he produces; (b) working* (*i.e.* from the act of producing); (c) *himself* as a producer; and (d) *other workers* or producers. To resolve these contradictions, Marx observed that the concept of a cooperative where workers themselves owned the cooperative was a viable mechanism through which the workers could no longer be alienated. Also, that way, the capitalist would no longer usurp the *surplus value* deriving from the workers' productivity.

The recent political developments in the Middle East involving public revolts against sitting national governments are indicative of the manifesting contradictions within the prevailing mode of production between the level of development of the forces of production and the relations of production. The increasing levels of poverty and the widening gap between the haves and have-nots, coupled with job insecurity and high unemployment rates, lead us to ask again: what if Marx was right? Indeed, how else can we explain these revolutions? It is a truism that many protests that are going on in different parts of the world are influenced by the underlying material and economic conditions of society. In the United Kingdom, for example, Dian Abbott, a Labour Party lawmaker from Hackney (quoted in the *Express*, Wednesday, August 10, 2011, p. 8 (a publication of the *Washington Post*)), commenting on the August 2011 riots in the southern parts of London, observes: "This did not come from nowhere", and that, "You have kids wondering if their mum will have a job. It's not all about race. But it's about rich and poor." Such striking observations lead us to ask one more time: what if Marx was right? The July 2009 labour unrests in South Africa provide further evidence of why Marx could have been right.

Describing the book, *Why Marx Was Right*, Amazon.com has the following to say on its website

(Accessed Online: July 7, 2011): "In this combative, controversial book, Terry Eagleton takes issue with the prejudice that Marxism is dead and done with. Taking ten of the most common objections to Marxism—that it leads to political tyranny, that it reduces everything to the economic, that it is a form of historical determinism, and so on—he demonstrates in each case what a woeful travesty of Marx's own thought these assumptions are. In a world in which capitalism has been shaken to its roots by some major crises, *Why Marx Was Right* is as urgent and timely as it is brave and candid. Written with Eagleton's familiar wit, humor, and clarity, it will attract an audience far beyond the confines of academia."

One of the independent reviewers of the book, *Why Marx Was Right*, writing on Amazon.com's website, observes (Accessed Online: July 7, 2011): "Terry Eagleton's 'Why Marx Was Right' is a wonderfully written and accessible introduction to the thought of Karl Marx. It is fashionable to dismiss Marxism as 'outdated' or 'irrelevant' as it pertains to contemporary economic and political problems. Eagleton provides a much needed correction to this ignorant viewpoint."

The same commentator continues: "Eagleton takes the many objections voiced by the enemies of Marxism (e.g. Marxism is 'great in theory' but only leads to bloodshed; Marxism is utopian; Marxism reduces everything to economics; Marxism is deterministic, etc.) and demolishes them one by one. Here is Eagleton's take on those who hypocritically condemn Marxism as 'bloodstained': 'Modern capitalist nations are the fruit of a history of slavery, genocide, violence and exploitation every bit as abhorrent as Mao's China or Stalin's Soviet Union. Capitalism, too, was forged in blood and tears; it is just that it has survived long enough to forget about much of this horror, which is not the case with Stalinism and Maoism.' (p. 12-13) Ever argue with someone who claims that socialism is an 'unrealizable utopia'? Here's Eagleton's answer: 'There is good reason that there can never be any complete reconciliation between the individual and society... Marx's claim in the Communist Manifesto about the free self-development of all can never be fully realized. Like all the finest ideals it is a goal to aim at, not a state to be literally achieved... Those who scoff at socialist ideals should remember that the free market can never be perfectly realized either... Some of those who claim that socialism is unworkable are confident that they can eradicate poverty, solve the global warming crisis, spread liberal democracy to Afghanistan and resolve world conflicts by UN resolutions…' (p. 87-88)"

Another independent reviewer of Eagleton's book, also posting on Amazon.com's website, observes (Accessed Online: July 7, 2011): "Eagleton's content is masterful. He does an excellent job of demonstrating how Marx's critics contradict themselves, how they (often intentionally) misunderstand and distort Marx's message into the exact opposite, and how they project many of the faults of capitalism – conformity and rigidity, among others – onto Marxism."

While the practice of Marxism per se, as seen in different parts of the world, and the different ideological interpretations of Marxism could have involved some departures from the scientific theory of Marxism, that in itself does not mean that Marxism is dead or outdated and should be confined to the archives. Even in public international law, not all States follow customary or conventional international law. Some States engage in State practice that departs from accepted norms of public international law, and we must understand that State practice can only qualify as public international law (*i.e.* customary international law) if it involves a widely practiced custom that is supported by the relevant *opinio juris*. By parity of reasoning, not all versions of Marxism have been reflective of the scientific theory of Marxism. Even more comforting is the fact that dialectical materialism remains a well-grounded philosophical guide to the understanding and interpretation of all human history. Perhaps, we can conclude by casting some reflective thought on the Marxian principle of 'labor' as a source of 'all' wealth, dating back to Adam Smith's *The Wealth of Nations*. Closely related to this, the Marxist distinction between 'exploitation' and 'oppression' is not only enlightening but also empowering. But for lack of space in this paper, we will not delve into such intricacies.

CHAPTER 77

GLOBALIZATION AND THE WITHERING AWAY OF NATIONAL CONSCIOUSNESS

It is almost fifty (50) years since Franz Fanon, a black Frenchman with African roots, wrote his famous book, the *Wretched of the Earth*. And 1961 was also the year in which that great philosopher, psychiatrist and revolutionary passed away while receiving medical treatment for cancer at a hospital in Bethesda, Maryland, USA. The *Wretched of the Earth* was not his only major work. He had previously published *Black Skin, White Masks* in 1952 as well as other works. But why bother about Fanon's ideas today when the world has changed so much? Many say socialism is dead and that the cold war is over. Others add that Marxism is a long forgotten and buried ideology, and that what we need now are not political ideologies but wealth creation. It is contended, for example, that not even China can claim today to be communist given its aggressive foreign direct investment policy in developing countries. Indeed, China has embraced private capital, with marked social class divisions within its society. China is today believed to be capitalist. It would be interesting to explore in a separate treatise how China became capitalist from the old communist State that we used to know. It is, however, not the purpose of this paper to indulge in such polemics or to revive the old Marxist debates. History, none the less, has a tendency to repeat itself. And the past often informs the present, while the present informs the future. In an interview with a correspondent of France-Soir on July 22, 1960, Patrice Lumumba was asked, "Some of your political opponents accuse you of being a Communist. Could you reply to that?" And Lumumba answered: "This is a propagandist trick aimed at me. I am not a Communist. The colonialists have campaigned against me throughout the country because I am a revolutionary and demand the abolition of the colonial regime, which ignored our human dignity. They look upon me as a Communist because I refused to be bribed by the imperialists." The charismatic Lumumba echoed further, "We are neither Communists, Catholics nor socialists. We are African nationalists. We reserve the right to choose our friends in accordance with the principle of positive neutrality."

I first read Franz Fanon's *The Wretched of the Earth* during my undergraduate student days at the University of Zambia almost twenty-five (25) years ago. I later lost my copy of that book, together with works of other scholars. Among them, I lost my copies of *Das Kapital* and *Lenin–Selected Works.* Over the years, I have accumulated so many other books, including some which I bought twenty (20) year ago as a graduate student at Oxford. Sometimes, I do not even know where to store all these books. Recently, I decided to buy an e-book reader to save storage space and to enable me purchase electronic copies of some of my old favourite books. And one of the e-books that I decided to buy and to read all over again is Fanon's masterpiece, the *Wretched of the Earth*. In particular, the chapter, *Pitfalls of National Consciousness*, read together with the *Foreword* by Homi K. Bhabha (*i.e.* in the 2004 edition of the book), remains a classic. It examines the psycho-affective condition of the local middle class that succeeded the colonial foreign bourgeoisie. Fanon weaves intelligibly certain aspects of Marxist ideology using a strong professional grounding in psychiatry to understand the psycho-affective condition of the indigenous class of African elites that took over from the white colonialists. Although Fanon's thesis has been criticized by some Marxists for focusing too much on psycho-affective issues rather than the actual material conditions that determine human consciousness, Fanon's contributions cannot be dismissed easily. Even to this day, we continue to see how the local elite in some parts of Africa are influencing the direction of domestic politics, notwithstanding the role played by international capitalists.

Closely related to Fanon's work are the indelible footprints of Amilcar Cabral, a Guinea-Bissauan revolutionary and intellectual luminary. In an address titled, *The Weapon of Theory*, delivered to the first Tri-continental Conference of the Peoples of Asia, Africa and Latin America, held in Havana, Cuba, in January, 1966, Cabral postulated as follows: "Our refusal, based as it is on concrete knowledge of the socio-economic reality of our countries and on the analysis of the process of development of the phenomenon 'class',... leads us to conclude that if class struggle is the motive force of history, it is so only in a specific historical period. This means that *before* the class struggle — and necessarily *after* it, since in this world there is no before without an after — one or several factors was and will be the motive force of history. It is not difficult to see that this factor in the history of each human group is the *mode of production* — the level of productive forces and the pattern of ownership — characteristic of that group. Furthermore,...classes themselves, class struggle and their subsequent definition, are the result of the development of the productive forces in conjunction with the pattern of ownership of the means of production. It therefore seems correct to conclude that the level of productive forces, the essential determining element in the content and form of class struggle, is the true and permanent motive force of history." Interestingly, one of the most cogent analyses of Cabral's work is a 1985 doctoral thesis written **by a Zambian scholar, the late Dr. Angel A.M. Mwenda,** and titled, ***Amílcar Cabral and the Theory of the Revolutionary African Petty-Bourgeoisie.* In that PhD thesis, submitted to and successfully defended at the University of Leeds, UK, Dr. Angel** Mwenda provides an excellent and coherent analysis of Cabral's work.

Though somewhat distinct in their respective ideologies, with Cabral espousing stronger Marxist-Leninist sentiments, both Cabral and Fanon fought in the wars of independence. Fanon fought in the Algerian revolution war whereas Cabral led African nationalist movements in Guinea-Bissau and the Cape Verde Islands. Cabral was sadly assassinated in 1973, a few months before Guinea-Bissau declared unilateral independence. These men were not just simple freedom fighters. They were actually leading intellectuals who believed in the nexus between theory and practice, writing and articulating erudite scholarship as well as leading policy dialogue on critical revolutionary issues.

In Southern Africa, Mozambique gave the world Eduardo Chivambo Mondlane who served as President of the Mozambican Liberation Front (FRELIMO) from 1962, the year that FRELIMO was founded in Tanzania, until his assassination in 1969. These were great men. They read widely, articulated issues intelligibly, and also wrote erudite and intellectually challenging works on the issue of class struggle in Africa as well as that of de-colonization. Mondlane was himself a PhD holder from a leading university in the USA, despite being engaged deeply in the fight for Mozambique's independence. In leading the liberation movement, Mondlane committed 'class suicide' in the Cabral sense, forgoing all the luxuries that he could have gained personally had he been an Uncle Tom to the Portuguese. Amilcar Cabral's theory of class suicide postulates that the petty-bourgeoisie has to make sacrifices for the class struggle against the imperialists. This entails, *inter alia*, forgoing a lot of materialistic and bourgeois tendencies that are likely to be in conflict with the interests of the proletariat.

With the demise of Mondlane came Samora Machel. Angola, too, had its battles. But that is a different story. Suffice it to say, one just has to read some of the speeches of Samora Machel. The continent was burning with issues-based debates. It was not just a question of contending ideologies of socialism against capitalism, but there was also a great awakening of the 'national' question among the masses. This awakening or consciousness was an African renaissance against imperialism. And the inspiring story of one Patrice Lumumba against the Belgians and their Western allies in the Congo DRC is one that has not been told fully to our young generation. These were men of courage and character. Their ending filled the hearts of many an African with hope. Even as Martin Luther King Jr. proceeded with his message of peaceful protest during the civil rights era, and as Malcolm X articulated the ideology of radicalism in order for man to win freedom, both Martin and Malcolm knew that they had equally well-enlightened brothers on the African continent dealing with similar challenges. Young Steve Biko at the University of Natal, studying for his medical degree, lost his life while pushing for equal rights.

Many universities in Africa were at the time incubators of revolutionary ideas and knowledge, with intellectuals such as Walter Rodney and many others committing more intellectual ink to paper to fight underdevelopment in Africa. Rodney, a native of Guyana, came to take up an academic appointment at the University of Dar-es-Salaam. Like Che Guevara's contribution in the Congo DRC, Walter Rodney came to Africa not as a foreign investor or missionary. These men were progressives against imperialism. And Africa was thriving. The colonialists had been overcome but were still hanging on to the last thread of hope in the name of neo-colonialism. And Franz Fanon was just beginning to write on these and many other issues when he passed on.

Today, with globalization coming on the scene, the political-economic landscape has changed somewhat. Although the agenda is the same, the approach is different. One thing, however, remains true. Fanon had rightly predicted that much of the local elite, in crying out for national consciousness, were only waiting to take over from the white colonizers. Indeed, not much has changed. We can draw parallels between the early post-colonial African State and the politics of today when many intellectuals and elites cry foul that there is need to have a new government. Whereas change may be good, change for the sake of change is not helpful. In the Marxian sense, change must involve a leap from quantity into quality, with fewer but qualitatively stronger opposition parties that are interested not just in the superficial change of political faces. Thus, real change must be about improving the living conditions of the people on the ground, and not about enriching a few elites.

The internationalization of capital, or globalization, as it is commonly known, has had many effects on the doctrine of State sovereignty. Today, it is almost illusory or utopian to talk of national consciousness when faced with globalization. The strategic de-nationalization of State sovereignty has political-economic ramifications on the concept of national consciousness. Globalization robs a nation of a broad-based indigenous national ideology. The so-called 'global interests', determined and defined in the West, take precedence in the form of a dominant foreign ideology spearheaded by the international capitalist. With globalization, there is ideological fragmentation internally within many developing countries as some nations begin to regress into tribal politics and ethnic psycho-affective sentiments, leaving room for a thriving dominant foreign ideology. Political parties begin to be formed along tribal lines as national consciousness withers away. The concept of tribe takes precedence over that of nation. This change favours mainly the interests of the international capitalist and those of their local surrogates. Political strategies are short-changed for simple and short-lived tactics. And the pace-maker of the international political economy shifts the debate from class struggle to that of fighting global terrorism, drawing attention away from the increasing levels of poverty amongst the inhabitants of the underdeveloped world. At the same time, the local elite in the poorer nations, being a reactionary and regressive social class and having no intent to champion any major cause predicated on national consciousness, are in it for themselves. It then becomes clear that Fanon's ideas are not dead or outdated. The pitfalls of national consciousness are still with us.

Africa has been a testing ground of many different political ideologies and development strategies. Post-colonial African States have experimented with different development strategies, including the accommodation, reorganization and transformation development strategies. Upon attaining political independence, some African States sought to transform their country's socio-economic institutions and structures completely, so as to break away from the yoke of colonialism, while others sought to retain much of the colonial socio-economic foundations, making only modest reorganizations to their institutional and structural set-ups. Yet, there is also another group of post-colonial African States that opted instead to accommodate almost all the socio-economic institutions and structures inherited from their colonial masters. Of the three groups, much of the transformationist camp embraced Marxist-Leninist ideology. By contrast, in the reorganizationist camp, a convoluted brand of socialism and some indigenous African philosophy, focusing on Afro-centric policies of economic development, began to emerge. The convoluted brand of socialism, with many of its proponents confusing State capitalism for scientific socialism, came to be known as African socialism. And African socialism included Ujamaa from Tanzania,

Humanism from Zambia and Négritude *from Senegal. Closely related to this was the idea of Pan-Africanism espoused by Ghana's Nkhrumah. Although inspired by scientific socialism under the ideology of Marxism-Leninism, Pan-Africanism never really applied itself seriously to proletariat class struggle.* In the post-colonial African States that pursued the accommodationist approach, the concept of a free-market economy was being inherited from the former colonial powers.

Over the years, Africa has weathered so many political economic storms, riding through the rough tides of massive privatizations into the era of globalization. In addition, different modernization theories, including theories of industrialization, as well as policies of economic diversification, export promotion and import substitution, have been propounded to try to understand the so many unanswered questions about Africa's economic quagmire. From the works of Samir Amin and many other Africanists to parallel developments in Latin America, as evidenced, for example, in Andre Gunder Frank's dependency theory, many Africanists have sought to find lasting solutions to Africa's underdevelopment. The liberal Africanists have not been shy to even invoke such sources as W.W Rostow's non-communist manifesto on the stages of economic growth as well as Joseph Schumpeter's theory of economic development. Even as economics becomes an increasingly mathematical and quantitative science, the major economic hurdles facing Africa remain unresolved.

In the United Kingdom, Daniel Johnson (*Standpoint,* Online: October, 2010), albeit writing cynically on Ralph Miliband, one of the intellectual luminaries of Marxist persuasion in that country, observes: "A century after Marx's arrival, his most devoted disciples were still convinced that the master was correct: once capitalism collapsed under the weight of its contradictions, the British would embrace a socialist revolution. One of the most prominent of these fundamentalists was Ralph Miliband. ...Like Marx, Ralph was a refugee; unlike Marx, he was fleeing persecution not for being a socialist but simply for being Jewish. Aged 16, he arrived on the eve of the Battle of Britain. Unlike most of his family and friends on the Continent, he survived the war and the Holocaust, but it never occurred to him to admire the political system of the country in which he had found sanctuary. The first place he visited in London was Highgate Cemetery, where he stood before Marx's grave and swore a clenched-fist oath of allegiance. For the next half a century, he never wavered in his determination..."

But such cynicism is not helpful when all it does is to try to deflect attention from the real issues on the ground. In many African countries, the petty-bourgeois middle class that is constantly trying to wrestle political power from the governing class is a mixture of opportunistic tendencies and some modest reformists. There is, however, not much difference between those that are governing now and those that want to govern. The opposition may throw accusations of corrupt practices at government structures, yet some of the opposition leaders have themselves served in the same government that they accuse of being corrupt. We must understand that corruption cannot be fought by those that benefit from it or those that have vested interests in it. Neither can corruption be fought by those that expect to benefit from it when they come to power. Corruption can only be fought by those that loathe it, with no desire to benefit from it whatsoever. These are the pitfalls of national consciousness. Matters of the stomach often take centre-stage when corrupt politicians ascend to power. And the nation is then drawn into the Dunning-Kruger effect where we begin to see some unskilled politicians, due to their cognitive bias, making poor decisions and reaching erroneous conclusions. Lacking magnanimity, these politicians' pride or incompetence denies them the meta-cognitive ability to appreciate their mistakes.

And as a result of this illusory superiority in rating their ability as above average, or as much higher than it actually is, the unskilled politicians will pontificate on complex issues that they hardly even understand, while the really learned and highly skilled underrate their own abilities due to an illusory inferiority complex manifested through what seems like the lack of self-confidence. In these parts of the world, the Dunning-Kruger effect often shows up when the average minds get confident, while the intelligent get doubtful. It is the Dunning-Kruger effect that helps to explain why some populist politicians, despite being unenlightened on many matters of governance, often hold out as experts and, also, why the electorate even votes for them. Such politicians only serve to fortify the pitfalls of national consciousness, entrenching deeply tribal and ethnic divisions. Charles Darwin once said: "Ignorance more frequently begets confidence than does knowledge." And Bertrand Russell made a closely related remark, observing that: "One of the painful things about our time is that those who feel certainty are stupid, and those with any imagination and understanding are filled with doubt and indecision."

CHAPTER 78

UNIVERSITY LEAGUE TABLES AND THE RANKING OF AFRICAN UNIVERSITIES

The recent ranking of universities worldwide has attracted much debate and controversy both within and outside academia. In particular, the credibility and reliability of some of the methodologies used to arrive at these rankings has been a major source of concern. Why are many universities in Africa not listed amongst the best universities in the world? A causal walk through most of the university rankings published on the internet lists only one or two universities from Africa. And, in our part of the world, Zambia, to be specific, we now have a number of public and private universities. Of these, only the University of Zambia (UNZA) appears on the rankings that are periodically published on the internet. Even so, UNZA appears not on the global rankings, but only on the continental rankings for Africa. In a 2010 ranking of top African universities, Webometrics ranked the following five (5), in their order of standing, as the best universities in Africa:

(a) University of Cape Town (UCT); (b) University of Pretroria (UP); (c) Stellenbosch University; (d) University of Witwatersrand (Wits); and (e) Rhodes University. These five are all South African universities. Understandably, South Africa has a stronger economy than many other countries in Africa. Our own UNZA ranks somewhere down the hierarchy as number sixty-seven (67), falling behind even much lesser known institutions.

The challenges facing higher education in Africa are gigantic and monumental. But we cannot give up. Even when universities in Africa are marginalized and not afforded decent space on university league tables, we still cannot give up. We must view university league tables as an opportunity rather than as a threat. If we can reinvigorate and strengthen our higher education system in Zambia, our universities will easily move up on the rankings. A paradigm shift here could occur where we are able to turn adversity into opportunity. Many individuals have a tendency to rank almost everything in life. For example, we sometimes rank men. At other times, we rank women. Don't we all know of many famous beauty pageants in the world today? We also have many singing contests. And we have several weight lifting and body-building contests. We also rank the best cars in town. And we rank the richest people in the world. We even rank boxers and athletes, or how nationals of a particular country are known to consume more beers than nationals of other countries. Very soon, we will be ranking churches and pastors as well as mansions and farms. As a people, human beings worldwide are obsessed with rankings. In Zambia, for example, many often worry about the ranking of our national soccer team. And in some foreign cultures, some people even rank toilet paper, preferring that which will not cause them harm or injury when they are at work.

In 2007, a famous ranking of African universities published Online by Topratings.wordpress.com listed the following five (5), in their order of standing, as the best universities on the African continent: (a) UCT; (b) Rhodes University; (c) Wits; (d) UP; and (e) Stellenbosch University. Again, these are all South African universities. And they comprise the same group of universities in the Webometrics ranking noted above. However, in the 2007 rankings compiled by Topratings.wordpress.com, our very own UNZA ranked slightly higher at number fifty-six (56). That said, instead of complaining about the inherent bias in the rankings, we need to understand what drives these rankings and how best we can position our institutions to get a better ranking. Others might argue that, after all, who cares about these dubious rankings! But we must care because the rankings have a signaling effect to the market in terms of public perception on the quality of education provided by our universities. Propaganda, like ideology, can shape or determine the legitimacy (and not just the "legality") of an institution as well as the public perception on the quality of education provided by that institution. Therefore, we need to work our way strategically in influencing the opinions of consumers and the public on such matters.

In general, the system of ranking universities, like that of ranking university faculties or academic programs, is very pedestrian and has a marketing and commercial function imbedded in it. Rankings contribute to the "commodification of higher education". Although many prospective students tend to apply to universities ranked highly on university league tables, most of the league tables have been widely criticised as not reflecting an objective, systematic and scientific ranking of universities (see, for example, Mwenda, 2007: 63-78; and Obasi, 2008: Online). The league tables, however, can persuade some prospective funding bodies to channel their financial resources to top rated research universities. Examining the role of university league tables, Obasi (2008: Online) observes that 'the ranking of universities today is traceable to the pioneer efforts of the Carnegie Commission on Higher Education in 1970 when it started the classification of US Colleges and Universities. But the present-day ranking of universities in a form of league table at national levels was started in 1983 by the US News and World Report, and was later followed in 1993 by The Times of London that concentrated on institutions in the United Kingdom.' According to Obasi (2008: Online), such ranking of universities at national levels (and until very recently at the international level) is a logical outcome of the functional transformation of universities towards meeting the demands of a global knowledge economy that ushered in a new era (or paradigm) of "academic capitalism". Obasi (2008: Online) observes that universities in Africa are as usual at the crossroads in the face of the challenges posed by the world university rankings that confront them with a double tragedy of experiencing a "mission in crisis" and "crisis of mission". For example, not many know that the recent ranking of universities internationally by Webometrics has been based primarily on the criterion of "web presence and visibility" of the universities (Obasi, 2008: Online). As such, 'one general and fundamental concern that have emerged from the issue of global rankings is that no single university in Africa has made it into the first top 200 universities in the world league table published by the *Times Higher Education Supplement* so far. Again, only four universities (all from the Republic of South Africa) were able to make it into the top 500 universities in the *Academic Ranking of World Universities (ARWU) by the Institute of Higher Education, Shanghai Jiao Tong University (SJTU)*. This disturbing revelation raised and still raises genuine concern about the level of perceived quality of some universities in Africa. But it also raises some critical questions that have to do with the ranking itself. First, why and how are these rankings done? Secondly, how valid and reliable are the ranking methodologies? And lastly, what is the motive of the entire ranking exercise?' (Obasi, 2008: Online)

Closer to home, why are institutions such as UNZA fairing badly on league tables of African universities? Established a few years after Zambia attained political independence in 1964, UNZA is undisputedly the most well-established and the most widely recognized Zambian university internationally, followed by Copperbelt University (CBU, which resulted from the merger of what was then known as the University of Zambia at Ndola Campus (UNZA-NDO) and the Zambia Institute of Technology (ZIT) in the late 1980s). Both UNZA and CBU are public universities. The third public university in Zambia is Mulungushi University, established only a few years ago. Thereafter, a slew of recently set up private universities follows. Yet, UNZA is the only Zambian university that features on such university rankings as Webometrics' top hundred (100) universities in Africa. But, wait a minute – we are not here judging the other Zambian universities, based on the idea that they are not ranked anywhere in the world. That is beside the point. We know full well that university rankings generally are quite subjective. The issue rather is why are African universities, and our own Zambian universities, in particular, not fairing that well on these university league tables?

Although most of our universities in Zambia are legally authorized by the relevant Government Ministry to provide university education, they can hardly boast of decent infrastructure to sustain and support the delivery of quality university education. For example, from the comfort of my home, I can easily search for a book in the libraries of many universities in South Africa, using their publicly accessible free Online library catalogues. But I can hardly conduct such search for a book at UNZA Library or CBU Library. Yet, even small universities like Swaziland and Lesotho have such IT facilities at their libraries. Be that as it may, in Zambia, the 'new' private universities appear less bureaucratic, and with minimal red-tape, than UNZA and CBU in the way they conduct business. And, unlike UNZA and CBU, they hardly have 'closures'. The new universities also seem to respond more quickly to market demands for higher education. By contrast, UNZA and CBU, although having better human capital resources and infrastructure, often struggle to meet the challenges of a changing business environment. And so, the question remains: why are our African universities fairing so badly on university league tables? There are a number of factors that can help to address the issue. Chief among them are the following:

(i) A good number of university rankings on the internet are based primarily on data that is publicly available on the internet e.g. via the respective universities' websites. So, if a university is slow in updating and maintaining the contents of its website, or if the actual design of that website is uninspiring and poor, the university might attract negative perceptions from those that deem themselves entitled to rank African universities. Much of the ranking business is about web visibility and presence. The assessors or rankers hardly ever visit these universities. They rely mainly on secondary data through print and electronic media. And the issue of web visibility points to a need for most of our universities to have effective strategies of knowledge management. A notable interface in today's world of IT between the consumer and the university is the university website. Indeed, a website can be an effective marketing tool. If, for example, staff profiles of academic members of the university are not well-documented, and the institution's website is poorly maintained, without any useful information on research output of the academic staff, obviously someone surfing the internet is left to wonder whether there is much research activity going on apart from teaching. The three core functions of an academic, in their order of priority, as I contend, are: (i) scholarly research and publication; (ii) teaching excellence; and (iii) administrative responsibilities and community service. And if we understand this point clearly, we will then be able to appreciate the correlation between good teaching and effective learning. And information pertaining to both has to be captured and marketed to the consumers strategically in order to not only gain favorable rankings, but also to attract research funding. If potential financiers out there do not know much about what you do, how do you expect them to finance your activities? And for public universities especially, they have to be pro-active to reach out to the business community so as to diversify from a mono-culture of state subsidies and government funding. Indeed, African universities should be making efforts to attract consultancies from the private sector. These consultancies often go to individual academics for their own personal profit, as well as to some private consulting firms. Yet, African universities have the human capital to deliver in such areas but for the poor management of institutional affairs and the lack of innovation and entrepreneurial zeal amongst the administrators.

(ii) Another useful example of how a well-maintained and updated website can help to position a university favorably relates to the showcasing of talent within the university community as well as in the alumni base. I was not surprised when Harvard University Law School highlighted, as a main news item on its website, the election of Barack Obama as President of the United States. President Obama and First Lady, Michelle Obama, are both Harvard Law School graduates. And President Obama was the first Black law student to serve as Editor-in-Chief of the prestigious Harvard Law Review. One would have thought that our very own UNZA Law School should have been proud of showcasing on its website one of its own outstanding alumnus, the late President Levy Mwananwasa, who was also a State Counsel, when he won the elections as President of the Republic of Zambia. Levy was and remains the first UNZA graduate to have held the highest office in the land – that is, the office of the President of the Republic of Zambia. The point being made here is that UNZA should have capitalized on the opportunity of recognizing President Mwanawasa as one of its outstanding alumni who had ascended to the highest office in the land. Through such measures, you quickly buy-in stakeholder interest of the party you are recognizing so that when the institution requires more funding, that person can lend you an ear. The politics of confrontation against the State as well as those of antagonizing the Government, over each and every small item, are politics of the past. Today, we should be thinking in terms of opportunities, as opposed to threats, when partnering with such key stakeholders as the Government. We have to understand that, although academic freedom is important in academia, a public institution such as UNZA is supported primarily through Government budgetary allocations. And it does not mean when you are honoring someone then you are selling out on your principles of intellect and academic freedom. Equally, not every UNZA graduate that becomes a Head of State deserves such honor. Levy was not only the first UNZA graduate to become the President of the Republic of Zambia. He also had behind him a decent record of professional competence and standing. And that is what makes a difference. Look, it did not have to take a foreign university to confer Mwanawasa with an Honorary Doctorate. As Zambians, aside from honoring our local musicians and artists, we are often quick at honoring people from other parts of the world who may not even have scored as much as Mwanawasa did either locally in Zambia or, at least, in the international community. The principle being espoused here is that even in a family, the strength of a family will be known by the strength of its family members. Indeed, the strength of a family does not come from outside. It comes from within. In short, you must find and claim a champion from amongst yourselves. Your champion will not come from outside or from your neighbor's home, but from amongst yourselves.

(iii) While UNZA and CBU have done a commendable job in respectively forging academic links and partnerships with universities in many parts of the world, it is not clear that the new private universities in Zambia have the capacity to do so. Although some of these institutions are satellites of foreign academic institutions, and others have collaborative links and partnerships locally with professional bodies in Zambia, the international stature of a university is expected to go beyond that. The accreditation and membership of these universities in various international and regional forums should be a must. Indeed, you have to hang out with the big boys if you want people to know that you are a big boy. It's that simple. Once you are in the group of the big boys, the peer mechanism within that group will signal to the world that you are now part of the big boys. Also, given the massive brain-drain from a number of African universities, mainly due to poor incentives, our universities should find innovative and flexible ways in which to attract external examiners and visiting professors from leading universities internationally. Unlike in the case of retaining full-time or adjunct academic staff, some of these initiatives do not require money. You can advertise or invite someone for a non-stipendiary appointment, especially an eminent and distinguished scholar. And you are likely to find many willing partners. I speak from experience, having taught in universities in the UK, the US, and

South Africa. It can work if only we can change our mindset in the way we do business. Now, the attraction of these eminent persons to a university for periodical teaching or research should come with a condition that in their scholarly work they should cite their affiliation with the respective Zambian university where they are affiliated. Here, if you are dealing with a big name in academic circles, you know already that you have captured an excellent marketing tool simply by having that person's name associated with your university. These are just some quick thoughts, but a large volume of work has been dedicated to this topic in my latest book – *K.K. Mwenda and G.N. Muuka (eds), The Challenge of Change in Africa's Higher Education in the 21st Century, (Amherst, NY: Cambria Press, 2009).*

CHAPTER 79

EMPLOYERS OFTEN RESPOND TO UNIVERSITY BRAND NAMES

In these trying times when the country is witnessing all sorts of self-professed political pundits, wannabes and charlatans, busy misleading wananchi just to secure their votes in the forthcoming Presidential and General elections, I seek to excuse myself. I choose instead to take a detour into an avenue that is more critical to human development than the usual ubiquitous politicking and maneuvers by those that want to secure their political fortunes. It is expected that, as time draws closer to the elections, different folks and strokes will be jostling, hustling, deceiving and betraying one another, all in the hope of securing their political fortunes. Indeed, this is what happens when poverty of the mind is too deeply entrenched in the politics of the day. It becomes a matter of personal survival. It's a time to perfect lies.

In this article, I want to address a very fundamental area of human development, namely, the higher education sector in Zambia. At the outset, it must be noted that the dictates of globalization, or rather the internationalization of capital, if I may, to use a euphemism, have brought about a paradigm shift in the way we do business. Whilst many are preoccupied with the politics of the elections in Zambia this year, I am concerned mainly with the future of higher education and its implications on human resource development in the country. But I am not saying elections are not important. It's the underlying politics that are unattractive. There is more to life than living off politics financially and materially. No wonder many an African politician are often not too keen to retire. What we are seeing in Tunisia, Egypt and many other countries should come as no surprise. Only noble and distinguished individuals like Neslson Mandela can rise above such selfishness and pettiness of not wanting to retire from politics.

Turning to the higher education sector in Zambia, we hear complaints from various sectors of society that some employers in Zambia prefer recruiting or employing graduates of certain Zambian universities to those from other local universities. In any event, this experience is neither surprising nor novel. The privatization of higher education has seen a plethora of many private universities spring up across the country. Suddenly, university education has become good business. But, then, why are some employers shunning graduates of some private universities? We surely don't have all the answers until we talk to each and every employer concerned. Be that as it may, we can hypothesize based on the responses gathered from many stakeholders in the higher education sector. These responses are not unique to Zambia, but apply also, almost mutatis mutandis, to many other developing countries with a liberalized higher education sector. In this respect, countries such as Kenya, Tanzania and Uganda are only but a few good examples.

Back in the days, a friend of mine working for the mines (ZCCM) in Zambia once told me of how engineers educated abroad, say, in the UK had better career prospects with ZCCM than their counterparts educated locally at the University of Zambia (UNZA). I dismissed this view as merely subjective inductive reasoning based on a few isolated examples. But with time, I began to see also how the accountancy qualification from the UK-based Association of Chartered Certified Accountants (ACCA) was being perceived by many employers as more useful than the Bachelors of Accountancy (BAcc) degree programme offered by Copperbelt University (CBU). Experience shows that BAcc graduates, among many others, are the ones that go on to study for ACCA, and not the other way round. But, I cannot profess to be an expert on accountancy studies. I am only highlighting what the experience has been based on my own observations and interactions. I concede, however, that there could be some good reasons for the elevated status of the ACCA qualification over the BAcc degree, but such reasons have not been publicly promulgated. In any event, that argument is beside the point. All I am saying is that such apparent prejudices will always be there. Perception matters a lot. So, as long as the new universities in Zambia do not brand themselves strategically in the marketplace, a number of their graduates, even good ones, will continue to have difficulties securing stable jobs. Branding is an important aspect of marketing. Professor Michael Porter of Harvard Business School sets forth three generic strategies which help to confirm this view of marketing. The three generic strategies relate to cost leadership, differentiation and focus. These strategies must be well understood along with the advantages and risks inherent with each strategic option.

The higher education sector is a service sector. We must understand the environment in which these universities operate. It's not just a question of setting up a university or getting a license from the relevant Government Ministry to operate a university. There should be more strategic thinking in the background on matters such as public perception, competition, market share, capital, and human resources, as well as other threats or weaknesses facing an institution. Ideally, branding of a product or service involves a paradigm shift in the way customers view that product or service. A university must distinguish itself through research excellence and quality teaching. Also, there should be a sustained focus in the area in which an institution is directing itself, with minimal distractions. And the cost implications of such an approach should be holistically and systemically internalised. Names such as Oxford, Cambridge, Warwick, Harvard, Yale, MIT, Stanford, Sorbonne, Wharton Business School or INSEAD did not just spring up from nowhere. There was obviously a lot of thinking done and time spent in building these brands. And the same goes for powerful clothing brands like Gucci, Louis Vuitton, Versace and so forth. A lot of strategic thinking has gone into these brands. Likewise, a number of our universities should consider moving away from the old concept of Strategic Planning into what Professor Henry Mintzberg of McGill University, Canada, calls Strategic Thinking. As Mintzberg observes, strategic planning is about analysis (i.e., breaking down a goal into steps, designing how the steps may be implemented, and estimating the anticipated consequences of each step) whereas strategic thinking is about synthesis, about using intuition and creativity to formulate an integrated perspective, a vision, of where the university should be heading. The latter is what is missing with many of our universities, old and new.

Not too long ago, we saw how some law graduates from a private university within Zambia won a court case in which they had sought the court's intervention to enable them to register for admission to the Zambia Institute of Advanced Legal Education (ZIALE) for the learner legal practitioners' course. Legislation has now been passed to codify the court's reasoning in that case. Initially, ZIALE was unwilling to admit these students. One would suspect that, perhaps, ZIALE was afraid that many graduates of these new private universities had not yet cut their teeth in law or that they would not meet the professional standards expected on the ZIALE learner legal practitioners' course. But it was all about perception since, until recently, there was no body or forum responsible for the accreditation of law schools in Zambia.

To change perception, we must influence the client's view. Power alone may not immediately win us much. But once we influence perception, we have a greater chance of succeeding. And that is how brand-names are built. They influence the clients' perception. In a sense, influence is a subtle form of power. Currently, State universities in Zambia, like those in many other African countries, are perceived by many employers to be producing better equipped graduates than private universities. Mindful that some superficial cynic might say, "Hey, wait a minute. UNZA and CBU have been around for a long time. These new private universities are still young, privately funded and should be given a chance...", I am awake to such cynicism. In response, I would ask: "How come we have some private hospitals in some cities within Zambia that do better than some public hospitals?" Where is the difference here? Is the health sector not a service sector just like the higher education sector? Time for excuses is over. We need a vibrant and well-regulated higher education sector. And notwithstanding arguments of nepotism and corruption in the hiring of fresh university graduates, many private universities should pull up their socks if they want employers in Zambia and elsewhere to accept their graduates as readily employable. It is not surprising that much of the fuss about the accreditation and ranking of universities has now gained momentum in the developing world after the privatization of higher education. The challenge is on how we respond to the present for us to be able to embrace the future.

- *Kenneth K. Mwenda*

CHAPTER 80

CHANGING LANDSCAPE OF PROFESSIONAL CAREERS IN A GLOBALIZED WORLD

Back in the days, when I took my undergraduate studies at the University of Zambia (UNZA), there were no computers for students. We all wrote our student essays on hand-written scripts. And there was hardly any room for greater margins of error if you had to get a good grade. Preparing different drafts and revisions was almost unthinkable. You had one good shot, and it had better be good. I hear even some of the best notable professors in our time wrote their PhD theses and books that way, giving great care to accuracy and precision since there was minimal room for error. In those days, you could only make a reasonable number of revisions to your academic work, if at all that was possible, given that there were no computers akin to the modern day cut-and-paste culture. Also, it was too costly to find someone to type your work or to make frequent revisions to the same. For example, to prepare the final work of your dissertation or thesis, you had to run it on stencil before printing it. But with modern technology today, all this is history. Type-writers and stencils are long gone. And those who were trained to work with type-writers and stencils have had to adapt quickly. You only have to ask my professional friends and colleagues in the journalism field.

Back in the days, there were no cell-phones or email facilities. We simply had to rely on 'oral tradition' forms of communication and letters. Occasionally, one would get the luxury of using a 'land-phone', as we would call it then. I first heard of a fax machine, for example, when I was about to graduate in the mid to late 1980s. I kept wondering what in the world it was, but did not want to expose my ignorance. Even credit cards and debit cards were a myth. Friends and colleagues would sit for accountancy (and/or commerce) exams where they had to, among other things, describe a credit card or debit card without ever having seen one before. Times have now changed. Many people have plastic in their wallets. Technology has ushered in a new era. Now, I can even surf the internet and check my webmail from the comfort of my bedroom using iPaD-2 or Blackberry. And I can even read e-books on my Nook while taking a leisure walk in the park. Such is the wizardry of technology.

The strategic de-nationalization of State sovereignty, known today by many as globalization, has transformed the way we do business. Globalization has also unfortunately affected many people's careers. For example, the role that an office secretary used to play back in the days has now been transformed into that of an executive assistant or special assistant, retaining only a few of the well-trained secretaries. The boss or manager can now type his or her work, especially when it comes to assignments that require his or her technical and specialized in-put. The executive assistant and the personal assistant are left to handle less technical work such as scheduling meetings for the boss and following-up on many other office chores. Indeed, today's boss is expected to know how to use all office machinery, including a fax machine and a computer. But what does this frenzy with capital intensive technology mean? It means job opportunities for many professionals are increasingly becoming threatened with the introduction into the labour market of more capital intensive technology. But, then, what do we mean by the term 'profession' or 'professionals'?

The American Heritage Dictionary defines the word 'profession' as 'an occupation, such as law, medicine, or engineering that requires considerable training and specialized study.' However, in our every day parlance, we often refer to many occupations or careers as professions. Thus, for our immediate purposes, the term includes academic disciplines that are not professions, strictly speaking. Indeed, while a profession should be capable of being practiced only by those that are professionally qualified to practice that profession, and whereas a profession is often regulated by a regulatory body that issues guidelines for professional practice and license, not every academic discipline enjoys such exclusivity. We must understand that even prostitution, as a profession, enjoys the exclusivity of those in the practice since only prostitutes have the courage and guts to prostitute.

In today's world, we are quickly moving away from labour intensive technology. Even for professionals such as lawyers, with increasing technological advancements pertaining to electronic apps, we will soon start seeing inventions of many apps that can easily generate all kinds of legal documents for which lawyers charge so much money. And this is already happening, as we speak. In many developed countries, for example, standard templates for commercial contracts are being developed and digitized, with the option of customizing these documents, such that you do not need a lawyer to prepare or draft a legal agreement. Even in the field of medicine, we are seeing many drive-through health clinics or pharmacies that are similar to such fast-food places as McDonalds. Except for complex ailments that require proper diagnosis and treatment within a hospital environment, many patients are likely to find it cheaper to get their medication off the counter, via the internet or through a drive-through clinic. Already Viagra can be procured easily over the internet. We are living in fast-changing times. More and more professional jobs are being threatened with the development of more new capital-intensive technology every day.

In general, professional skills are not expected to be easily substitutable or replaceable. But with the changing landscape of professional careers in a globalized world, this may not necessarily hold true all the time. Many professional jobs are being outsourced. And the casualization of labour is becoming a common trend in many labour markets. So, we have to think futuristic in order to remain competitive. To put issues in context, many young people that I have mentored over the years have asked me this question: "Do I have to do a Masters degree after I complete my undergraduate studies?" There is no one-size-fits-all answer to this question. A more cursory look would suggest that an individual does not need to do a postgraduate degree in order to practice a profession. Although many professionals do, however, proceed to get postgraduate degree qualifications, a first degree alone, plus professional certification, suffices to practice a profession, notwithstanding that an individual with a first degree only may not be as competitive as a holder of postgraduate qualifications.

In contrast to professional fields, in academic fields that are not professions in the strict sense, it is almost imperative that an individual goes all the way up to PhD level, or at least up to Masters level. In these fields, there is no professional certification or licensing. The individual just has to distinguish himself or herself through, say, postgraduate education. We are, however, mindful that there are some nuances that ought to be spelt out here. In certain professional fields, such as medicine, especially for those medical doctors that are educated in Commonwealth countries, prior to getting certified to practice medicine, they will have earned three Bachelor degrees, namely, a Pre-Medicine Bachelors degree, a Bachelors degree in Medicine and a Bachelors degree in Surgery. Likewise, their counterparts in the US follow a similar tradition, although the latter two Bachelor degrees are referred to jointly as the Doctor of Medicine (MD) degree. Closely related to this, at almost all American Bar Association (ABA) accredited Law Schools, the study of law alone, excluding the non-accredited post JD degrees, takes three years after completing a four years Bachelors degree. So, typically, an American trained lawyer will take seven (7) years of university education to obtain his or her Juris Doctor (JD) degree whose equivalent in many Commonwealth countries is the Bachelor of Laws (LLB) degree, whether offered as an undergraduate or graduate degree.

While experiential learning can at times be a good substitute for formal education, and that there are some folks out there who feel strongly that academic degrees alone will not equip you with the relevant managerial or technical skills in times when jobs are hard to find, one cannot place his or her hopes on simply gaining experiential learning without acquiring first some relevant qualifications on which to base that experience. Experience must be grounded in sound and relevant theory in order to remain meaningful. To contend with globalization and the changing nature of the professional job market, many professionals have to employ some form of strategic thinking. For example, today's accountant cannot afford to be just an accountant. He or she must understand the evolving trends in the job market and how he or she will be able to adapt to these challenges.

To remain competitive today, one cannot stick rigidly to a single or monolithic area of specialization when the job market is volatile and not looking certain. Systems Thinking implores us to continuously evaluate and assess our strengths and weaknesses against some of the options, opportunities, threats, costs and risks that are in the market. We need to audit trends in the market to be able to generate viable scenarios through scenario planning. In short, we need to engage in strategic thinking, as opposed to strategic planning. If, for example, there are no jobs for lawyers, a lawyer must be ready to meet the challenges by entering into a new career. A good MBA degree, for example, can be a good conduit for the lawyer to do this.

Likewise, if, there are no clinical jobs for medical doctors, a medical doctor must be equipped to move into, say, a managerial position in the financial sector or into managing a hospital. But clinical experience alone will not provide the medical doctor with the requisite experiential learning or credentials to run a stockbroking firm or a pharmaceutical firm, for example. The medical doctor needs to have more than just clinical skills. The same reasoning applies to a lawyer who can no longer rely solely on litigation or legal drafting skills when law firms are no longer hiring. Some engineers have pursued effective strategies of diversification by acquiring, say, an MBA or accounting professional qualifications such as the British ACCA or the American CPA, ending up as excellent financial and auditing professionals. That way, they are somewhat insulated against the impact of the shrinking job market since they are more fungible and can easily move from one corporate department to another or from one industry to another.

But diversification through combining academic degrees or professional qualifications should not be done randomly. We have to be mindful of what it is that we want to achieve in life. If, indeed, one feels that he or she has reached the level of self-actualization on Maslow's hierarchy of needs, especially those living in well-to-do economies, then perhaps he or she can go mountain climbing or consider diversifying into poetry, drama or classics. However, for those in poverty-stricken economies, the primary goal is likely to be one of careers that bring bread and butter on the table. For this latter group, there is really no time to dream. And the multi- and interdisciplinary fields chosen by an individual must be somehow related strategically. Although the skills-set need not fall within a monolithic domain, since they are expected to be diverse, it is, nonetheless, important to maintain a meaningful link between the various multi- and interdisciplinary skills.

In developing careers for the twenty-first century, we must realize that as more and more companies endeavor to cut-down on costs, they are looking for employees that can carry out many different specialized tasks. If they can get a lawyer who understands compliance, for example, as well as anti-money laundering, that lawyer can wear the different hats and save the company from hiring compliance and anti-money laundering experts. Here, all that is needed is to expand the scope of the lawyer's responsibilities as well as that of the job description to include compliance and anti-money laundering. We are moving into an era of multi- and inter-disciplinary skills. Just as we know that a key strategy for any organization is to be able to survive, so it is with individuals. But, of course, we are not saying the world out there is perfect. There will always be some discriminatory tendencies, such as nepotism, racism, tribalism, regionalism or ethnic prejudices, which might militate against a well-executed strategy for multi- and inter-disciplinary skills. For example, we know full well that sometimes even good performance evaluations are not a guarantee for 'some people' to get a promotion or to survive down-sizing in times of economic distress. But, at least, one is better off trying than not trying.

CHAPTER 81

MAKING SENSE OF PHDS FOR THE ACADEMIC WORLD

Not too long ago, a screaming alarm was sounded in Nigeria's academic circles: "Public and private universities in Nigeria were recently reminded by Professor Julius Okojie, Executive Secretary of the National Universities Commission, that by 2009 all lecturers must possess a doctoral degree – or lose their jobs." (T. Fatunde, "Nigeria: Lecturers without PhDs to lose their jobs," March 30, 2008, available Online). According to this 2008 media report, "This directive, supported by the federal government, has generated a great deal of controversy in and outside higher education. But both supporters and opponents of the idea are unanimous about one thing – to prevent instability and uncertainty in the fragile university system, the qualifications deadline should be extended to allow affected academics to obtain their PhDs."

The said media report sank the hearts of many. It went on to add: "In an address to the Association and Committee of Vice Chancellors, the NUC's Okojie referred to a regulation called the Benchmark Minimum Academics Standard, or BMAS, which relates to the basic qualification a university teacher must possess. He said: '*If you don't have a PhD, you cannot teach. It has been an old regulation in the university system. If you graduate with a first class or second class upper, we take you as a graduate assistant. You are a trainee fellow. You are not a lecturer. When you earn your masters, you become an assistant lecturer. You are still not a lecturer…*'."

According to Okojie (see: Ibid), a lecturer is an examiner, and that "*the day you obtain your PhD, even if you have never worked before, your first appointment is lecturer grade two.*" Okojie argues further, "*What has happened in the past is that because of the dearth of PhD holders, universities employed those with mature masters as a lecturer grade two.*" Okojie notes forcefully that an academician without a PhD cannot be an examiner and should be excluded, among other things, from board of examiners' meetings (see Ibid.). Here it must be stressed that the PhD qualification (i.e. Doctor of Philosophy in a particular field) should have been earned from a legitimate and well-recognized university.

Understandably, the experience of Nigeria on the proposal advanced by Professor Okojie does not provide us with an article of faith. Each society goes through different socio-economic motions and will thus experience different emphases of socio-economic development. However, we can learn something from contemporary developments in parallel jurisdictions or societies. Indeed, both Nigeria and Zambia are Commonwealth countries. And our higher education systems are similar, with a heavy dosage of British colonial influence in both cases. Further, while there may be disparities or peculiarities distinguishing the two countries, I would like to posit that there are also a number of commonalities that help to inform the debate. Against this background, I begin by asking: is it feasible in Zambia today to put across a policy recommendation such as that propagated by Professor Okojie? Mindful that Nigeria has had many universities compared to Zambia, and that a good number of these Nigerian universities are much older than ours, it is also a truism that, like everywhere else in the developing world, Nigerian universities are struggling – and struggling hard, too. A question then follows: what can we learn from each others' experiences or predicaments?

It would not be too ambitious to state that a good number of our local universities in Zambia, like those in Nigeria and elsewhere in the developing world, might be shut down if we were to adopt Professor Okojie's proposal. But that is not to say our Zambian universities are not trying. They are trying. And I have no doubts whatsoever that our two leading universities, the University of Zambia and Copperbelt University, are by far much better academically than much of what I have seen on the African continent north of South Africa. But we must not relax or become complacent. We must constantly seek to improve the status quo. And if Professor Okojie's proposal sounds too harsh, we must find better alternatives or a middle ground. But, then, research and teaching are fundamental core functions of any decent university. We cannot run away from this fact. As a result, the number of PhD holders among faculty members in an academic department, although not an end by itself but certainly a means, is a helpful indicator of the critical "scholarly" mass that the academic department enjoys. To administer PhD programmes effectively, there must be well-funded PhD programmes with a critical mass of qualified people to teach and supervise research. But what happens if the funding is not forthcoming? What to do now, as they would say in Russia?

Let it be known that we concede that there are some brilliant professors out there without PhDs who have guided many junior colleagues to PhD awards. It is very possible, though increasingly rare, especially in Africa, for someone with a first degree only, or with a first degree and a Masters degree, to ascend on the echelons of academe to the rank of Full Professor and to supervise PhD students. Such an individual must be a well-established scholar in his or her field, although this practice is frowned upon in some academic disciplines.

In essence, while Professor Okojie's submissions are well-grounded, I would like to argue that instead of simply placing emphasis on our academicians getting PhDs, we should be factoring in the constraints and limitations that they face. To that end, I would like to recommend that where an academician has no PhD but has, notwithstanding the financial constraints, through his own entrepreneurial zeal, successfully churned out sufficient and impressive scholarly work, he should be given an opportunity to validate that scholarship through a *PhD by Submission of Published Work.* Many of our universities in Africa, unfortunately, do not make provision for such an award in their academic regulations. The route to a PhD by Submission of Published Work is a long-standing tradition in many British, Australian and New Zealand universities. The applicant would have to submit a portfolio of his or her best published scholarly work for examination for a PhD degree. And the standard to which the PhD examiners will carry out the examination is expected to be exactly the same as in the traditional sense where a PhD student has been working on a doctoral thesis under academic supervision. But, then, a PhD by Submission of Published Work should not be confused with or mistaken for a Higher Doctorate. Higher Doctorates, or Senior Doctorates as they are sometimes called, are very rarely awarded. They are reserved only for those who have made exceedingly substantial, original and significant contributions to a science or body of knowledge through exceptionally insightful and distinctive scholarly publications, earning them recognition as international authorities in the field of research that forms the basis of the degree. In many Commonwealth countries, for example, appellations pertaining to Higher/Senior Doctorates include the degree of Doctor of Laws (LLD) for very senior legal scholars, the degree of Doctor of Science (DSc) for very senior natural scientists, the degree of Doctor of Letters

(DLitt) for very senior social scientists and the degree of Doctor of Medicine (DM) for very senior medical scholars.

Be that as it may, the concept of a PhD by Submission of Published Work would encourage those academicians without a PhD to look into possible ways of working harder to develop their skills and credentials. In the UK and the other countries listed above, the PhD by Submission of Published Work route is available also to alumni of the university. But, of course, certain minimum standards must be met before one can proceed. Also, not any type of publication will fly under this rule; that is, certainly not newspaper articles or cut-and-paste consultancy reports! Only work appearing in scholarly and peer-reviewed academic journals and scholarly books, especially monographs, but not Edited Volumes or Casebooks, would qualify. The work selected for submission must also be on a related theme or related themes. That way, scholarly research in our universities can be encouraged instead of frightening our academicians with ideas of possible dismissal. Through such an approach, those churchmen, businessmen and politicians who are in the habit of accessorizing themselves with honorary doctorate degrees will not find it easy. Only serious scholars will be able to muster enough courage to attempt a PhD by Submission of Published Work. But it will not come easy, though. And in many African countries, the academic regulations of our universities must be revised in order to provide for a PhD by Submission of Published Work. There is also a need for a paradigm shift so that the whole system is not abused by those pre-occupied with settling scores with adversaries.

It is important to observe that, when ranking universities, among some of the common criteria used by rankers is the number of PhD holders on the full-time academic staff of a university as well as their scholarly research output, in addition to factors such as how many PhDs have graduated from that university in a particular year, how many undergraduates got Distinctions or First Class, and the employability rate of graduates from the university. Indeed, we all stand to gain by examining international best practice with a view to assessing the viability of adopting or adapting some of these practices to our own context. Currently, many EU countries are pre-occupied with the Bologna process to create a European Higher Education Area through making their academic degree standards and quality assurance standards more comparable and compatible throughout Europe, in particular under the Lisbon Recognition Convention 1999. So, what is the future for Africa?

CHAPTER 82

SCRUTINIZING THE SCRAMBLE AND CRAZE FOR MBA DEGREES

The Master of Business Administration (MBA) degree is undoubtedly one of the most highly sought after graduate degree programmes in the world today. The student demand for MBA degrees has increased dramatically in the last twelve to fifteen years. Many universities and colleges are now offering MBA degree programmes. While the US is, arguably, the pioneer of MBA degree programmes, Britain, too, has caught up quickly. And many other countries, including former socialist countries in Eastern Europe, are now offering MBA degree programmes. Many MBA students perceive the MBA degree as a key to a successful high paying job. A general but somewhat contentious view prevails that, except for a few isolated examples, many MBA programmes are pursued by highly ambitious individuals that want to get to the top quickly. It is even argued that that is why MBA degrees are now a fashionable thing among business elites. Even lawyers, accountants, engineers and medical doctors are opting for MBAs. Why is there such a big fuss about MBA degrees? It is not surprising to find that even individuals that already have, say, a PhD still opt to pursue an MBA. So, what is it that drives people to seek MBAs? Is there something special about an MBA that is missing in other university degree qualifications?

In many parts of the world, several young and middle-aged professionals are busy looking for ways through which they can ascend to the higher echelons of the corporate ladder. This view might sound ridiculous to some, but that is the real world we live in. Whether through hook or crook, many young and middle-aged professionals would also like to get to the top and earn that fat salary. They hear stories of how Mr. XYZ or Ms. ABC, a now wealthy corporate executive, first went to Harvard Business School or London Business School to get an MBA before landing his or her dream job. The MBA is thus seen as a passport to the often imagined dream job. Almost invariably, the majority of these MBA students feel that an MBA will guarantee them financial success and catapult them into a fast-track career for a senior management position. Yes, it might work for some, while for many others things might end up in disillusionment. But, let us take a more reasoned look.

Not all MBA degree programmes are worth the money and effort that people invest in. Many employers are busy looking for valuable work experience of the job applicants before considering anything else. Of course, an MBA earned at an elite Business School in the world will impress most recruiters. But the MBA should be accompanied by something else that is equally valuable on the résumé or curriculum vitae – that is, valuable work experience! Further, the MBA must aim to support or build on a primary profession. It should not be a standalone qualification. Put simply, it is best to have a primary profession before seeking an MBA. The MBA alone is not enough. It must rest on some established profession and valuable work experience, unless the concerned individual is coming on to an MBA programme straight from undergraduate. Additionally, whether we like it or not, the university or school where one obtained his or her MBA degree matters a lot. The metaphor of how the same bottle of beer can sell at different prices depending on the affluence of the 'place' where it is sold is not far from the truth. The name of the university or school can, at times, make or break your long awaited post-MBA dreams. It is no use picking an MBA from an unknown or unaccredited school, unless that MBA will only be put to use in a country or place where most people do not know anything about the accreditation of MBA programmes or the ranking of Business Schools. But even then, one must exercise caution here since some jurisdictions and countries have outlawed the use of such qualifications for obtaining employment.

Generally speaking, MBA degree programmes come in many different forms and shapes. In the UK, for example, the MBA degree programme is obtained by many students through full-time study over a period of ten months to twelve months. By contrast, many full-time MBA programmes in the US last over two years. The two year period in the US includes a six months work placement in industry to carry out a project-based assignment. Other variants of the MBA in both the UK and the US include the distance-learning MBA degree programmes, the Executive MBA degree programmes, evening-class MBA degree programmes (i.e. part-time or full-time), and Online MBA degree programmes (akin to the distance-learning MBA degree programmes). Quite often, the curriculum of a distance learning MBA degree programme follows closely that of a full-time MBA degree programme within the same specialty and school, unless otherwise specified. The Executive MBA, by contrast, will often involve a lesser number of modules and/or courses than a full-time MBA, and is usually taken on a part-time basis. At many Business Schools, Executive MBA students attend classes, say, on one or two weekends every month, and are fairly advanced in their career paths.

Over the years, I have spoken with many individuals that have pursued MBA degree programmes to get a sense of what motivated them to pursue the MBA degree. Some, especially those professionals without a business management background, argue that they wanted to get some business sense of how to run their practice or company. Others argue that they did not want to end up with a single-track career or single specialty in these difficult and turbulent economic times. Yet, there are also those that are blunt enough to admit that they wanted to get to the top faster and that the MBA was therefore a surest way of getting there. I must be candid here in saying those that go for an MBA degree just because everyone else around them is doing so are likely to end up disappointed. There should be a good reason why you have chosen a particular degree programme instead of just following blindly what others are doing. People should ask themselves if an MBA really makes sense for them or their circumstances. In certain instances, one does not really need an MBA.

But how does one go about choosing a suitable MBA degree programme? I remember reading a very interesting advert in the Economist magazine some years back. It was an advert put out by the University of Warwick, stressing that: “It is not the letters after your name that matter, but the name after those letters!” In short, the advert was saying that it matters where you got your MBA degree from. More recently, I have seen an advert by Cornell University in one of the local US newspapers, postulating as follows: “Want an Ivy League MBA?” In essence, it is the same message of where you got your MBA degree. Such adverts might sound snobbish to some people, but that’s the real world we live in. We all want the best, not so? And that is why not all MBAs can cut it in the job market. You need the right MBA brand, that is, if you can afford one.

Understandably, many factors can and do affect or determine people’s choices of an MBA degree programme. These factors include: (a) the availability of funding to study for a good MBA programme; (b) the tuition fees demanded for that MBA programme; (c) the city in which the university offering the MBA is located; (d) the ranking of the said MBA programme on MBA League Tables; (e) the accreditation of the MBA programme by well-known international accrediting agencies (e.g. AMBA and EQUIS (i.e. UK and EU accreditation of MBA programmes, respectively) or AACSB (US accreditation of MBA programmes mainly)); (f) whether the MBA programme is too quantitative to a point where the applicant feels somewhat intimidated and would rather look for an MBA programme that is less quantitative; (g) the requirement to pass the GMAT exam by some Business Schools, especially some top schools in the US, before enrolling for the MBA programme (including the GMAT score obtained by the MBA applicant); (h) the strength of the applicant's undergraduate degree and/or work experience; (i) the availability of some MBA scholarships which often come as a waiver of part of tuition fees; (j) the reputation of notable MBA alumni that you may have heard of or that you know; (k) the adverts that you see or read in the media or via the internet; (l) the guidance from career counselors and mentors; (m) the decision to be taught by a notable or renowned professor at a particular Business School; (n) whether the applicant is in full-time employment and his or her employers are willing to provide study-leave; (o) whether the applicant is married to a supportive spouse who is willing to allow her or him to go for further studies; (p) whether the applicant is a single parent with relatives that can help to look after that person's children when he or she goes back to school for an MBA; (q) the availability of modern technology such as reliable internet connection for Online learning; and, (r) the availability of good local MBA programmes within the home country of the applicant. These are some of the tricky issues that affect our choices for an MBA.

Now, it is not for me to confirm which ones are the best MBA degree programmes out there. Neither is it for me to affirm which ones are the best Business Schools. Various schools have different strengths and weaknesses. Some schools are strong, say, in MBA programmes with a focuss on Finance, whilst others are better at MBA programmes focussing on Marketing. There are many areas of focuss on different MBA programmes. For example, one can take a General Management MBA programme, covering a whole range of courses and modules in general management and business administration. Lately, we have seen some schools offer MBA degree programmes tailored specifically for such Healthcare Professionals as medical doctors, dentists and so forth. Other MBA programmes place much emphasis on Project Management, especially those that are tailored for individuals with an engineering professional background. Yet, there is also an MBA strand that is increasingly becoming popular, focusing on Strategic Management.

In conclusion, I leave the reader with the following message: (a) do a background search on the ranking of the MBA school or MBA degree programme so that you can get a sense of some public perception of that school or MBA degree programme (please note that, although many university rankings are not that objective, they do, however, help to shed some light on public perception); (b) do a background check on whether that MBA degree programme or school is accredited by a reputable and recognized accrediting agency; (c) go for an MBA that best complements or augments your current strengths or areas of expertise, unless you want to divert or change career paths altogether; and, (d) evaluate the cost of investing in an average-rated MBA degree programme at a foreign university against the prospects for recovering that investment afterwards, and then contrast that option with the benefit of targeting a good local MBA programme offered locally within Zambia. Finally, in terms of the prestige attached to various MBA programmes, I would opine that the Harvard MBA has a good ringtone. A similar ringtone can also be heard when it comes to the MBA degree from, say, MIT (US), Wharton Business School (University of Pennsylvania, US), Kellogg Graduate School of Management (Northwestern University, US), London Business School (UK) and INSEAD (France). These are top brands. You can also aim for the overall name and strong reputation of a leading university such as Oxford or Cambridge, Yale or Stanford. That, too, will turn heads. In the UK, for example, after London Business School, two of the strongest and most reputable MBA programmes are the University of Warwick MBA programme and the Cranfield University MBA programme. In Africa, the University of Cape Town, the University of Witwatersrand and the University of Pretoria have some of the strongest and most reputable MBA programmes. I would also want to believe that MBA programmes at the University of Stellenbosch and Rhodes University follow closely in the strong reputation of the three South African MBA programmes mentioned above.

CHAPTER 83

BUILDING SUSTAINABLE CAREERS FOR THE TWENTY-FIRST CENTURY: A HUMAN RESOURCE MANAGEMENT (HRM) PERSPECTIVE

From a human resource management (HRM) point of view, the effective crafting and execution of strategies of diversity and inclusion provide a fulcrum of enhancing economies of scale and scope for HRM efficiencies within an organization. And the strategies of diversity and inclusion often refer to issues of minorities in the workplace. Further, minority groups could be construed along gender lines, ethnic backgrounds or race relations. But the execution of such strategies requires courage from the organization's leadership as well as from all those affected by the desired change. And change does not come easy. It sometimes requires a paradigm shift, moving away from the status quo and disturbing other people's comfort zones. And so it is with careers. Sometimes, we have to move away from our comfort zones in order to survive. In a sense, diversity and inclusion should be understood as percolating to the spheres of employees' skills-set. It should not be seen to refer only to issues of race and gender.

The world today is arguably different from what it used to be some thirty to forty years back. There are now many new technological inventions and scientific discoveries. Science and technology have come up with innovations and discoveries that have improved people's quality of life, albeit the persisting poverty in many parts of the world. In the 1980s, for example, when I took my undergraduate degree studies, many universities worldwide did not have computers for students to use when researching or writing their academic essays. I remember vividly that I would submit all my undergraduate essays in handwritten format. And each time we, the students, would write our essays, we somehow knew that there was nothing like a first draft or a revised draft. That very first submission had to be the first and final version of the essay. So, we learned how to pay greater attention to detail, and how to get it right the first time. We had to be meticulous from the outset, knowing that there was not much room for any margin of error. Looking back today, I would imagine how tedious and difficult it was for those who took, say, their PhDs in the 1970s and 1980s when revising and re-typing the respective chapters of their thesis or dissertation. I can only imagine that the type-writer must have been constantly clicking all night, and one probably needed many stencils to re-type the corrected and revised versions of his or her research. But, today, thanks to science, the modern computer has made it easier.

I also hear that post offices worldwide are struggling with declining business because email has taken over from postal mail. The volume of what used to be bulky postal mail has now been superseded by emails, or by attachments to a short email message, that can reach its intended audience within seconds of pressing the button on your computer keyboard. The transmission of electronic mail, or email, as it is often referred to, is even faster than that of express courier services. It does not matter the distance between the sender and the receiver of the email. Transmission is almost instantaneous. So, you can imagine how much business the postal services and the courier services are losing as a result of innovations such as the introduction of email. And you don't have to walk or drive to the post office any more. You can simply send email from the comfort of your home, while sipping some coffee, or from your office, as you multi-task on other assignments. Computers have even cut-down the costs of hiring secretaries since many bosses can type their own work. Thus, the function of a secretary has had to be re-designed and re-focused into one of a more demanding role of personal assistant, administrative assistant or executive assistant. Thanks again to modern technology and computers.

Today, people can even publish books electronically, as e-books. They can even send photos to friends electronically, without having to print them out in readiness for postal mail delivery. And the use of skype to place international telephone calls has cut down drastically on the costs associated with such calls. Thirty to forty years ago, the concept of a cell-phone, Blackberry or i-phone was unimaginable. Today, you can place a telephone call while shopping or while taking a leisure walk to the park. You don't have to wait until you get to a land-phone. Also, in the yesteryears, we used to have great and admirable encyclopedias on the book shelves. I remember that, in the early 1970s, when my father returned from his studies in Canada, he brought along with him many books that included iconic encyclopedias and dictionaries. But all these hard-texts are now superseded by electronic media, with Wikipedia and others providing abundantly, and at almost no cost, information that was only available through print media. Besides, the content of websites can be updated promptly and at a lower cost, as opposed to updating or correcting the contents of print media. We are living in a different world altogether. So, how then does that impact on or shape our choices of building careers for the twenty-first century?

Inter- and multi-disciplinary skills

We begin by assuming that every person is a hard worker and that there are no issues affecting their ability to perform technically in their areas of expertise. And we are mindful that different people have different aspirations in life. In general, however, we all make decisions based on our own view of the world. And such viewpoints are often influenced or persuaded by intrinsic and idiosyncratic values as well as by external influences and actors. The environments to which we are exposed, whether as children or as adults, and the dynamics of socialization that come with these environments, determine the degree of emphasis we place on certain choices and values. I have watched with kin interest how the process of globalization is affecting career choices of many people. Today, thanks to technology, one can even telecommute between two different continents. But that is not all there is. The global economic meltdown in many parts of the world has seen many people lose jobs. In many developing and developed nations, a number of employers are increasingly hiring employees less and less on permanent and pensionable basis. Rather, the norm is moving towards contractual fixed-term or temporal jobs. A study on how this affects productivity in terms of employee motivation is perhaps outside the scope of this paper and better left to industrial psychologists. When I took my MBA, I begun to see a different world from the world I had known all along as a lawyer. I was accustomed to thinking in terms of legal rules. But studying management and executive leadership opened the horizons of my mind to issues beyond those of legal rules. Organizational behavior, for example, is not something one would reduce to a complex set of rules or principles. Issues of corporate culture, too, like those of strategic management, go beyond mathematical models or legalistic rules. And this applies not only to lawyers but to many other professions as well. Let us take a reasoned example of the medical profession. Many a medical doctor may have strong and well-honed clinical skills, but they often lack the necessary managerial skills to run a medical practice such as a hospital. To equip themselves with managerial skills, medical doctors that are aspiring to be managers can benefit from pursuing courses such as an MBA degree or some executive leadership programs. Closely related to MBA degree programs are MPH degree programs, although the latter programs tend to focus principally on public health issues. That said, without a strong grounding in management, a medical doctor may not find it easy to run an established medical practice. In developed countries, many lawyers and medical doctors with established firms or practices tend to hire professionals from relevant fields to attend to the administrative aspects of the firm or practice.

While it is appreciated that experiential learning can at times be a good substitute for formal education, and that there are some who feel strongly that academic degrees alone will not equip you with the relevant managerial or technical skills, in times when jobs are hard to find one cannot place his or her hopes on simply gaining experiential learning without acquiring first some relevant qualifications on which to base that experience. Experience must be grounded in sound and relevant theory in order to remain meaningful. But we concede, too, that there are some exceptional and isolated cases where some individuals can make good managers without any formal managerial training or education. Be that as it may, there are also many other individuals that have no 'political' connections or networks to give them a chance to try out a managerial position even though they do not have the requisite managerial qualifications and experience. Such individuals are less likely to find sympathetic employers who are willing to take a gamble on them. Besides, many employers today are trying to cut-down on costs. Porter's generic strategies, although designed primarily for industries, help us to understand how best we can position ourselves not only for managerial positions alone but also for other careers that can help in fulfilling our ambitions. We must think outside the box from a human resource management (HRM) perspective.

The three generic strategies articulated by Porter are: (a) cost leadership; (b) differentiation; and (c) focus. From an HRM perspective, specialization and division of labor has been the mantra for a great many of us. Grounded, to some degree, in Ricardo's theory of comparative advantage, as well as in Porter's strategy of 'focus', the concept of specialization and division of labor has suffered an affront in the wake of globalization. To remain competitive today, one cannot stick rigidly to a single or monolithic area of specialization when the job market is volatile and not looking certain. Systems Thinking implores us to continuously evaluate and assess our strengths and weaknesses against some of the options, opportunities, threats, costs and risks that are in the market. We need to audit trends in the market to be able to generate viable scenarios through scenario planning. In short, we need to engage in strategic thinking, as opposed to strategic planning. If, for example, there are no jobs for lawyers, a lawyer must be ready to meet the challenges by entering into a new career. An MBA may be a good conduit for the lawyer to do this. Likewise, if, there are no clinical jobs for medical doctors, a medical doctor must be equipped to move into, say, a managerial position in the financial sector or into managing a hospital. But clinical experience alone will not provide the medical doctor with the requisite experiential learning or credentials to run a stockbroking firm or a pharmaceutical firm, for example. The medical doctor needs to have more than just clinical skills. The same reasoning applies to a lawyer who can no longer rely solely on litigation or legal drafting skills when law firms are no longer hiring. Some engineers have pursued effective strategies of diversification by acquiring, say, an MBA or accounting professional qualifications such as the British ACCA or the American CPA, ending up as excellent financial and auditing professionals. That way, they are somewhat insulated against the impact of the shrinking job market since they are more fungible and can easily move from one corporate department to another or from one industry to another. But diversification through combining academic degrees or professional qualifications should not be random and ill-thought. We have to be mindful of what it is that we want in life. If, indeed, one feels that he or she has reached the level of self-actualization on Maslow's hierarchy of needs, especially those living in well-to-do economies, then perhaps he or she can go mountain climbing or consider diversifying into poetry, drama or classics. However, for those in poverty-stricken economies, the primary goal is likely to be one of careers that bring bread and butter on the table. For this latter group, there is really no time to dream. And the multi- and interdisciplinary fields chosen by an individual must be somehow related. Although the skills-set need not fall within a monolithic domain, since they are expected to be diverse, it is, nonetheless, important to maintain a meaningful link between the various multi- and interdisciplinary skills.

In developing careers for the twenty-first century, we must realize that as more and more companies endeavor to cut-down on costs, they are looking for employees that can carry out many different specialized tasks. If they can get a lawyer who understands compliance, for example, as well as anti-money laundering, that lawyer can wear the different hats and save the company from hiring compliance and anti-money laundering experts. Here, all that is needed is to expand the scope of the lawyer's responsibilities as well as that of the job description to include compliance and anti-money laundering. We are moving into an era of multi- and inter-disciplinary skills. Just as we know that a key strategy for any organization is to be able to survive, so it is with individuals. However, political lobbying and networking alone, as a strategy for climbing the corporate ladder, are not sustainable strategies for survival in the long-term. Once the grand-father or the grand-mother leaves the company, you become open to vulnerabilities and insecurity because there is nobody to protect you. Indeed, as an unprotected species, you are open to attack from adversaries that have long waited for your protector to leave. You become a homeless person or an orphan within the organization. But with a well thought out investment strategy in multi- or inter-disciplinary skills, you can take on Porter's strategy of differentiation to distinguish yourself from your competitors as a more valuable asset to the organization. But, of course, we are not saying the world out there is perfect. There will always be some discriminatory tendencies, such as nepotism, racism, tribalism, regionalism or ethnic prejudices, which might militate against a well-executed strategy for multi- and inter-disciplinary skills. For example, we know fully well that sometimes even good performance evaluations are not a guarantee for 'some people' to get a promotion or to survive down-sizing in times of economic distress. But, at least, one is better off trying than not trying.

The name after the letters matters more than the letters themselves

With the privatization of higher education in many developing countries, a number of unaccredited universities and colleges are springing up in these countries. And these types of institutions can also be found in the developed world. A number of them are not even recognized internationally and can be quite aggressive in marketing their services through means such as a strong internet presence, adverts in the media, unsolicited mail, and so forth. Most of these institutions are Diploma Mills. Therefore, in pursuing strategies of diversifying one's portfolio of skills-set, it would be ill-advisable to target Diploma Mills. Gradually, many employers are beginning to know more about phony universities and schools. For example, the internet has useful information on the ranking and accreditation of different schools.

Although some critiques may argue against the issue of ranking universities and the credibility of the methodology for these rankings, Diploma Mills have never enjoyed any decent rankings.

Quite often, and depending on the culture of a particular country or employer, the reputation of the university or college you attend matters a lot. One can call it a form of discrimination, but that's just what happens. The name of the university you attend tends to be given much weight than, say, the title of the degree you get from an unknown university. Further still, in countries where the regulation of certain professions is strong, you want to avoid getting a degree that has no favor of professional regulation or recognition, even though the degree is from a good school. Such biases and prejudices are common in many developed countries.

Also, the predominant nationality, race, gender, tribe or alumni base in a particular company is likely to favor the replication of its own value systems by recruiting mainly from among those with similar backgrounds. Many people, naturally, tend to feel comfortable with a kind of their own. So, if, for example, a company that operates in Country Y as a multi-national from Country X is looking at recruiting from, inter alia, citizens of Country Y, it may concentrate on a pool of candidates with ties to Country X. If for example, you are a citizen of Country Y, but studied in Country X, you stand a better chance of getting a job with that company than a fellow citizen of Country Y with the same qualifications and experience but who did not study in Country X or who is not married to a citizen of Country X. The idea really is that you would be seen by the recruiters to be more 'acceptable' in terms of culture and ethos (as well as in sharing jokes), consistent with the interests of those in senior management at the company, especially that much of the senior management are likely to be from Country X, anyway.

Conclusion

Recognizing the limited value of 'political' lobbying, networks and connections within the corporate set-up, especially for minority social groups, this paper has posited that, as we move into the twenty-first century, the issue of building careers of multi- and inter-disciplinary backgrounds becomes more acute than ever before. This strategy, it was argued, is particularly important for minority social groups that are often vulnerable and less protected in workplaces. By contrast, those with political powerbases that are firmly anchored in the dominant culture within the organization, or those from social groups that are more protected than others, can afford to survive easily without going an extra mile. All they need is a grand-father or grand-mother in the company to protect them. And they can also feed off from the value system and the dominant networks of those in power. However, in order for the vulnerable to mitigate such risks and threats, they have to adopt strategies of diversifying their skills-set as a helpful way in which to enhance their potential for survival. This is particularly important for those minorities operating in politically-charged corporate environments or in economically-depressed job markets.

- *Kenneth K. Mwenda*

CHAPTER 84

DEVELOPING SOUND LEGAL AND REGULATORY FRAMEWORKS FOR FINANCIAL AND PRIVATE SECTOR DEVELOPMENT IN AFRICA

This article aims at identifying and examining pertinent policy issues in the development of sound legal and regulatory frameworks for financial and private sector development in Africa. At the outset, it should be pointed out that the article does not profess to be a priority list of policy recommendations for all African countries that follow the English common law. It should certainly not be misconstrued as an attempt at spelling out an exhaustive list of policy recommendations. Rather, the article seeks to stimulate debate around critical issues that are of wider application to many African countries with a common law background. Admittedly, some issues may not be as that critical in one jurisdiction as they would be in another. Law, it must be emphasized, does not exist in a vacuum. Its relevance must be understood within the context of each and every country's socio-economic and

---

- *Kenneth K. Mwenda*

political background. Indeed, as one famous English judge, Lord Denning, put it succinctly in *Nyali Ltd v. Attorney General* [1956] 1QB 1, at pp. 16-17, regarding the applicability of the English common law to the African continent, while sounding a warning that extended to other parts of the world,

> "Just as with an English oak, so with the English common law. You cannot transplant it...and expect it to retain the tough character which it has in England. It will flourish indeed, but it needs careful tending. ...In these far off lands the people must have a law which they understand and which they respect."

Against this background, the article stands back from untested academic theory, focusing instead on pragmatic lessons of experience informed by the author's vast experience and expertise in the fields of international and comparative corporate law and financial services regulation. The article brings the reader to quick speed on salient features of the law for developing a sound financial sector as well as an attractive investment climate.

Placing Africa's legal systems in context

In many parts of Africa, the legal system of a particular country is either based on the English common law or some civil law traditions. The legal transplant of jurisprudential norms from the western world to many developing countries has followed a historic pattern. As such, the transplanting of legal norms from the English common law world (in the West), or from the French and German legal systems, to African countries has depended, in part, on which western power had previously occupied a particular African country. Many African countries have tended to borrow heavily from the jurisprudence of their former colonial masters. Thus, a good number of former British colonies and protectorates have adopted the English common law whereas many former French, German and Portuguese colonies follow the civil law. It is important to take such factors into account when undertaking legal reforms in Africa. Certain features of the common law are unique to common law jurisdictions only. And certain aspects of the civil law are unique to civil law countries only.

Factoring in the role of African customary law

In addition to many African countries inheriting a primary jurisprudence from their former colonial masters, almost all African countries have retained a form of secondary jurisprudence which lingers around the periphery of western legal thought. This secondary jurisprudence – that is, African customary law – more often than not operates in the shadows of western jurisprudence and, therefore, does not have a significant impact on modern commerce or finance. The duality of legal traditions in many African countries does not, however, pose major threats along the lines of conflict of laws in some western legal systems. In many African countries that follow the English common law, precepts of African customary law are only valid in so far as they do not infringe upon public policy, or are not contrary to legislation, or are not repugnant to natural justice, good conscience and equity.

Hybrid legal systems

It is important to point out also that there are other African countries whose legal systems have attributes of both the common law and the civil law. Cameroon is a case in point. Cameroon's legal system is composed of attributes of both the common law and the civil law, including tenets of African customary law. Nigeria, too, has a hybrid system comprising tenets of the English common law, African customary law and Islamic law. Such hybrid legal systems have evolved as part of the legacy of colonialism. Likewise, South Africa, Lesotho, Zimbabwe, Namibia, Botswana and Swaziland all boast of having attributes of both the English common law (in the area of corporate law, for example) and Roman-Dutch law (in certain other areas of the law), including attributes of African customary law.

Creating an enabling environment through the development of efficient and effective legal and regulatory frameworks

What is missing in Africa's legal systems to help develop robust and sound financial and private sectors? Some critical areas to consider include the following:

(a) a number of African countries need to examine the efficacy of their laws relating to land title registration, with a view to harmonizing and improving these laws (especially where legal and equitable interests in immovable property fall either

under statutory law or the common law or African customary law);
(b) a number of African countries need to examine the efficacy of their laws relating to different forms of commercial security, with a view to improving such laws (and this includes the need to find out, for example, the costs and benefits of moving to a centralized and automated registry system for the registration of different security interests);
(c) a number of African countries need to examine and strengthen the institutional capacity and independence, as well as the accountability, of the judiciary, financial sector regulators, the lands registry, the companies registry, and the office of the official receiver (for insolvency matters);
(d) a number of African countries need to address the issue of weak, and sometimes a clear absence of, anti-money laundering laws, including the marked absence of anti-money laundering regulations and codes of practice to be promulgated by different regulatory agencies that oversee financial intermediaries and gatekeepers such as banks, other licensed financial institutions, stockbrokers and securities firms, insurance companies and brokers, bureau de change, building societies, pension funds, lawyers, accountants, real estate agents, casinos, and many others;
(e) a number of African countries need to examine the efficiency and effectiveness of their payments system and the laws governing such systems so as to facilitate the growth of national, regional and international trade for a particular country;
(f) a number of African countries need to strengthen their legal and regulatory frameworks for insolvency

and creditor rights so as to promote intermediation between the sectors of the economy in need of finance and those that have the ability to finance; and,

(g) a number of African countries need to examine the efficacy of laws relating to the regulation of all forms of financial services, including insurance, pensions, banking, micro-finance, taxation and securities, with a view to improving such laws, especially that the potential for economic growth in Africa's informal sector remains relatively untapped and underdeveloped.

Salient features of corporate governance and directors' liability

A good number of common law countries in Africa have Companies Acts which are versions of the old English Companies Act 1948. Yet, England has moved on. The current UK Companies Act 2006 was preceded by the English Companies Act 1985, with several amendments thereto, as reflected, in part, in the Companies Act (Amendment) 1989. As a result of this lag in modernizing company laws, a number of African countries have not adapted to international best practices dealing with, say, the disqualification of company directors who are guilty of such statutory offences as fraudulent trading while a company is insolvent. These are some of the areas in which African legal systems should move fast if they are to provide an enabling environment for commerce and finance to thrive. How do you make recalcitrant directors liable for acting in their own interests even where they ought to have known that the company's books of account are in the red?

And how do we deal with issues of cross-border insolvency? Are there treaties, such as mutual legal assistance treaties, between and among many African states? If not, what is the way forward?

Shortcomings of placing less emphasis on trusts law

Although the concept of trusts law is essential in modern commerce, and in spite of the fact that most common law systems, unlike their civil law counterparts, benefit from doctrines of equity, many common law countries in Africa do not have a well-developed 'indigenous' jurisprudence of trusts law. If anything, there is need for capacity-building in areas of advanced commercial law so that the judiciary, the legal profession, the accounting profession and many other stakeholders can benefit from and learn about contemporary issues relating to modern commerce in a globalised world today. The current underdeveloped state of the legal infrastructure and institutions in many parts of Africa can be attributed, in part, to the underdeveloped state of most African economies and also to the lack of emphasis on such important areas of commerce as trusts law in the legal education curricula of many African universities.

Conclusion – turning theory into practice

While a good number of African countries have done considerably well in introducing modern pieces of legislation for their emerging markets, compliance with and enforcement of the laws remains relatively weak. There are many reasons for such developments and they include such shortcomings as endemic and systemic corruption, poor governance frameworks and culture, bad economic policies, weak institutional capacity in many public bodies and regulatory agencies, and inadequate and insufficient economic incentives to overcome the debilitating effects of poverty on the morale and motivation of the workforce.

Although many countries in Africa have today adopted modern legislative instruments to support the development of their financial and private sectors, they still need to address the vexing question – what do they do about the issue of poor compliance and enforcement? As a general rule, the development of a good law in the financial or private sector should not be an end in and of itself. It should be supported by institutional capacity-building to bring about sustainable development of that sector. And the development of good laws should not only be premised on the policy objectives underpinning such laws, but also on the size, structure, functions and organizational set-up of the business institutions and markets regulated by these laws.

Also, the legal framework should be seen to mitigate possible risks that could arise from information asymmetry in cases, for example, where a consumer lacks much information on a regulated entity or market. While self-regulation may not be an immediate answer, most African countries have shied away from models of self-regulation, relying heavily instead on State-driven regulation. Indeed, there is very little evidence to suggest that self-regulation, in addition to any other system of regulation, is a top priority for African countries. The culture of State control still lingers on and a number of African countries are only now beginning to grasp concepts of a market economy.

A common argument against self-regulation in developing countries is that these countries have weak compliance and enforcement cultures, and that they therefore need a central commanding authority to enforce compliance. It is argued that although regulatory bodies may set regulatory standards and norms, the bulwark of investor protection lies in what the legislature says. This could explain why some regulatory bodies in Africa do not have statutory powers to mete out criminal sanctions against culpable parties. Such powers are left in the hands of the State. But, in State-driven regulation, there can also be the danger of over-regulation by the State or a threat of over-concentration of regulatory and supervisory powers in some state institutions, thereby giving rise to opportunities for corrupt practices by some employees of that state institution.

CHAPTER 85

LIMITATIONS OF THE 'LAWYER-CLIENT PRIVILEGE' POSITION AND THAT OF CLIENT CONFIDENTIALITY BY BANKS AND ACCOUNTANTS IN THE FIGHT AGAINST MONEY LAUNDERING

What happens in a case of suspected money laundering where a gatekeeper such as an accountant or lawyer is implicated? Does the Prohibition and Prevention of Money Laundering Act 2001 or the Bank of Zambia Anti-Money Laundering Directives 2004 say anything? Both the Prohibition and Prevention of Money Laundering Act 2001 and the Bank of Zambia Anti-Money Laundering Directives 2004 Act are largely silent on the need to regulate such gatekeepers against money laundering. Yet, time and again, we have seen that accountants do serve as financial and investment advisers to many corporations and individuals. Also, accountants and lawyers do provide trusts and company services to many business houses, and these services include company formation and incorporation, providing advice on how to avoid and optimize tax situations, and carrying out powers of attorney on behalf of a customer. But, then, what happens in a situation where some accountants or lawyers are implicated in the commissioning of an offence of money laundering while providing advice to customers or while carrying out their usual business functions on behalf of a customer? Should such accountants and lawyers be protected by the law even if they are facilitating money laundering?

In an effort to resolve the lacuna in the Prohibition and Prevention of Money Laundering Act 2001 and the Bank of Zambia Anti-Money Laundering Directives 2004, the Zambian parliament enacted the Financial Intelligence Centre Act 2010. However, notwithstanding that some statutory provisions in the Financial Intelligence Centre Act 2010 overlap and repeat some of the statutory provisions in the Prohibition and Prevention of Money Laundering Act 2001, section 29 of the Financial Intelligence Centre Act 2010 provides that an institution regulated by a supervisory authority and required to make suspicious transaction reports (i.e. a reporting entity), or a director, principal, officer, partner, professional or employee of a financial institution, that suspects or has reasonable grounds to suspect that any property constitutes proceeds of crime, or is related or linked to, or is to be used for, terrorism, terrorist acts or by terrorist organisations or persons who finance terrorism, should, not later than three working days after forming the suspicion, submit a report setting out the suspicions to the Financial Intelligence Centre. The same statutory provision, section 29, covers also situations relating to attempted suspicious transactions. And section 29 establishes legal obligations on any legal practitioner, notary public or an accountant to submit suspicious transaction reports if: (a) the legal practitioner, notary public or accountant engages, on behalf of or for a client, in a financial transaction associated with an activity specified in relation to such professionals under the Financial Intelligence Centre Act 2010; and (b) the relevant information upon which the suspicion is based was not received from, or obtained on, a client in the course of ascertaining the legal position of the client, or in performing their task of defending or representing that client in, or concerning judicial, administrative, arbitration or mediation proceedings, including advice on instituting or avoiding proceedings, whether such information is received or obtained before, during or after such proceedings. In essence, what this entails is that section 29 of the Financial Intelligence Centre Act 2010 does not alter or reverse the common law principle of client confidentiality regarding the attorney-client privileged position even where the information at stake relates to money laundering. Section 29 covers only those situations where a lawyer or accountant is working with another party, say, in a business partnership, and then the lawyer or accountant stumbles across suspicious information concerning the business or the other party.

However, at common law, the duty of confidentiality relating to communications between a lawyer and his or her client is not absolute (Gabriel: undated, Online). For example, the privilege does not apply where a client is seeking advice from a lawyer in order to commit a crime or to aid someone to commit a crime (see: *Ibid*). If it were, every criminal would first discuss his intentions with his lawyer in order to work out a flawless plan before committing the crime (*Ibid*). Without this limitation, the lawyer would not be able to turn in such criminals (*Ibid*). However, the lawyer should, in fact, report such a person's intent to commit a crime. While a lawyer should report future intended crimes by a client, the lawyer cannot and is prohibited from reporting past completed crimes (see *Patton v. United States*, 281 U.S. 276, 306, 74 L. Ed. 854, 867 (1930); *Funk v. United States*, 290 U.S. 371, 385, 78 L. Ed. 369, 377 (1933); *Williams v. Chapman*, 118 N.C. 943, 945, 24 S.E. 810, 811 (1896); and, *Locke v. Alexander*, 8 N.C. 412, 417 (1821)).

In short, should an accountant or lawyer in Zambia be allowed to provide financial or legal advice, as the case may be, that facilitates money laundering or organized crime without facing any legal sanctions whatsoever? What about criminal funds that have been placed in a client account run by a lawyer on behalf of his or her client? Can such funds be reached by the Anti-Money Laundering Investigations Unit, a statutory body established by the Prohibition and Prevention of Money Laundering Act 2001, or the Financial Intelligence Centre, also a statutory body established by a different and competing piece of parallel legislation, the Financial Intelligence Centre Act 2010? Or, should the lawyer be allowed to protect the funds under the argument that the funds, together with any other information and document in the custody of the lawyer, are protected by a fiduciary duty of confidentiality and the lawyer-client privileged position? What does the Law Association of Zambia (LAZ) have to say, as the mother body of the legal profession and also as the professional body responsible for the regulation of professional ethics in the legal profession? And what does the Zambia Institute of Certified Accountants (ZICAS) have to say, as the mother body of the accounting profession and also as the professional body responsible for the regulation of professional ethics in the accounting profession? Are there any standards or codes of practice on such matters in Zambia?

With specific regard to money laundering matters, no major standards or codes of practice have ever been promulgated by LAZ or ZICAS (Mwenda, 2005: 95-99). In the American case of *In re Grand Jury Proceedings Under Seal*, 947 F.2d 1188, 1189-91 (4th Cir. 1991), an accountant was initially hired to provide business and tax assistance. Later, the accountant worked with a client in presenting relevant information to the attorney. The court held that the communications between the client and the accountant, in preparation for communications with the attorney were protected by the attorney-client privilege. A similar ruling was passed in *In re Beiter Co.*, 16 F.3d 929, 939-40 (8th Cir. 1994), holding that communications between an independent consultant hired by a client and a client's lawyer were protected by the attorney-client privilege where the purpose of the communication was to seek legal advice. In another American case, *McCaugherty v. Siffermann*, 132 F.R.D. 234, 239 (N.D. Cal. 1990), it was held that communications between a client's attorneys and a consultant hired by the client were protected by attorney-client privilege.

Closely related to the US position, the UK's International Compliance Association, in its training manual, the *International Diploma in Money Laundering Manual*, (p. 60), observes that: "...lawyers are attractive because they can offer launderers and their communications with them the protection of legal professional privilege (sometimes referred to as 'attorney client privilege'). *Legal professional privilege*, which has its foundations in English common law, *provides that no legal adviser can be compelled, without the express consent of his client, to disclose statements made to him by his client in professional confidence or to produce documents made in the same circumstances*. The attraction of legal professional privilege to money launderers is obvious."

Notwithstanding the strong arguments in favour of the 'attorney client privilege' norm, the American case of *Scott Paper Co. v. United States*, 943 F. Supp. 489, 499-500 (E.D. Pa. 1996) demonstrates that a defendant can be denied a claim of attorney-client privilege where it is unclear whether documents for which the defendant seeks privilege 'were maintained in files subject to open review by all members of the IRS (i.e. the equivalent of the IRS in Zambia is the ZRA) or whether they were maintained with an expectation of confidentiality'. In another American case, *United States v. Kelsey-Hayes Wheel Co.*, 15 F.R.D. 461, 465 (E.D. Mich. 1954), it was ruled that: "It is difficult to be persuaded that these documents were intended to remain confidential in the light of the fact that they were indiscriminately mingled with the other routine documents of the corporation and that no special effort to preserve them in segregated files with special protections was made."

In Zambia, what then is the legal position regarding the 'attorney client privilege' rule in matters of money laundering? Both the legislative and regulatory frameworks are silent. And the courts of law are yet to be faced with such a challenge. The situation of money laundering is also likely to be exacerbated by the plethora of poorly regulated real estate agents that keep popping up in the real estate industry. In spite of the existence of a law to regulate real estate agents in Zambia, that is, the Estate Agents Act 2000, the real agents need to be regulated properly and effectively. A number of these real estate agents are a potential conduit of money laundering to conceal ill-gotten wealth in properties such as a chain of houses, mansions, apartment buildings, pleasure resorts, farms and so forth. As the *Zambia National Broadcasting Corporation (ZNBC)* reports in an article titled, "ZIEA pounces on fake agents," and dated, May 17, 2011:

"The Zambia Institute of Estate Agents...pounced on illegal real estate agents in a joint operation that was conducted with the help of the council police in various parts of Lusaka. The operation dubbed Sanity saw about eight illegal estate agents rounded up and their posters destroyed. The agents have been given 28 days to register with the Zambia Institute of Estate Agents or face the law. Zambia Institute of Estate Agents Publicity and Communications Chairperson Raphael Thole says the operation was intended to enforce the provisions of the Estate agents Act. Mr. Thole says under the Act, all real estate agents are supposed to be registered, trained and regulated by the Zambia Institute of Estate Agents. He is saddened that members of the public have continued to lose huge sums of money to illegal real estate agents..."

What about financial intermediaries such as stockbrokers and dealers? They, too, need directives or a code of conduct to guide them against committing offences of money laundering. And what about banks and the issue of confidentiality over customer accounts and customer information, especially where examples are cited pointing to practices in jurisdictions such as Switzerland where arguments in favour of non-disclosure are quite strong? Article 28 of the Swiss Civil Code protects a bank account holder's right to privacy. This statutory provision codifies the concept of bank secrecy in Switzerland. In that country, the bank account holder's right to privacy over his account extends to both individual account holders as well as businesses. An exception to bank secrecy is, however, made where a report is required pursuant to anti-money laundering legislation in Switzerland.

In Zambia, how does the Prohibition and Prevention of Money Laundering Act 2001 or the Bank of Zambia Anti-Money Laundering Directives 2004 fair? Both the Zambian Act and the Bank of Zambia Directives are largely silent on the matter (*Cf.* Section 29 of the Financial Intelligence Centre Act 2010. Also, the Bank of Zambia issued a directive on December 10, 2008, in order to enhance the usage of the Credit Reference Bureau Africa Limited (CRBAL), compelling all credit providers to provide or disclose credit data to CRBAL and not to grant new loans without reference to the CRBAL. But this development alone has nothing to do directly with money laundering). Neither is section 29 of the Financial Intelligence Centre Act 2010 that helpful. However, at common law, the duty of confidentiality owed by banks to their customers, and the exceptions to this duty, were set out in the case of *Tournier v. National Provincial & Union Bank of England* [1924] K.B. 461. In that case, it was ruled that banks owe their customers a fiduciary duty of confidentiality extending at least to information concerning account transactions. This duty of confidentiality extends beyond the date when the banker-customer contract terminated. And exceptions to the duty can be seen where the disclosure is under compulsion of the law, or where there is a duty to the public to disclose, or where interests of the bank require such a disclosure, or where the disclosure is made with the express or implied consent of the customer. It could be argued, therefore, that section 14 of Zambia's Prohibition and Prevention of Money Laundering Act 2001, which reads, 'It shall not be unlawful for any person to make any disclosure in compliance with this Act', falls under some of the exceptions to the general rule in the *Tournier* case, namely, that disclosure is permissible where there is a duty to the public to disclose, or where interests of the bank require such a disclosure.

It is, however, doubtful whether section 29 of the Zambia's Financial Intelligence Centre Act 2010 or section 14 of Zambia's Prohibition and Prevention of Money Laundering Act 2001 (as amended by the Prohibition and Prevention of Money Laundering (Amendment) Act 2010) can be used to compel a lawyer to divulge information that is protected by the lawyer-client privileged position. We have already looked at section 29 of Zambia's Financial Intelligence Centre Act 2010. By contrast, section 14 of Zambia's Prohibition and Prevention of Money Laundering Act 2001 does not create a statutory duty on any person to disclose information, but merely offers legal protection where such a person decides, in compliance with the Prohibition and Prevention of Money Laundering Act 2001, to disclose relevant information to the investigative and prosecuting authorities. So, what to do now, as a Russian friend of mine would ask. LAZ and ZICAS should pass regulations, respectively, pursuant to section 12(4) of Zambia's Prohibition and Prevention of Money Laundering Act 2001 to regulate the legal and accountancy professions, respectively, on matters to do with money laundering! The said section 12(4) read as follows: "A Supervisory Authority shall issue such directives as may be approved by the Unit (*i.e.* the Anti-Money Laundering Investigations Unit) which may be necessary for the regulated institutions to prevent and detect money laundering."

And then section 2 of that same statute defines a 'Supervisory Authority' as any one of the following: (a) the Bank of Zambia; (b) the Registrar of Building Societies; (c) the Registrar of Banks and Financial Institutions; (d) the Registrar of Co-operatives; (e) the Registrar of Insurance; (f) the Securities Exchange Commissioner; (g) the Registrar of Companies; (h) the Commissioner of Lands; (i) the licensing authority under the Casino Act; or (k) any other authority established by law as a Supervisory Authority. Here, in regard to paragraph (k) of section 2, the establishment of LAZ and ZICAS as the supervisory authorities over the practice of law and accountancy, respectively, is evidenced in the Law Association of Zambia Act 1973 (as amended through to 2006) and the Accountants Act 1982 (set to be repealed and replaced by the Accountancy Bill 2008).

CHAPTER 86

STRENGTHENING THE INSTITUTION OF MARRIAGE THROUGH THE INTRODUCTION OF ALIENATION OF AFFECTION LAWS

Having been away from Zambia for more than twenty (20) years, albeit my intermittent yearly visits to the country, I have often found myself at a loss when it comes to some Zambian lingua articulated amongst the Zambian socialites whenever I visit my beloved country. Although I have spent a good half of my life in Europe and the USA, I do miss my native country, Zambia, very much. A phrase or term that I heard recently in Zambia was that of "MBAs", meaning a lady or man that is "Married but available." Indeed, our world is either changing fast or it is getting crazier by the day. When I left Zambia soon after President Kaunda lost elections to President Chiluba, I would not have imagined that there would one day be phrases such as "Married But Available" or "MBAs" in Zambia. And that Zambia professes to be a Christian nation, as proclaimed and promulgated by many charismatic evangelicals, is a reason that we should look into the role of law in effecting social change. Of course, nobody, and no society or country, is perfect. Yes, "MBAs" can be found everywhere in the world. But when we proclaim ourselves to the world that we are a Christian nation, are we not placing ourselves on a peddle stall? Indeed, is it really necessary to make such public proclamations, especially where we choose to enshrine such religious dictates in the Republican Constitution? This article does not in any way purport to argue in favor of or against the declaration of Zambia as a Christian nation. Neither does the article advance a male chauvinistic view of the world on "MBAs". Rather it seeks to deconstruct that bias, arguing instead for the curbing of the common vice in men – that is, that of initiating and perpetuating extra-marital affairs! Cognizant of the fact that many decently married women (as well as some highly disciplined single ladies), unlike many married men, hardly ever engage in extra-marital affairs, the article stands back from gender politics and sets forth a challenge to those that support the declaration of Zambia as a Christian nation. The article is not an indictment on any mortal being or any gender persuasion, but rather it offers a secular approach of how we can help inform the discourse of declaring Zambia as a Christian.

At the outset, it should be pointed out that law does not operate in a vacuum. Its relevance must relate to the common aspirations and values of a people. And if a nation professes or aspires to be a Christian nation, it is expected that the moral and social fabric of that nation should espouse principally such values, without, however, stifling out competing heterogeneous values and religious dictates. After all, that is what a democracy is all about – to put up with others! But some cynics may be uncomfortable in their seats and may be too quick to argue that there is no need to regulate people's moral conduct, and that it is up to people themselves to control their morals. If that be the case, then we might as well forget about criminal law and criminology since people can just control their behavior.

Many divorce attorneys have pondered the relevance of some ancient common law doctrines, such as the tort of alienation of affection, in some US jurisdictions. Put simply, alienation of affection is a tort action brought about by a deserted spouse against a third party who is believed to be the cause of the failure of the marriage. To illustrate, a Mrs X can bring about a civil action for alienation of affection against her husband's extra-marital lover as long as Mrs X can show, inter alia, that the defendant is the adulterous spouse's lover. In some instances, employers of the cheating husband or cheating wife can also be sued. The argument here is that the workplace is where the cheating spouse met his 'secret' office-lover, and that the cheating spouse's employer should have known, or should not have allowed or entertained such illicit affections in the workplace. And, in the US, closely related to the tort of alienation of affection is the action of **criminal conversation which normally occurs**

where an adulterer convinces his or her spouse to forgive him or her. Here, the injured spouse need not forget, and he or she can later bring an action for **criminal conversation**. Criminal conversation allows a loyal spouse who has suffered through an affair of a cheating spouse to sue the interloper even if the marriage stays intact (see *Thomas v. Siddiqui,* 869 S.W.2d 740 (Mo. banc 1994)). Doesn't Zambia as a Christian nation need such laws in order to curb the moral vice of infidelity? Of course, every country in the world has similar moral vices, but they have not declared themselves a Christian nation. And we recognize and admit that God has given each one of us the moral choice to sin or not to sin. But, then, the Government can also pass laws to help us keep our promises to God truly faithful, not so? It's called regulation. And regulations come in many different forms and shapes.

In the past, many nosy family members, as well as gossiper-neighbors or church elders, who may have advised a spouse to seek divorce have been sued for alienation of affection. That said, today, many states in the US have legislated against this tort, abolishing it entirely (see also *Thomas v. Siddiqui,* 869 S.W.2d 740 (Mo. 1994); *Townsend v. Townsend,* 708 S.W.2d 646 (Mo. banc 1986); *Wyman v. Wallace,* 615 P.2d 452 (Wash. 1980); and *Fundermann v. Mickelson,* 304 N.W.2d 790 (Iowa 1981)). However, the tort is still recognized – and is still justiciable – in the states of North Carolina, South Dakota, Utah, Mississippi, Hawaii, New Mexico and Illinois. In comparison, we have in Zambia, under African customary law, several judicial decisions of the

Zambian Local Courts pertaining to 'interference in marriage' where a cheating spouse is said to have engaged in extra-marital affairs. Although the Zambian Local Courts are not a court of record, and mindful that these courts have now been decreed not to entertain such cases, there is still ample evidence that under African customary law our Local Courts have passed rulings on marriage interference. The argument that Local Court rulings on marriage interference actually militate against the notion of the potentially polygamous nature of a marriage contracted under African customary is a dubious one. Claims relating to marriage interference have not always been confined to marriages under African customary law. Except in cases of divorce-related proceedings which are normally confined by statute to the High Court or the Supreme Court, the Local Court could deal with issues of marriage interference where there is a Christian marriage or a statutory marriage (i.e. one contracted under the Marriage Act 1918, as amended through to 1994), especially that the defendant here is not a party to the marriage. And both these marriages are required by law not to be potentially polygamous, but only to blossom under monogamy. That said, an interesting viewpoint that attempts to explain why cases of marriage interference are no longer entertained by the Local Courts is that perhaps many folks in the political circles fear that they, too, would eventually be caught up in such cases due to their notorious extra-marital affairs.

Be that as it may, it is important to point out that the Zambian Local Courts have no jurisdiction over criminal matters. To that end, issues falling in the domain of the Local Courts, regarding the adulterous conduct of a spouse through extra-marital affairs, are of a civil law nature and akin to the common law tort of alienation of affection. And if our Zambian customary law has been in tandem with the common law tort of alienation of affection, why not have such a tort codified under a piece of legislation in Zambia to give full weight to the declaration of Zambia as a Christian Nation? After all, aren't Christians supposed to respect and uphold the institution of marriage, especially if they are anointed with the Holy Spirit and claim to be prophets within their charismatic evangelical movements or if they partake in Holy Communion, say, at a Catholic Church? In both cases, are Christians not required to uphold the institution of marriage, especially if they are to lead a secular or religious flock? Besides, is that not what God's people are supposed to do when faced with a choice between laws that encourage divorce, on the one hand, and laws that strengthen the institution of marriage, on the other? How Christian can we be if we shy away from laws such as the common law tort of alienation of affection? That tort ensures that those that try to get in-between two people that are legally married face the wrath of the law. And we can learn from our own Local Courts in Zambia. They seemed to be on the right track until they were told to refrain from holding adulterers accountable. It is, however, not clear whether, for Zambia, as a Christian nation such a move was meant to promote forgiveness, just as in the case of the Biblical story where the Lord Jesus Christ forgave that lady accused of engaging in prostitution.

Although some critics maintain that archaic laws such as the common law tort of alienation of affection, tenable mainly in the US, are no longer relevant to the modern world, due to the increasing rate at which divorce is taking place, that very view is the reason why actions pointing to the tort of alienation of affection should be retained at common law – to preserve the institution of marriage! Divorce, as many social workers can attest to, often leaves the children in a worse off situation (see *Larson v. Dunn*, 460 N.W. 2nd 39, 45-46 Minn. 1990). And as Christians, I am sure even those who espouse the notion of declaring Zambia as a Christian nation agree that the tort of alienation of affection is very Christian in intent and spirit. It has a deterrent element against promiscuity and infidelity. Besides, marriage is a contract under which two parties agree that it is an exclusive union between them until "death do them part (as opposed to 'until divorce do them part')." But because we live in a world where we like to compromise and justify our own actions, we have reversed this dictate of natural law and replaced it with our own positivist view of the world in the name of 'divorce can be granted where a marriage has broken down irretrievably.' But then, we keep saying we are a Christian nation, yet we uphold laws that appear un-Christian in nature. Yes, Zambia professes to be a Christian nation. Isn't it right then to argue that the common law tort of alienation of affection works in tandem with Christian values that favor the sanctity and inviolability of the contract of marriage? It is important to observe that an action for alienation of affection does not require proof of extra-marital sex. The party suing (i.e. the plaintiff) must simply show that: (a) his or her marriage to his or her spouse involved some degree of love between them; (b) the spousal love between them was alienated and destroyed; and (c) the malicious conduct by the extra-marital lover of the cheating spouse led to or caused the loss of marital affection.

In making his or her case, the plaintiff is not required to show that the extra-marital lover of his or her cheating spouse set out to destroy the marital relationship. All that is required is for the plaintiff to show that her husband's extra-marital lover, or his wife's extra-marital lover, intentionally engaged in acts which would under reasonably foreseeable circumstances affect the marriage. Viewed from this angle, the extra-marital lover has very few defenses to fall on. He or she can, however, defend himself or herself if it can be shown that he or she did not know that the person he or she got involved with affectionately was in fact married. But rarely does it happen that an extra-marital lover does not know that the person she is dating is married. Pretty often, the extra-marital lover will simply shut her eyes to the obvious hoping that one day the man will leave his wife and marry her. Such incidents are common where, for example, a chronically lustful married man, when provided with extra-marital sex by a lady of limited financial means, becomes the economic messiah and savior of that lady – and sometimes the economic messiah and savior of her immediate family as well, irrespective the Christian values espoused by the lady or her family. This "commodification of love" is a common occurrence in many parts of the world today. Sometimes, the economic messiah in the relationship will be an elderly married woman who, desiring more sexual gratification outside her marriage, pounces on a destitute and indigent young man of limited financial means. So, how can we tell if a party knew that the other party is married? Surely, there ought to be some degree of suspicion, not so? Let us take a more reasoned look.

Whereas the concepts of *actual knowledge* and *actual suspicion* import a subjective test, the concepts of *constructive knowledge* and *reasonable cause to suspect* import an objective test. In the subjective test, it has to be shown that the defendant/accused actually knew what was going on. By contrast, in the objective test, the focus is on the totality of circumstances and whether it would be reasonable to impute knowledge to the defendant/accused. But, then, how do we define the term knowledge for purposes of determining whether a person had actual or constructive knowledge that the person he or she was dating is married? Should we apply a criminal law standard or a civil law standard in defining *knowledge*? Adulterous cases in Zambia, like the tort of alienation of affection in the US, are in the civil law domain. In the English case of *Selanghor v. Craddock (No.3)* [1968] 2 All ER 1073, Ungoed-Thomas J., defining the term 'knowledge', was of the view that 'knowledge' meant 'circumstances which would indicate to an honest and reasonable man that such design was being committed, or would put him on inquiry'. The test applied by Ungoed-Thomas J. is an objective test of a 'reasonable' man. In *Re Montagu's Settlements*_[1987] Ch. 264 at 285, another civil law case, it was held that 'knowledge' is not confined to actual knowledge, but includes actual knowledge that would have been acquired but for shutting one's eye to the obvious, or wilfully and reckless failing to make such inquiries as a reasonable man would make. Again, the objective test of a 'reasonable' man was applied. And in *Baden Delvaux and Lecuit v. Societe Generale,* [1983] BCLC 325, a civil law case, too, it was pointed out that knowledge can comprise any one of five different mental states: (i) actual knowledge; (ii) wilfully shutting one's eye to the obvious; (iii) wilfully and recklessly failing to make such inquiries as an honest and reasonable man would make; (iv) knowledge of circumstances which would indicate the facts to an honest and reasonable man; (v) knowledge of circumstances which would put an honest and reasonable man on inquiry.

The ruling in *Baden Delvaux and Lecuit v. Societe Generale* imports both an objective test and a subjective test of 'knowledge'. To satisfy the subjective test, unlike in the objective test, the intention of the defendant/accused must be proved. Paragraphs (i) and (ii) relate to the subjective test which requires the plaintiff to show that the defendant/accused had 'actual knowledge' or that he 'wilfully shut his eyes to the obvious'. By contrast, paragraphs (iii), (iv) and (v) relate to the objective test of how a *reasonable man*, when placed under similar circumstances, would have reacted. With this background information, we can then estimate if an extra-marital lover 'knew' that the person he or she was dating is married.

Turning to the concept of suspicion, in seeking to determine whether or not the extra-marital lover ought to be, or was expected to be, suspicious of the marital status of his or her illicit lover, one would be tempted to ask: what would constitute *reasonable cause to suspect* that a man is married? And what does the word *suspect* mean? Lord Devlin in the English Court of Appeal decision in *Hussein v. Chong Fook Kam* [1970] AC 942 defined *suspicion* as follows: "Suspicion in its ordinary meaning is a state of conjecture or surmise where proof is lacking: '*I suspect but I cannot prove....*'". Suspicion must not be confused with speculation or a hunch, or gut feeling, because suspicion may sometimes take a while to formulate and it falls only short of proof based on firm evidence. It seems that, in the case of suspicion, there must be a factual basis upon which it can be founded. But, of course, there is a subjective test and an objective test of *suspicion*. The objective test is usually formulated as: *where a person has reasonable grounds to suspect*. Akin to the objective test of *knowledge*, the objective test of *suspect* imports the concept of a *reasonable man* and how this reasonable man would have reacted.

It is, therefore, no good defense for an extra-marital lover to argue simply that she or he did not know that his or her illicit lover was married, especially where the extra-marital lover is caught up in the definitions of 'knowledge' highlighted above. Equally it is no good defense for the extra-marital lover to argue that it is actually the cheating spouse that went after her. But in some occasional cases, though, and depending on the evidence before the court of law, it might be a defense for the extra-marital lover to demonstrate that she was not the active and aggressive seducer. That said, it is no good defense for the extra-marital lover to argue that pre-existing marital problems that were being encountered by the person she got involved with point to an absence of affection between that person and his wife, unless such unhappiness had reached a level of negating love between the spouses. All said and done, what is our take as a Christian nation? Shall we shut our eyes to the truth and to the obvious, ignoring the moral and social decay in contemporary society of our so-called Christian nation? Law can, indeed, be an effective instrument of social change where it is designed, implemented and enforced thoughtfully.

PART - B

CHAPTER

87

UNEDITED EXTRACTS FROM THE MEDIA

Hitherto, we have explored and examined critically a number of contemporary issues in the *Law and Social Sciences* discourse through the prism of public intellectualism. We have endeavoured to break down complex ideas and concepts into easily discernible but critically insightful analyses. In doing so, we have not compromised on the quality of the analyses, but have actually enhanced the value of the arguments with subtle and useful humour to help the average guy on the street appreciate the ideas coming from the ivory tower of academia. That said, we are mindful that some people can be too sensitive and, thus, may not take too kindly to some views and analyses expressed in this book. But, as Kanye West would say, "They say I talk with so much emphasis... Ohhh, they're so sensitive!"

Before we turn to the concluding sections of this book, let me add that we are living in strange times. You may be wondering what I mean by this. You only have to turn to the media to read or listen to the news about strange stories of human misbehaviour. For a number of these news items, not even psychologists, social workers or criminologists can offer convincing solutions. Indeed, why do some people behave the way they do? Could someone explain to me why we have chronic haters in this world from time immemorial? They just keep on hating, and sometimes even hating on people that they hardly know. Is that normal? How can someone hate a person that they do not even know, but only hear about or read about? But that is the reality of the world we live in. Haters will always be there. But why should it be that way?

Because we are living in strange times, I was not too surprised when someone told me that for an individual to work for a certain coveted company or institution, "You have to know someone there, notwithstanding, or irrespective of, your good qualifications and impeccable work experience!" This guy stressed emphatically, "I have all the right qualifications and experience, and have been trying all these years to get in there, but it has not been possible." But then, let us take a more reasoned look. There can be a few isolated exceptions to the general rule, admitting meritocracy over personal connections. But, these are few and apart. Admittedly, the general rule tends to favour cronyism at many workplaces. So, the focus here is not on the isolated bona fide cases of meritocracy, but rather on the general rule of cronyism and mediocrity hiding under the guise of promoting a homogenous culture of team-work. But when did 'knowing someone' ever become a part of an individual's CV or required skills-set? Does 'knowing someone' speak to an individual's technical and functional competences as a performer? Yet, we often absorb and accept such prejudices as normal behaviour in our societies. And we tend to see them as part of our day-to-day ordinary life.

A few years ago, I was talking to an ambitious and overzealous African brother who openned to me on his own personal strategy of getting ahead of others at his workplace. And somewhere in the earlier chapters of this book, I have shared a similar story. Anyhow, the guy went on, referring to his workplace: "When I joined this company, the first thing I did was to find out which ass I was going kiss to climb the corporate ladder! Look, everyone does it. Nobody should cheat you that they just made it on merit. They all had to kiss ass!!!"

I tried to explain to the brother about the importance of genuine mentoring and coaching, as I had learned the same on my MBA degree years back. And I tried to highlight that good 'networking' need not be about 'kissing ass.' But he pushed back sharply, saying: "Look, I do not need a mentor or a coach in my life. I don't need that. All I need now is a 'sponsor' who can connect me to powerful people that can lookout for me in the company against any vultures!" Somewhat, what he was saying was beginning to sound as though it was making sense, although it was not philosophically appealing to me. He continued, none the less, "If you don't kiss ass, my brother, when the company is not doing too well, or if they just do not like you, they will target you for a prejudicial redundancy, literally throwing you under the bus, because you are too proud to kiss their ass. They want total loyalty even if they say 'let us discuss' or 'please feel free to express your views'. At the end of the day, they want conformity! These folks have a natural liking for brothers and sisters who kiss ass. I am just trynna be real and trynna survive. I ain't Uncle Tom, though. I am just trynna survive. That's all..."

Now, the legitimisation of cronyism and mediocrity is not only a preserve of the corporate world. It is also found in the world of politics. But then, is 'kissing ass' the 'right' thing to do in order to survive or to get ahead of others? Someone once said: "You cannot eat morals! At the end of the day, I need to feed my family. And how I do it is nobody's business..." But what happened to issues of morality in our philosophical enterprise? Does 'hunger' rob us of all manner of erudite thought? I am sure there are some exceptions to the general rule, but the majority of cases – I am afraid to say – end up like in the picture appearing hereunder (that has been doing some email rounds but whose source remains undetermined).

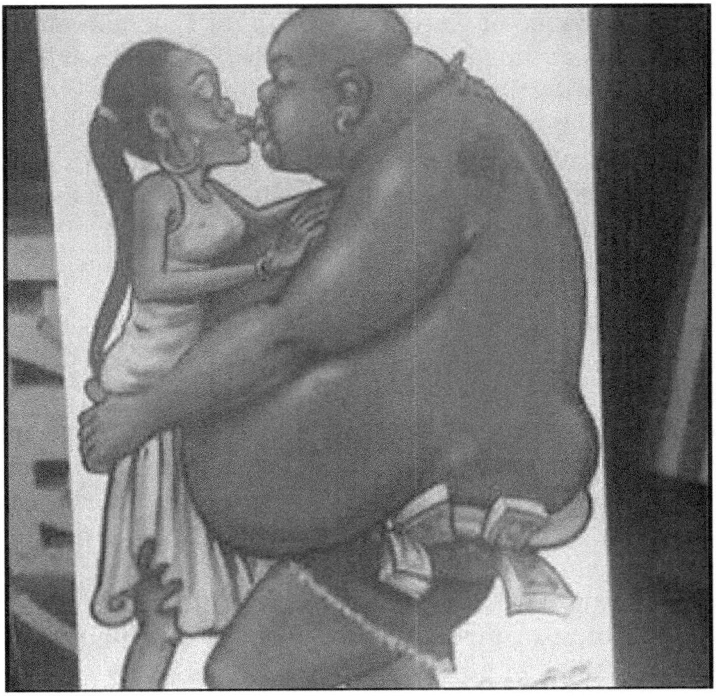

Back in the days, the old folks would say, "Money talks!!!" But today, money actually shouts!!! We are living in strange times.

A headline of a leading Zambian newspaper, the *Post*, on Friday, January 24, 2014, read: "Police want law to criminalise sensual or suggestive dancing". I am not, however, qualified to state whether or not the police were moving in the right direction. Suffice it to say, we are living in strange times. The *Post* newspaper article continued: "POLICE are waiting and crying for the day Parliament will enact a law to criminalise sensual or suggestive dancing, says deputy Inspector General of Police Solomon Jere. Speaking at Parliament...when he appeared before the committee on legal affairs chaired by Monze UPND Member of Parliament Jack Mwiimbu, Jere said police had noticed with great concern the different styles of dancing that had become common nowadays, which he said were different from the ones practiced in the olden days. 'But it is very difficult for the police to do something about controlling the way people dance unless Parliament comes up with an Act to criminalise certain types of dancing. It will become easy for us to move in and pounce on certain types of movements which are very suggestive. So for now, we are legally tied as we watch certain types of expositions in different outlets of drinking. For the police, we are also waiting and crying that one day, there will be something to control the nature of dancing. We cannot at present do anything in terms of how people are supposed to be controlled on how they should dance,' Jere said."

On Tuesday, January 21, 2014, the Zambia *Post* newspaper, in an article titled, " 'Sex for fish' killing men in Senanga", reported that: "WOMEN from Lusaka and other urban places are fond of trading sex for fish with fishermen in Senanga, according to assistant social welfare officer Victor Walubita. 'There is what is called 'sex for fish' in Senanga. Some women from Lusaka and many other places come to buy fish in bulk from fishermen at the Zambezi River for reselling in their respective places. Unfortunately, some of these women don't want to use money. They want to use their bodies and most of these fishermen are vulnerable people so they sleep with these women and they get infected just like that,' he said. Walubita said many fishermen had died and left orphans, who were turning to the Department of Social Welfare for help."

It is not only in Africa that some people use sex to get what they want. It is everywhere, except in Heaven. To put matters in context, the music and movie industries in developed countries are not short of people who have been known to use sex to get their record deals or movie roles. In Uganda, that country's *Daily Monitor* newspaper reported Online in an article dated September 15, 2013, and titled, "Lecturers' tale of students offering sex for marks", that: "Whenever soliciting for sex at the university is mentioned, what quickly comes to mind is lecturers wanting or even demanding sexual favours from their students. At all public and private universities in the country, there have always been reports of students complaining about their lecturers demanding sex from them in exchange for academic favours. There is, however, another side to this story – the story of students offering and pleading to give the lecturers 'anything they want' so as not to re-sit an exam, test or coursework."

The Ugandan report continues: "It is a story that has rarely, if at all, openly been told. But some lecturers at Makerere University, on condition that their identity is concealed, were willing to divulge the female students' sex schemes at this prestigious institution. One of them is a lecturer at the School of Computing and Informatics Technology (CIT). He is a young man in his early 30s. For purposes of this story, we shall call him Batte (it's only coincidental if there is a lecturer at CIT called Batte)... Batte says, 'Way before the semester begins, female students find out what lecturer will be teaching which course unit. Once they have acquired this information, they weigh their options and make decisions accordingly. They will know who is a no-nonsense lecturer that they will not bother with their crafty schemes. They will go for that one they suspect can easily succumb to their appetising offers.'..."

We are, indeed, living in a strange world. And there are more questions than answers in people's minds but for lack of courage to voice out. In Malawi, for example, the following media article stunned many readers.

CHILEKA MAN CONCEALS EX-WIFE'S PRIVATE PARTS AGAIN

August 27, 2009

FRANK NAMANGALE STAFF REPORTER

Police in Chileka, Blantyre have rearrested Samuel Mayinga for concealing his ex-wife's private parts through magic for going out with another man, almost two years after he was arrested on same allegations.

The ex-wife, Edina Lasitoni, reported to Chileka Police last week that after assurances by his ex-husband in 2007 that he would free her from the magic spell, she only had sex with her new man for a couple of days before Mayinga allegedly 'locked' her again. Chileka Police Station spokesperson Stella

Ndelenga said police rearrested Mayinga last week and charged him with conduct likely to cause breach of peace. He is on remand at Chichiri Prison and will appear in court on a date to be decided later.

Ndelenga said Mayinga did not meet the assurances he made to police and in court in 2007 that he would free his ex-wife of the magic spell. The Chilangoma Magistrate's Court in Machinjiri withdrew the case in October 2007 after Mayinga made the assurance. Ndelenga said Lasitoni only enjoyed her conjugal rights with her new husband for about three days before She was 'locked' again. She said last December. Lasitoni ended her relationship with the other man and reconciled with Mayinga on the understanding that he would 'unlock' her as per Mayinga's demand.

"Surprisingly, after their reconciliation, every time Mayinga wanted to have sex with her, her private parts kept disappearing. Fed up with the situation, the woman chased Mayinga away," Ndelenga said, suggesting that Mayinga was failing to undo his magic.

Ndelenga claimed Mayinga, on his rearrest last week, pleaded with the police to accompany him to the bush to look for the concoction to unlock her. She said police refused because last time they did the same but it did not work.

In Zimbabwe, some locals have invented a local "African blue-tooth" that not even the CIA or KGB could invent during or after the Cold War! This African blue-tooth gives the patent owner, usually a male, or a male licensee, remote wireless access sexually to the genitals of an unsuspecting female. Now imagine if such technology were to fall in the hands of an irresponsible or truant young man who happens to have a very bad or poor working relationship with a female boss at work. In no time, she would not know what has hit her!

In an article dated January 9, 2014, and titled, "Mubobobo: The Bluetooth version of rape," the *Zimbabwe Financial Gazette* reported Online that: "In recent years, there have been numerous stories in the media, involving cases that have been alleged to have happened around the country, where some men have been lynched by crowds or chased from villages after being accused of practicing mubobobo. Simply put, mubobobo is a form of witchcraft where a man possesses a charm for the purposes of magic that gives him power to have sex with a woman without her consent and without any contact. The latter has earned mubobobo the nickname 'bluetooth sex' or 'wireless sex'. Some charms that have been in the press involved use of women's underwear."

The report in the *Zimbabwe Financial Gazette* continues: "There are two types of mubobobo. The first type is practiced in broad daylight where the victim, (a woman) feels sexually aroused in a public place, or like there is someone having sex with her. The second type of mubobobo is nocturnal, the victim dreams of sexual intercourse taking place near her by people or animals or sees a man masturbating... The theme is the same, there is no contact whether by day or by night. Daylight mubobobo should also not be confused with perverts who ejaculate in queues, masturbate in public or steal women's underwear from washing lines. The men who possess these charms do it for a variety of reasons that include but are not limited to enhancing wealth, exercising power over women or a certain woman (and their male partner/s) or to gain extraordinary physical strength to execute manual jobs. The bottom line is that mubobobo is *witchcraft.* Some women are not affected by it because they have the spiritual protection against witchcraft. Interesting though is that if a man fails to execute their mubobobo they end up hating their target and one can catch them unhappily staring at her."

So, what to do now? Do we have pieces of legislation that are robust enough against practices of witchcraft in many parts of the world? And what is the weight of evidence required in such cases to secure a conviction, or are these cases relegated to some lower courts of law with no system of proper records, involving mainly African customary law? Further, can we criminalize acts of witchcraft or similar acts from other sects that practice closely related 'publicly unwelcome' and 'mystic' rituals? Indeed, where do we draw the line when someone that subscribes to such mystic rituals or practices cries foul that any attempt at enacting or enforcing legislation against his or her suspicious act or sect is an infringement of his or her constitutional right and freedom of conscience, especially in situations where it cannot be proved that the accused person has actually harmed or intends to harm anyone (*e.g.* by trespassing on the person of another)? Even where a confession is obtained from the suspect, as in the Malawi case above, how reliable is such a confession when there is little other evidence to support the confession? We are living in very strange times. Against this background, let us now turn to some cognate items in the concluding sections of this book.

The Post
The paper that digs deeper

Friday, April 21, 2000

Political WATCH:

ENLIGHTENED DICTATORS

By

Dr. Kenneth K. Mwenda

As I sat in my first class seat, flying from Moscow to London, and sipping some mild Chardonnay with a light dip of some prawns into avocado cream, I wondered into some undisciplined thinking and began pondering over the political milieu in my beloved country, Zambia.

What next for a president? A lawyer, a businessman, a preacher, or a thug? What next? Perhaps, a lady would do. After all, our women are not as lamentable in thug and political-rogue behaviour as our men.

As at now, I have not heard of any woman seriously scheming to take over Plot No.1 . Our mothers and sisters are too honourable to dip their hands in such political mess!

But, democracy should not discriminate on the basis of gender. FTJ will soon hang up his boots after his last cap for the national team this season. I am mindful, however, that the man might take up a full-time coaching job to help out his team.

KK, too, has finally retired after playing for his team and winning quite a number of international caps. He has finally lived up to expectation.

KK is now bidding farewell to all the pretenders in African politics. Amidst such good gesture from Zambia's top two political figures we are now left with an abundance of pretenders and a few good players. The phony ones are busy schemming and gnashing teeth, outdoing each other left, right and centre and busy trying to outfox kin and kith over who takes over the remains of political power.

The little time we are left with before next year's presidential elections is to be occupied by divisive and cunning tactics, shrewd and treacherous machinations, and moribund, decaying henchmen tactics to please the master - with a hope of succeeding the throne. Opportunism will rise to its greatest height and we shall witness players on the political playing field trying to take free-kicks even when the ball has just gone out for a throw in!

Both in the ruling party, MMD, and in the opposition UNIP in particular - there is a serious power vacuum for the hot seat. MMD had Great Chilu to take the Great Kalu free-kicks. So did UNIP find comfort in their captain, Super Ken.

The two are now about to hang up their boots. But, both MMD and UNIP still have to go to the Africa Cup Finals to meet the Pastor Mumbas and the Mazokas of this world who are eagerly waiting.

Let us hope that the referee will be fair and that no off-side goals will be allowed, especially if taken from a Chilu free-kick! UNIP and MMD, the parties now struggling to find replacements for their top players, must seek a ball-wizard to take the free-kicks, otherwise Andy will take the candys home.

The race is now hot. In his time, Great Chilu took his free-kicks cunningly, and that is what politics is all about ... in a Machiavellian sense, if you will. If KK, while in power, played gracefully on the international arena, but lethal domestically, then likewise he has the hallmark of a good international diplomat because he could shield the ball from other players and thus conceal some of the domestic weaknesses from the international audience.

Indeed, he played with great wizardry, finesse and the aura of a great player. But, good players internationally have one thing in common: their game is similar although they maybe be taught by different teachers. Yes indeed, my trip to Russia was very fulfilling. President Putin had just been elected to office. Personally, I felt as if I was coming from a pilgrimage. Although I am not a Marxist-Leninist, nor strictly speaking a rightist, I do sympathize with leftist thought. However, I still extend a cordial and warm handshake to rightist ideology. In the world of diplomacy, things are never in black and white. It's a world full of grey shades, and with time we all begin to learn. But even in that greyness, one must learn to be a man of his own definition and character. For me, it was a great honour to visit Russia for I grew up on Marxist-Leninist literature throughout my undergraduate days at the University of Zambia.

So, as I sat in my first class seat on that flight from Moscow I could see in my mind's eye what Africa possibly needed. It had nothing to do with Russia. Rather, it was something conceived out of my own intellectual and ideological biases, if you will. I had by now switched from my Chardonnay to gin and tonic and had re-focused my thoughts, while reclining from undisciplined thinking into my usual structured thought. Africa needs some extremely enlightened dictators. I mean really 'Eenlightened' ones! Democracy, as espoused by the West, seems to be a difficult thing for us to grasp. Maybe it's not just for us. We must therefore find something which is of our own.

The West might call ours dictatorship, but that is

how our forefathers lived. Chiefs are born as chiefs and there are no elections or coup d'etats in the village. But that in itself presents a unique form of democracy and we cannot deny it. Extrapolating this analysis, structured and highly enlightened dictatorships seem the only way forward. Look, what do you do when you have tried something and it is not working? Have we not tried Western ethos of democracy and what has come out of it? Nothing! Let us not be too academic by arguing that we need first to change the institutional and structural arrangements before democracy can work. That is a lame and duck excuse. We need a system that is workable, one that can work to bar forms of anarchy which are masked as democracy.

The system must, however, preserve the dignity and well-being of mankind, while placing an emphasis on state and individual responsibilities. This is what we need in Africa. It may sound too harsh, but I admire great men like Shaka Zulu who surged forward on the basis of a disciplined army that did not tolerate laziness. Judged by the times when the Mfecane wars were fought, Shaka was an enlightened dictator who built a kingdom that amassed great wealth. But, I concede that times are now different. Be that as it may, concepts such as Shaka's still apply and all we need to do is adapt them to a different context and time. What we need is pragmatism, originality, versatility, adaptability and realism. Please don't get me wrong, but get me right instead: I am not calling for a

return to the old times. But history has a tendency of repeating itself. We can only predict the future if we know where we are coming from, notwithstanding any external forces, and if we accept our present shortcomings politically and economically. Somewhere in between, and from what experience has taught us, we must find a niche to surge forward. This is an era of enlightenment in which the African renaissance is taking place, and truly, the only free man is an enlightened person.

- *Kenneth K. Mwenda*

TIMES
of ZAMBIA
forward with the nation

Thursday, March 11, 1999

'DON'T HAVE AN INFLATED EGO'

By

Dr. Kenneth K. Mwenda, in Accra, Ghana

THIS piece is dedicated to the youth of Zambia. The dilemma in which many young African intellectuals find themselves today poses very interesting questions that can only be answered by rocking towards a paradigm shift.

In our pursuit of social justice, ought we not to bring prudence and good reasoning to both the young and the old? Ought we not to break the barriers that shield intellect from wisdom?

Africa's young intellectuals have often found themselves ostracized from the mainstream of social governance. We must define what an intellectual is. The term intellectual is not confined to one who simply wields a university degree.

No, not all. An intellectual is one who is guided chiefly by intellect rather than by emotion. An intellectual thinks before he acts. An intellectual can engage constructively and creatively in open debate and criticism.

Objectivity is the hallmark of his or her trade. An intellectual pursues a line of thought objectively and systematically and does not hide behind senseless phrases such as 'that is your opinion' whenever he or she is found wanting in intellect.

An intellectual stays away from mediocre forms of discontentment, such as the following phrase: 'Ire, ni mfulwa sana! Ku mutima kwa fina sana!' (Translated as: I am very upset. There is so much darkness over my heart - without really applying any sound reasoning to such proclamations, e.g. why has the upsetting thing happened? Is there any contributory negligence on my part? What are the lessons to be learned if at all I am part of the problem?)

Indeed, other forms of mediocre expressions which are often devoid of intellect include:

'Ala, kalya na li ka pata! Na ka pata fye!' (Translated: kaja ni ka zonda! Or, I hate him! I just hate him - without applying any sound reasoning at all).

Yet we often hear these sentiments day in and day

out from our people, some of whom even claim to be Christians and intellectuals. Whenever inflated egos of these individuals are deflated, by unexpected criticism, they cease to think properly and become emotional.

They lack rationality of any kind and only see that which they desire to see – hate! Then, we know that we are dealing with lowly and poorly cultivated souls.

Indeed, intellectualism points to a nexus between theory and practice. It is that link which distinguishes an intellectual from mere breeders of palm tree justice.

In the commonwealth mundane of mankind, where mortals with limited faculties want to reign, the notion of social justice is then relegated to norms which are dispensed only by 'old age' underneath a coconut tree. In such cases, society ceases to perceive intellectualism as a creative and interactive science.

Wisdom, if at all it is there, is then elevated to circumscribe issues within the sole monopoly of 'old age'. These are the 'attitudes' that rest and brood beneath the 'coconut tree of social justice'. Who dare question? The inquirer will be accused of falling short of cultural expectations. He will be labelled insolent and rude. But this is how we live in Africa. We run away from facts.

We run away from the truth and we compromise because we want to be in good books with everyone at all times. This is our senseless way of social justice. But life teaches us that you cannot win that way.

You must first be honest with yourself. What is important is to know that what you are pursuing is the truth. As a fable would tell you, a man whose home is run by his cruel wife will leave his own house to go hunting or drinking when his wife is upset, irrespective of who has annoyed her.

The man will only return late in the night or after some days (if he has gone hunting) with a hope that the woman has now calmed down.

His relatives will also stay away from his home because they loathe the way he fears his wife. But, as the fable shows, this is not a clever man. He sees running away as the means to solving his problems. He fails to confront his wife for a solution because she is guided by emotions rather than by intellect and reason. But, he who fights and runs away lives to fight another day.

Indeed, not long ago, I was flying to Africa. I sat next to an old man, on my right, and a young lad, on my left. Both were Zambians. It was a pleasant flight for I could switch into my Zambian dialectics easily. The old man kept everyone in the first class awake with his story of how during the colonial days they (he and his colleagues) threw stones at the colonial masters to gain Zambia's independence.

His story went on and on. I could not tell him to stop making noise for that would have been deemed rude. However, I was quite uncomfortable. But that is our notion of social justice; to keep quiet. Interestingly, however, the young lad seated on my left sprung up to his feet, after taking some good shots of gin and tonic, and interrupted the old man:

"Imwe ba mdala... (Translated: Hey, old man), you mean there was no one among you, those days, who was sensible enough not to throw stones! Only small kids throw stones! Elderly folks shouldn't throw stones. They ought to think!!!"

The old man was ostensibly very upset and he roared with anger:

"Ala, ine ku mu time kwa fins!!! (Translated: My heart is really clouded with darkness)"

The man began shaking with anger. I knew that he felt insulted by the young man's comments. It was then that I stepped in to mediate. I told the young man:

"Truly young man, you ought not to have said that! That was not very nice of you."

But no sooner had the old man risen to go to the loo, I continued whispering to the young man:

"Wa chita fye bwino mwaiche (You did well young man). Ala, teti tula le no tulo ati pantu fye bale pose ama bwe (we can't even enjoy some sleep simply because he threw stones)!"

When the old man returned from the loo, I picked myself nicely and reprimanded the young man again for offending the old man. I knew that the old man's ego was badly injured. I had to help him rejuvenate his ego and pride. Having done that, I knew that it was now time to talk to the old man.

I politely turned to talk to the old man. I could tell that the man was a Bemba, merely by looking at his once 'inflated', but now 'deflated' ego (kalya aka chi pale ni nshi na Ica pwa).

I then continued: "Imwe ba md'ala... How can you run on to the battlefield without a 'Red Cross' flag? When you do that, as you have just done, the enemy will open fire at you and you should not complain at all that 'ulya mwaiche ta kwata umu cinshi'

(Translated: The young man is very disrespectful)! You ought to realize that 'mwi kala pata lala, mwine apa tala lika!' If you behave nicely, the young man will not bother to attack you. He is only human and you have already been irritating him! You started the fight! Keep your ideas to your own head if you cannot take criticism!"

There was utter silence. The man did not know what had hit him. But I knew deep within myself that the man got the message loud and clear. I then advised the young man to apologize, for courtesy's sake, even if by being loud the old man had waved his 'old age' immunity from criticism. Indeed, often, or rather always, elderly folks enjoy the 'old age' immunity from humiliating criticism.

But these folks must not begin to exploit and abuse that immunity by imposing their views on the young, save for views which are progressive and objective (but not for misplaced and self-interested views). Old folks should realize that society is heterogeneous and culture is dynamic.

The young folks are being exposed to all sorts of new ideas and you do not expect the young to 'cage' those ideas under a lid so that they begin to think as if they are seated beneath a coconut tree. But of course, the young have to be respectful of culture.

Make no mistake about that. But, change is also inevitable since culture is dynamic and it occurs at various recursive levels of sub-cultures and dominant cultures.

Thus, when we see university students agitating for social change we must begin to appreciate their sociology of knowledge. We cannot afford to close our eyes to the truth and let palm tree or coconut tree justice take hold over good reason and sound conscience.

TIMES
of ZAMBIA
forward with the nation

Saturday, October 25, 1997

CHILUBA'S MASTERS DEGREE LEGITIMATE - WARWICK DON

By

Dr. Kenneth K. Mwenda, in Warwick, UK

A LOT of interesting stuff has been written on Mr Chiluba and his masters degree from the University of Warwick. From the bio-data of Mr Chiluba, available on internet, it is not disputable that Mr Chiluba has no first degree. However, it is not my aim here to comment on the pre-MPhil degree qualifications held by Mr Chiluba.

It must be observed that it is perfectly legitimate for a person who has no first degree to pursue a masters degree in a field related to his occupation, career or profession.

For example, a lawyer who originally trained as a Barrister without having acquired a law degree, but 0 has significant experience in the profession e.g.

rising to the post of High Court Judge, can, in my view, proceed directly on to a Master of Law degree programme.

His or her professional experience culminates into valuable knowledge that cannot be discounted simply because he or she does not have a first degree. Indeed, there are various ways in which this can be done in different disciplines.

First, the concept of accreditation of prior learning (APL) indicates that if an applicant can satisfy the

admitting institution that he or she has already fulfilled some of the assessment requirements and will be able by completing the remaining requirements to fulfil the objectives of the program and attain the standard required for the award, he or she MAY be given credit for this.

Secondly, the concept of accreditation of prior learning achievement (APLA) shows that credit will be granted on the basis of the completion of a related program or discrete part of a program (such as a module or course), upon production of SUITABLE EVIDENCE.

This may include claims based on credit accumulation and transfer (CATS) points already awarded. Thirdly, application for credit may also be awarded by an institution of higher learning on the basis of prior experiential learning (APEL). The

APLA and APEL mainly fall under the jacket umbrella, APL.

The concept of APL must not be seen as taking away the value of qualifications of those of us who have pursued their studies in the straight line route of bachelors, masters and then doctorate. APL simply recognizes that there are many experienced people who operate at levels that are far higher than their paper qualifications.

Such persons, on production of evidence in a portfolio, must be given the opportunity to gain credit for their experience. Each institution of higher learning has its own policy on such matters.

So, if Unza, for example, has a mature entry exam for undergraduate "matures", which Mr Chiluba could have been required to sit for, Mr Chiluba could have been lucky in that a State House scholarship went begging to enable him avoid Unza and pursue a masters degree abroad.

He certainly acted wisely. In the 1997 UK Times League table of top research universities in the United Kingdom, the University of Warwick, was rated in the TOP FIVE out of approximately 97 universities in the United Kingdom.

Warwick was ranked far ahead - and has been for some time - of many famous universities. Indeed, the other universities in the top five this year included

Oxford, Cambridge, Imperial College (London), and London School of Economics (LSE).

In the light of the foregoing, it comes as no surprise that Mr Chiluba, like many other people today the world over, succeeded in getting a masters degree without a bachelor's degree.

It is perfectly lawful and legitimate for a person without a bachelors to obtain a masters degree as long as the admitting institution has diligently applied itself to standards of accreditation of prior learning.

Indeed, Mr Chiluba, like Dr. Kenneth Kaunda, the first president of the Republic of Zambia, has been in politics much of his life.

Mr Chiluba's masters degree does not depart in any significant manner from what the man has been doing all his life. Real knowledge is not gained in the closet but in the real world!

There is no doubt too that despite the heavy intellectual criticism - mainly from the Marxist and leftist thinkers - that Dr. Kaunda's humanism faced, a thinking process in Dr. Kaunda's ideology had been set in motion. Whether that thought process was right or wrong that is a question for the social sciences to answer on the fringe of value judgements. It is pointless being cynical over anything we are not happy about or do not agree with.

We must instead try to find the little merit, if anything, in what we disagree over so that littleness can be constructively criticized and re-worked into a better idea. Absolute dismissiveness is destructive as it thrives mainly on values of obscured "objectivity" imbedded in a conceited sense of all-knowing. That can be a serious danger in dealing with the ideological construct of things.

The author is a UK-based Zambian, a Rhodes Scholar and Lecturer in Law at the University of Warwick (UK).

The Post
The paper that digs deeper

Tuesday, December 7, 1999

Political WATCH

A PEOPLE'S HISTORY MUST BE PRESERVED

By

Dr. Kenneth K. Mwenda

That a people's history must be preserved to be passed on to generations to come is not in itself a euphoric symbol of mere sentimentalism or nationalism.

Rather, it is a fundamental norm upon which national cultures are born. In this article, I propose to salute the good efforts of some of Zambia's best; the names run from all corridors of life. Generations to come and those still with us will, undeniably, find role models in these people.

It is the role of society to provide role models and for the public media to promote these models so as to offer our youths a milieu of ethical and moral suasion. All progressive cultures and peoples have developed through a sense of belief in themselves. At closer circumspection, the discussion herein is akin to a 'Who's Who of Zambians in the ending Millennium'. But the idea is far from being one promoting or advocating elitism.

Rather, the idea is to try and write some melodious notes and chords of a historical nature for our people. This, it is hoped, is a way forward in building a sense of self-esteem and confidence amongst our youths.

Indeed, the article highlights some of the nation's own great names so that those who care to hear and those that care to listen will know where we are coming from and where we are going. Although the article does not claim to include all the names that the audience would like to see, there is an attempt, at least, to recognize and honor the efforts of most of these men and women.

At the very outset, His Excellence, the President of the Republic of Zambia, Frederick Jacob Titus Chiluba, must be commended for his role in bringing peace to the region of Southern Africa. Chiluba has done well in this area and clearly his efforts complement those of his predecessor, Dr. Kenneth Kaunda. Although the MMD government had started off a note that did not appreciate the idea of spending the country's resources on supporting peace/liberation efforts outside Zambia - since this is what Dr. Kaunda's government had spent much of the national resources on – the MMD government later realized that Zambia cannot exist as an island in this process of globalization. So, the Kaunda stand was adopted both in the case of the Congo and Angola conflict resolution efforts.

But Kaunda too, and Nyerere, as we shall see below, were students of Nkrumah's Pan-Africanist ideology which placed much emphasis on foreign policy and less on domestic policy.

Every time I travel to various parts of the world the one interesting item that often pops up in conversations - once I introduce myself as a Zambian - is the name and works of Zambia's former president Dr. Kenneth Buchizya Kaunda (hereinafter referred to as KK). This man, KK, undeniably, is a great political figure.

The history of Zambia and the continent as a whole cannot be told without mentioning the name KK. Books have been written on this man showing how he, together with the people of Zambia, made great sacrifices to liberate the Southern African region.

Everywhere I have been people are fond of KK. I can understand why. Apart from his charisma, charm, good personal attributes and a warm personality, KK spent 27years investing heavily in international politics and relations. Somewhat, this had its negative effects domestically and it also had its good sides internationally.

But there is little doubt that KK, like the late Dr. Julius Mwalimu (teacher) Nyerere of Tanzania, were students of the late Dr. Kwame Nkrumah of Ghana. I visited Ghana sometime this year. Nkrumah's legacy still lives on.

Indeed, Nkrumah was himself a great intellectual and probably one of the greatest political figures to have come out of Africa. His political ideology of Pan-Africanism, adopted mainly from early African-American political activists, is now being revived amongst several Africanist scholars as the 3African Renaissance2. Although Nkrumah was such a phenomenal figure, Africa has produced many more great names of which KK, Nyerere, Senghor, Sekou Toure and others remain prominent. But in Eastern and Southern Africa alone, perhaps the only contemporaries to KK are Nyerere and Madiba.

Although we have had many younger heads of state in the region, who even possess stronger academic credentials, they still do not match up. Indeed, they have a lot to learn. Politics is an art. Political science, by contrast, is a science that you can study in a classroom. Politics is that which you live with by the day and it is characterized by 'conflict'.

Those of you who have read political philosophy will agree, for example, that the Machiavellan style of leadership is sometimes exhibited by politicians who have never read political philosophy. It is all about the art of managing conflict. Some have the natural flair and gift to manage conflict into agreement and policy. From a purely Machiavellanist, one would acknowledge that Africa's dictators know very well how to hold on to power through the use of force. But of course, the democrat will have misgivings here. Even so, who am Ito disagree with the democrat? I am only a commentator and scholar.

In my humble view, and undeniably, the right and most honorable Dr. Nelson 'Madiba' Mandela remains the most respected and popular political figure of this century. The world cannot take that away from him. He has earned his respect. When top UK universities, including Oxford, Cambridge and Warwick, chose to honor Madiba with doctorate degrees it was indeed an event unprecedented by any worldly standards.

Sunday Mail

Sunday, July 18, 1999

TO WHOM DOES AFRICAN CUSTOMARY LAW APPLY?

By

Dr. Kenneth K. Mwenda, in Accra, Ghana

IN the depths of quietness, legend has it that in one Local Court case, which dealt with an issue of pregnancy, the following dialogue transpired:

The Local Court Justice asking the pregnant teenager, while pointing at the accused, a next door neighbor (married man) to the complainant:

"Is he the one responsible for the damage (pregnancy)?"

The young lady responding shyly: "Yes, he is the one..."

The Local Court Justice continues: "Tell this court what happened exactly!" After shedding some tears the young lady gathers courage and responds:

"Ni na kana festi then ba ni uza ati: 'okay, umutwe

fye... please'!"

(At first, I refused then he said: [Zambian English] "okay, just the 'pink head'..., please"!)

But this is African customary law we are dealing with here. African customary law continues to evolve in a flux, yet the subjects to which it applies often have difficulties deciphering the 'what it is' from the 'what ought to be'.

To whom does African customary law apply? Who can claim the benefit of African customary law? A number of scholarly studies and academic theses have been written on the nature of African customary law, yet the answers to some of the problems and challenges paused by African customary law are not easily discernible.

In this article, I will address some of the issues affecting African customary, at an ordinary prudent man's level, to try and show that the political economy has invaded the corpus of African customary law with a view of marginalizing the law and equating it with desperate individual aggrandizement in a deprived economy.

So, what is African customary law and how has this law been received in various parts of Africa? The integration of African customary law into the legal systems of many post-colonial African states has varied considerably.

But that is not the aim of this work. Suffice it to say that African customary law can be explained in simple language as that consistent practice of societal norms and values which are recognized within a reasonably wide community as having the force of law.

Here, consistency requires evidence of a reasonable time. We must therefore distinguish African customary law from mere traditional practices that lack the force of law. To do this, let us consider the following points.

1. African customary law is only opposable (applies only) to parties who have lived by that very custom. Thus, for customary law to apply to any party, the claimant must show that the subject, that is, depending on the nature of the claim (either the claimant, the accused or both) has not been a persistent objector to the custom and that, indeed, the custom in issue is one which obtains in his or her culture or community.

To illustrate, a Lozi man marrying a Bemba woman cannot be forced into such Bemba traditions as "uku lasa imbusa!" because there are no such traditions in bu Lozi land.

The Bemba family he is marrying into should not and cannot insist that 'nye ka fye umwana wa mu Lozi alase imbusa' (until the Lozi man spears the 'mbusa', we shall not proceed).

The mbusa tradition is very serious business ka! Here, I have only referred to it as an example where customary law finds itself at cross-roads. Exceptions, however, could be seen, for example, not only where the Lozi man has lived amongst Bembas and by their culture, but also where his life has been governed by Bemba culture elsewhere (e.g. because his step-father is Bemba).

Thus, not even a court of law will order 'specific performance' of the mbusa custom if it can be seen that the party contesting the custom is far removed from that custom. But, because most cases of African customary law are settled outside the court room, if the Lozi man is not strong enough 'pa ka mwa (that is, good enough in talking)' he may be forced to succumb to the Bemba custom of 'uku lasa imbusa'.

If, however, he refuses uku lase imbusa, the Lozi man might be regarded by the Bemba party as 'having insulted them!' For often a time that is how we treat dissent in African societies, although this feature does not constitute African customary law, but mere intimidatory tactics to weaken the opposition.

And, thus we then find ourselves, out of ignorance, saying 'mukwai eeh ntambi' (that is the culture) for the Lozi man 'uku lasa imbusa'. No, that is not true! Instead, what is being projected here is simply the Bantu practice of 'ubuntu', which has no binding legal force whatsoever.

Indeed, by arguing that 'ubuntu' (this term is loosely used here without any political philosophy connotation) is synonymous with 'intambi' one could end up either not being honest enough or simply not knowing our African customary law well enough.

'Intambi', under African customary law, applies only to those that have lived by that custom or whose life has been governed by such custom. The only common denominator in all African cultures, I contend, is 'modesty' and 'mutual respect'.

Suppressing dissent is not part of African customary law, particularly to a party that has not lived under such practices of fear and intimidation.

2. The analysis I have provided above helps to show how the learned men of the law, dressed in their elegant robs that suffix their wisdom, approach the polemics surrounding the legal force of customs and culture.

Whether we should change the process and substance of the law here is another issue altogether.

All we know is that when a judgement is passed

against a customary claim for some inchoate form of specific performance and the applicant decides to disobey the judgement by forcing the Lozi man in the above example to 'lass imbusa' the consequences of contempt of court would be quite severe. Ala, don't even think about it... don't even go there (smile)! The same applies in the case of, say, a Ngoni or Bemba man who is about to marry a Luvale or Lunda lady.

The Luvales or Lundas cannot lawfully insist to [inspect] his "manhood" to prove if he has been circumcised or not! No, they cannot do that. If they insist, I have little doubt that the Bemba man will quickly cry foul [and very loud indeed] that: "Ala na tukwa mu kwai" (I have been insulted)!

By contrast, perhaps, the Bemba man's cousin, the Ngoni man, playing "muzungu wanga" type of "utu chawa" (that is, pretending to be Mr. Nice) would succumb.

But, this is just a thought. He, too, could rebel!

3. There is a second thread to the argument on African customary law. In many Anglo-Saxon common law jurisdictions, including Zambia, municipal law (legislation) often provides something like 'African customary law is valid to the extent that it is not repugnant to natural justice, good conscience, and equity'.

What, then, is good conscience or equity? It is all a

matter for the Whiteman's education and culture, imposed on the African peoples, to interpret what constitutes good conscience and equity. We still live with these biases today! Ala, bwa fya!

So, to illustrate, a man that is lawfully married under the Whiteman's notion of a white wedding, that is, at the Civic Centre (statutory marriage) or at church (same effect here) cannot go ahead to take on another wife so long as his wife lives and their marriage has not been dissolved by the High Court.

If he takes another wife, he will be committing the criminal offence of bigamy for which the law can visit him. But, because he is often the bread winner at home, his wife will seldom think of ever taking him to court pantu kuti mwa lala po fye insala (you can just end up starving if the bread-winner is locked up).

This is how the political-economy permeates the cultural and legal spheres. But even then, we cannot call these developments, in themselves, African customary law. They are simply Bantu practices of ubuntu!

4. Another illustration of how certain customary practices can run contrary to the colonially handed down notion of good conscience and equity is the idea of female circumcision today, and other related practices that are not the privilege of the public to

know. “Ala, ca fina mukwai” (*English translation*: “The information is too sacred to be paraded in public.”). These African practices are shrouded in mystery and mysticism and they remain part of our culture.

Then the Whiteman's handed down law tells us that the practices in issue are barbaric and repugnant to natural justice and good conscience. Who is right then?

The beauty of it all is that these traditions are handed down by old age and the Whiteman's law cannot even enter at the invitation of the student/complainant. If the student complains about these society-wide approved ceremonial practices, she will have no witnesses to support her case.

All the elders involved will simply walk away, ati: "Ta fundwa uyu mu kashana!" (*English translation*: “This lady is not well tutored for the purposes of marriage”) because it's normal to have some of these practices in place so that when 'inspection time' comes..., (I cannot explain 'inspection time' beyond the quotation marks)!

In this way, we find that even the force of law and religion are both watered down. (To be continued next week on lobola, wealth and evidence in adultery).

- *Kenneth K. Mwenda*

The Post

The paper that digs deeper

Tuesday, September 7, 1999

Political WATCH

AFRICA'S DEVELOPMENT

By

Dr. Kenneth K. Mwenda

As Africa and the rest of the world begin to surge forward towards the next millennium, the question whether Africa will break loose from the york of underdevelopment still looms large.

Attempts at African socialism have been tried. Attempts at adopting schools of thought such as the international structuralist approach, or even Marxist-Leninist doctrinal analysis have been made.

Now it's bourgeois ideology all over Africa, and wrongly grasped for that matter! But what will provide Africa with a poignant solution to its problems? The dialectics are hardly effusive. It is a sweet journey, as an African, to learn to love oneself, to accept oneself, to respect oneself, to forgive oneself, and above all, to believe in oneself. To many others, most of these developments fall at the superstructural and ideological levels where economic determinism will have already inscribed some dictating norms. But even then, is it not correct to say that there is a correlative motion oscillating in the counter-direction, if only we choose to consciously swing the pendulum that way?

Indeed, the thought process must be user-friendly if I have to communicate. Listen folks, it all starts with attitudes towards ourselves, attitudes towards work, towards our very existence and towards our very well-being. Indeed, in an interesting e-mail note, a colleague of mine from Zambia once wrote:

"Being Zambian is a serious issue. In SA (South Africa), when a person sees another person driving the latest model Mercedes Benz, they dream of the day they will buy one (with the exception of thieves, of course). When a Zambian sees another Zambian driving the same car, they dream of the day they will meet the guy walking just like him." Upon reading this statement I wondered if that could be true. What sort of world our living in? I have had some elusive and fading hesitation to accept the foregoing as a factual representation of our attitudes. It is said that Zambia is a peaceful and Christian nation, unlike many other countries. But then, in that peace, Christianity and tranquility, is the silence and calm all that merry?

One other Zambian observer, responding to the sentiments of my colleague, noted: 3This is a very accurate and vivid portrayal of events amongst our people, both in Zambia and abroad. When I say 'people', it includes university-level educated individuals. Please, I mean no disrespect here! But there is so much of a projection of poverty of the mind which is illuminated either out of a deprived childhood or out of exposure to intense levels of abject poverty. One need not circulate questionnaires for a field trip exercise to determine levels of jealousy, envy and hate amongst a number (not all) of our people! Every time a friend works hard and tries to rise above the rim, they pass silly comments, tell lies about him or her, they put spanners in his or her way, mention it! It's pathetic! And they never give a pat on the back to say we are with you brother/sister all the way! Very rare, if you ever get such honest treatment. But this is all because of poverty! When I say 'poverty' it includes the uncultivated behavior of both the learned and unlearned! Almost everyone is busy fighting for space and recognition!

In economic terms, it is this scarcity of resources which raises transaction costs because getting to agree is difficult and often the costs relating to misinformation are high because the insider market players are using asymmetric information to skew the information and misguide potential competitors!

This is how we survive in our societies! We are eager to see a 'friend' fall. Indeed, that is why statements such as, 'We'll see when he/she trips! We've seen others trip before!' are made with utmost malice. But that is how we live in our societies. Vengeance and vendettas, spite and poverty. Very sad! I hate to be honest about it, but that is the way our people operate. They want to compete even when they have absolutely no comparable strength. Kitchen parties..., it's competition; dressing at church..., it's competition; weddings..., it's competition; cars..., its competition; building houses..., it's competition; politics... worse! Don't even go there! Yaak! It's sickening! We compete even over basic commodities and essentials of life! Lack of exposure could be a major factor in many cases! I'm sorry to be so blunt!'

For once, I chose to get into some undisciplined thinking, away from the books and the intellectual biases, and tried to see it from a Johari Window (as psychologists would say – though again this is intellectual; I can't help it, mwe!) so as to get it from the commentators' points of view. But it is hard to make pronouncements on such issues, yet this is where development starts from. It all starts with the mind. We must de-colonize our minds. Maybe my friends had a point after all. Until, we, as Africans, begin to have confidence in ourselves and in what we do, and not just waiting for some alien to come and rescue us from poverty or to show us the way out of our own problems, until we begin to change our attitude towards work, towards life, towards unity and collective development efforts, we have quite some work to do.

Civil wars, tribal squabbles and secessionist movements are all such counter-productive matters on which we expend countless efforts of energy just to champion our own selfish ends. But my submission here does not exonerate those in power (that is, the state) from blame. Sometimes, the state itself can encourage these divide and rule tactics in order to weaken the opposition and perpetuate its own existence. A fragmented opposition, in my humble view, is often a complete waste of time and energy. But, Africa must find its feet and come out of all these vices which are sometimes (and in many cases) triggered externally. The social class that represents these external forces must be checked. Time for selfish individual efforts is over! There are just too many problems in Africa and one wonders what the hell is going on out there! It all starts with the mentality of the people. Just take this small example: You go to see a top civil servant at a government ministry, after having made an appointment through his secretary earlier in the week, only to be told that:

"The boss says you come tomorrow because he is in a meeting or he is busy."

And when the poor visitor is just about to walk out of the ministry's premises, he sees the so-called boss driving out, in his GRZ Toyota Canny vehicle, with a pretty young lady seated in the front seat! That mentality must come to an end. People have to learn to be responsible; to honor time and to honor appointments!

A SUBMISSION TO THE HUMAN RIGHTS COMMISSION: ENSHRINING

COMMUNAL RIGHTS IN AFRICAN CONSTITUTIONS.

By

Dr. Kenneth K. Mwenda

Washington D.C., USA.

Formerly Lecturer in Law, University of Warwick and Visiting Professor of Law, University of Miskolc, Hungary.

While a state of nature is not necessarily a state of injustice, it is of necessity a state devoid of justice for when rights are in dispute there is no competent authority to render an impartial verdict. Such a state manifests itself in the contemporary Third World when political might and weight begin to oscillate luxuriously. But isn't justice 'ensouled' in the bosom of a judge? Is it not the judge that bringeth reason to the ordinary prudence of mankind? Is it not he/she that articulates and postulates the normative corpus of reason and right as the raison d'etats upon which the notion of social justice is born? In the commonwealth mundane of mankind, is it not good law (and enforcement) that governs civil behavior of mortals; from a medical doctor wielding a blade over his patient in the theatre to an accountant whose books must reflect a true and fair view of the company? Is it not the law, as inscribed by morality, ethics and aesthetics that forms the very Grund norm upon which our civil behavior is based? If this be the case, as I contend, and our traditional African societies have time immemorial recognized their own form of law, that is, customary law and rights, are we not justified in revisiting the social and intellectual discourse upon which the common good is based? Is it not the judge that defines the spectrum and facets of reason and right alongside the parenthesis of social justice? But, then, ought we not to seek a common good in judicial activism and constitutional re-engineering? If that be the case, and if you will, permit my indulgence here that the common good upon which the wise and the prudent rest their hopes must be shared with the beggar and the sucker. Many a time, African scholars begin their analysis of human rights from a Euro-centric standpoint which often encapsulates schools of thought such as Kantian moral philosophy through to leftist Marxist doctrinal analysis. But then, are human rights to be viewed solely in that 'replicative' sense? I am mindful, as a serious minded scholar, that there is an act of faith that opines that there is nothing as practical as a good theory. It is against this background that I now plunge into the intellectual depths of my analysis.

It is, indeed, my humble contention that African

- *Kenneth K. Mwenda*

states (I can only speak of Africa since that is home) must begin to consider seriously the importance of enshrining within their Republican Constitutions a duty upon the state to refrain from corrupting its own citizens. The superficial cynic will readily warm up to my argument as an academic thesis. But only when the cynic begins to appreciate that positivist jurisprudence, as espoused by Hans Kelsen, shows that legislation such as the Corrupt Practices Act and the Penal Code does not supersede provisions of the Republican Constitution – in a state which does not practice parliamentary sovereignty – does he or she begin to appreciate the depths of my analysis. Besides, the aforesaid statutes do not even deal with the issue of 'communal rights'. To many, communal rights are a novel idea as far as human rights are concerned. There is need for African peoples to respond to issues of state corruption by placing constitutional restraints on the state. These limits must be enshrined in the Grund norm, that is, in the Republican Constitution while principal legislation on the matter must remain intact.

In my mind's eye, I do contemplate a common good which would candidly and honorably permit the High Court to have original jurisdiction in matters of such a nature. Enshrining a constitutional clause, as I have proposed above, would ensure that 'communal rights' of the citizens are protected! We are in an era in which civil and human rights of individuals should no longer be seen as the sole camera of democracy. Our societies, through African customary law, have for a long time recognized the concept of communal rights. Citizens, therefore, as a community, must be afforded the communal right to ensure that their government (and future governments) does not corrupt them or engage in any other form of corrupt practices. Here, it must be proven that the 'state' did conspire to corrupt. Indeed, the state must be seen to have conspired. It is for the courts of law to give ordinary constitutional law meaning to the word 'state'. The petitioner, who could be a group individuals or an individual, must be permitted to petition the state (and not just the law offender/state official) in the High Court. As this would be a 'communal action', the issue of locus standi could then be easily overcome. On conviction of the state by the High Court, the state would have a right of appeal to the Supreme Court.

If the Supreme Court upholds the ruling of the High Court, the government in power would have to step down, at least not later than thirty days from the date of the ruling. I know that this sends tremors in the hearts of those thirsting for power. But we all know that when lions are feeding on a carcass, the hyenas and vultures eagerly wait on the side lines. That is what politics is all about, be it for those in power or those in the opposition. The opposition, once in power, like their predecessors, simply get into the lion's shoes. Change becomes symbolic and it remains cosmetic. If anything, the lack of honesty; the lack of a well committed leadership; and the lack of well-articulated ideologies, is often what manifests itself in personal vendettas of African politics. But to curb this vice and to give some hope for the future generations, African peoples must begin to re-engineer their Republican Constitutions to make the state more accountable.

The Post
The paper that digs deeper

No. 1449, Monday Edition, March 27, 2000

Political WATCH:

NEW DRAFT CONSTITUTION

By

Dr. Kenneth K. Mwenda

Kindly permit my humble indulgence in making this my noble contribution to the silent debate on next year's presidential elections in Zambia.

While interested parties and persons agonize in fear and worry about possible gains and losses from the forthcoming elections, and while those aboard the ship worry as to whether the ship will sink or it will reach the shore, the treacherous are busy skimming how to abandon one political party for another at the eleventh hour. It's called the 'moral hazard' inherent in the 'free-rider' problem.

Opportunists are ever in search of financial and political security even at the eleventh hour. Let us wait and see. It shall come to pass.

The ramifications of poverty in the political milieu cannot be underestimated. Principles and values arc lost. Theory and practice are de-linked.

Ethics and morals are watered down and compromised. We are left wondering wherein lies the solution to bringing sanity to the unending quest for power in man. Indeed, some (Fate' in the UNIP era and they are still 'eating' in the MMD era. Others want to 'eat' again after falling out of favor with the MMD government But when will-they-ever listen?

I hear calls that Dr. Kenneth Buchizya Kaunda should retire from active politics. Laudable as this view may seem, but is it only Dr. Kaunda who should retire from active politics? Did he start his political tenure alone? Of course, other colleagues of his have retired, but not all of them. There are lots of others, both in the MMD camp and in the opposition, who (Bate' with KK in the first and second republics, and they are still eating today while others hope to 'eat' again after 2001. These folks started off in the UNIP era, through to the MMD era. Yet, they forget their own inequities of old age, and see only that of their friend, KK. Yes, these folks even hope to 'eat' in the government of 2001, whether from within or outside the system.

Indeed, poverty erodes even the minimum levels of principle and ethics. It can even affect one's thinking, relegating all forms of sanity to political opportunism. But when will our people ever listen?

My major worry, though, is far above these mortals, but with the immortality and fate of the Republican Constitution; that is, the sanctity of the 'sacred' nature of the Republican Constitution for which we are all called to defend. Why do I say so?

Although it might seem ludicrous, one hopes that the opposition parties have not started drafting their own versions of a new Republican Constitution.

But again, I am not saying the present constitution cannot be reviewed objectively on non-partisan, fair and good grounds. My worry, by converse, is with these guys who come to power (or are already in power), with a lawyer-friend of theirs, standing dutifully right behind them and wielding the draft of a new Republican Constitution! This is common place in developing countries.

Perhaps, I should not be too harsh, as a lawyer, for who knows... tomorrow I could be asked to draft the new Republican Constitution, or to strengthen it (if the incumbents retain power). But let's think about it seriously.

The Constitution is not one document you just dream of changing after eating Nshima and yawning the whole afternoon. It's one big contract that binds the entire nation and peoples of that nation.

So, let me rest my case here and beseech the indulgence of the reader to think through this submission and see if we are headed for another Constitutional Review Commission after the presidential elections.

AFRICA FREEDOM DAY: A TRIBUTE TO PATRICE LUMUMBA

Daily Mail of Zambia, Saturday, 27th May 2000.
By

Dr. Kenneth K. Mwenda

As I look at my bookshelf, I see some specs of dust gathering on my old collections. There, on the bookshelf, sits volumes of works by Walter Rodney, Franz Fannon, Karl Marx, Vladimir Lennin, Plato, Babu, Dan Wadada Nabudere, Issa Shivji, Mamood Mahmdani, Amilcar Cabral, and many others. I sigh and then begin to ponder and wonder into some undisciplined thinking. Yes, the great names of Amilcar Cabral, Dr. Eduardo Mondlane, Samora Machel, Dr. Kwame Nkrumah, Dedan Kimathi, and Sekou Toure, all bring memories of irreplaceable African revolutionaries. These men fought for African freedom with honor, with a heart and with all their all. Their names will live on in the historical hail of fame in Africa and in lands far beyond. And yes, added to this list and giving the final definition of African freedom is the life history of the very right honorable Dr Nelson 'Madiba' Mandela, who lives on, in my humble view, as the rightful "Man of the Century." I take heart also to salute the great efforts of such other sons of Africa as Kaunda, Kenyatta,

Nyerere, and Senghor. These men, too, fought for Africa's freedom with a heart. Indeed, no person is perfect and nothing is really completely perfect. But above all else, these men had a concept of African freedom that remains elusive and shadowy in many of today's crop of African leaders. Perhaps, and only perhaps, there could be some hope from Tripoli. Indeed, all revolutionaries know that the wheel of revolution never comes to a permanent halt. It only suffers a temporary setback.

On this day, 25th May 2000, Zambia is celebrating Africa Freedom Day. But what does freedom mean to us, as an African people? Is freedom a synonym for political independence or does it equate with multi-partyism that only breeds politics of greed and hunger? Is freedom to be defined only within the context of elections that are monitored by outside observers and declared by them as free and fair? What is freedom for us African people? Will the African story continue to be a history and legacy of endless misery and suffering? But when will the truth be told and when will these people ever listen? At this point, I must stop and take time to salute and pay tribute to one of Africa's most moving political figures of the century. His name is Patrice Lumumba. I cannot introduce him any better than the following words quoted from the internet (*Source and disclaimer*: The original website where this article was extracted from is no longer available, and this author does not claim to be the source. However, the contents of what follows below are widely cited in the writings of many other pundits):

"'Lumumba: History will one day have its say'

Finally the chickens are coming home to roost. Thirty-nine years after the Congolese prime minister, Patrice Lumumba was assassinated on 17 January 1961, the truth is finally emerging. A book based on newly declassified Belgian archives has firmly pinned Belgium in the dock. The revelations, including the fact that Lumumba's body was cut into pieces and doused in sulphuric acid to erase the evidence, are so startling that the Belgian parliament decided on 9 December 1999 to set up a commission of inquiry into Lumumba's death and Belgium's responsibility in it. A can of worms, likely to touch Washington, is about to be opened... Belgian feelings (in the early 1960s) were very much shared by the US government which, itself, was eager to prevent Lumumba from calling on Soviet troops to help him retake the secessionist provinces of Katanga and Southern Kasai which declared unilateral independence on 11 July and 8 August 1960 respectively. The American president, Dwight D. Eisenhower, had long given the green light for the CIA to plan the elimination of Lumumba, according to Madeleine Kalb in her book, Congo Cables, published by Macmillan in 1982 based on leaked

State Department cables. Kalb wrote that Robert Johnson, a member of the US National Security Council, testifying before the Senate Intelligence Committee in 1975, revealed that during a meeting of the NSC on 18 August 1960, 'President Eisenhower said something – I can no longer remember his words – that came across to me as an order for the assassination of Lumumba.' Minutes of the NSC subcommittee on covert operations of August 1960 were more categorical: It was finally agreed that planning for the Congo would not necessarily rule out 'consideration' of any particular kind of activity which might contribute to getting rid of Lumumba.' On 26 August 1960, says Kalb, Richard Bissell, the CIA special operations chief, asked his special assistant for scientific matters, Dr Sidney Gottlieb to prepare biological materials for possible use in the assassination of an unspecified African leader. Gottlieb arrived in Kinshasa on 26 September but the plan eventually failed. Gottlieb later told the Senate Intelligence Committee that he had dumped the poison in the Congo River on 5 October, because the CIA station chief in Kinshasa had been unable to find a secure enough agent with the right access to Lumumba, and also because there were concerns about the potency of the poison which should have been put into Lumumba's food or in his toothpaste."

The above introductory note is only a snippet for

those who care to read and understand the history of a continent that has for a long been belabored as the 'dark continent'. But, perhaps most touching, and with a startling appeal to our notion of freedom for Africa, was Patrice Lumumba's last letter to his wife (*Source*: **Patrice Lumumba, *The Truth about a Monstrous Crime of the Colonialists***, (Moscow, Foreign Languages Publishing House, 1961), pp. 230-231). Lumumba, the first Prime Minister of the Congo, wrote this moving letter, in mid-January 1961, (shortly before he was assassinated) to his wife Pauline. Here, we pay tribute to this son of Africa by revisiting his last words:

"My dear wife, I am writing these words not knowing whether they will reach you, when they will reach you, and whether I shall still be alive when you read them. All through my struggle for the independence of my country, I have never doubted for a single instant the final triumph of the sacred cause to which my companions and I have devoted all our lives. But what we wished for our country, its right to an honorable life, to unstained dignity, to independence without restrictions, was never desired by the Belgian imperialists and their Western allies who found direct and indirect support, both deliberate and unintentional amongst certain high officials of the United Nations, that organization in which we placed all our trust when we called on its assistance. They have corrupted some of our compatriots-and bribed others. They have-helped to distort the truth-and bring our independence into dishonor. How could 1 speak otherwise? Dead or alive, free or in prison by order of the imperialists, it is not I myself who count. It is the Congo, it is our poor people for whom independence has been transformed into a cage from beyond whose confines the outside world looks on us, sometimes with kindly sympathy but at other times with joy and pleasure. But my faith will remain unshakeable.

I know and I feel in my heart that sooner or later my people will rid themselves of all their enemies, both internal and external, and that they will rise as one man to say no to the degradation and shame of colonialism, and regain their dignity in the clear light of the sun... As to my children whom I leave and whom I may never see again, I should like them to be told that it is for them, as it is for every Congolese, to accomplish the sacred task of reconstructing our independence and our sovereignty: for without dignity there is no liberty, without justice there is no dignity, and without independence there are no free men. Neither brutality, nor cruelty nor torture will ever bring me to ask for mercy, for I prefer to die with my head unbowed, my faith unshakeable and with profound trust in the destiny of my country, rather than live under subjection and disregarding scared principles.

History will one day have its say, but it will not be the history that is taught in Brussels, Paris, Washington or in the United Nations, but the history which will be taught in the countries freed from imperialism and its puppets. Africa will write its own history, and to the north and south of the Sahara, it will be a glorious and dignified history. Do not weep for me, my dear wife. I know that my country, which is suffering so much, will know how to defend its independence and its liberty. Long Live the Congo. Long Live Africa!"

Sunday Mail

Sunday, July 25, 1999

POLITICAL ECONOMY HAS INVADED THE CORPUS OF AFRICAN CUSTOMARY LAW

By

Dr. Kenneth K. Mwenda,
in Accra, Ghana
(Continued from last week)

THE third political-economic dilemma confronting African customary law manifests itself in 0 dowry. Today, moneys demanded for 'indalama sha mpango', as is commonly known in Bemba, as part of the dowry tradition, has a structural adjustment programme (SAP) connotation.

Whereas originally dowry payment in many African cultures was some kind token of appreciation to the in-laws (in both matrilineal and patrilineal cultures) and it could be in the form of cattle or some property or little moneys, today dowry ranges in millions of Kwacha and has been converted into pension supplements/grants to some in-laws.

It matters less that the brides family is not, say,

Tonga, where herds of cattle can be demanded. Besides, even where the bride is not pregnant the moneys demanded still sound like 'damages'.

Everyone is now demanding monetary gains, and making excuses that, that is what everyone else is charging.

Clearly, the law handed down to us by the whiteman in the colonial days, and still in force in Zambia today, would deem such extortionate bargains as repugnant to natural justice, good conscience and equity.

The present day forms of dowry payments have an effect of monetarizing a marriage relationship and this, in turn, waters down the rights of a woman in a relationship because the man feels he has already paid for the woman.

But when will our people ever listen, especially in a Christian nation like ours? Again, the economy has a great telling here and this is far removed from African customary law!

So, then, how is computation of dowry done today? Here are some clues:

Arbitrary figures are slapped on the man and they are based on elusive factors such as the level of education of the lady/bride (even though the man might be more educated than the lady and, in addition, Kaunda's schools were free and thus it would be fallacious to talk about moneys spent on educating an individual), inflated opinions of the kind of wealth on the lady's family, and many other such idiosyncratic values.

By contrast, factors such as the man is in 'most' cases the major bread-winner and that given the lack of effective social security in our societies the man will on many occasions be called upon, by tradition, to 'extend his arm' (generosity) to his in-laws are totally over-looked.

What comes to the fore immediately is the price of the woman. But this is justified if the woman is well educated and then she decides to marry a nut!

Obviously, the nut becomes a liability and not an asset in the balance sheet. This is how a market economy operates.

Sadly, though, the discipline of economics tells us, ceteris paribus, that when there is excess supply of goods and services in the market the price of these goods and services will obviously go down.

In such a case, it would be wise to read the market forces properly in order to reach an optimally efficient 'offering' price. If this were well considered, as I contend, the result would be in line with the dictates of African customary law which say dowry or lobola payment is only token.

Indeed, in many cases it is not so much that the man is unable to pay the sums demanded. Rather, it is the motive behind the astronomical figures that is being questioned; that is, the signal that is being sent out to the public by slapping such huge figures!

This is a very crucial point to consider in African customary law! It is not the inability or ability of the man to pay that is at issue, but rather the message that is being sent out to the public. Again, African customary law does not recognize inclusion of currency devaluation or monetary inflation in the computation of lobola or indalama sha mpango. Sooner or later, the law will begin to strike down such extortionate bargains, which exceed, say K1 million, as being repugnant to natural justice, good conscience and equity!

Another thread of African customary law that provides some exciting thought here is that of an individual's education or wealth. Under African customary law, an individual's education or wealth belongs to his people as well.

Thus, the fruits of his or her education or wealth are not his or hers alone! They are to be shared by all, including free-riders! Indeed, there has been case law in the past in some African countries supporting this argument.

It must be noted that this norm of family ownership

of education and wealth grew out of the fact that historically the extended family had to harvest their yield collectively in order to send an individual to school. But today, the nuclear family concept is looming large and economic hardships are simply constraining.

Again, African customary law finds itself at cross-roads here with the political-economy.

The fifth thread of African customary law is on issues of evidence. It suffices to prove adultery, for example, in many cases, when the accused is seen coming from a house/room with a female.

The duo need not be found entangled in the heat or passion of the moment. African customary law here, unlike the common law, places heavy responsibilities on individuals to refrain from hiding under the presumption of innocence whenever we are faced with cases of cross-gender 'closed level' interactions.

Indeed, customary law places a presumption of guilt, triggered by some weight of evidence from the plaintiff, on a preponderance of probabilities, against the accused. The accused must then show that he did not commit the offence of adultery.

In short, the burden of proof shifts to the accused! Equally, where a married woman is confronted by another woman concerning her husband that could be good enough evidence to prove a case of adultery.

It is for the man to come out in the open and show that really he has nothing to do with the other woman and he does not even know her.

But, sadly though, African customary law continues to reflect a gender bias as it upholds that 'African marriages' (that is, under customary law) are potentially polygamous! By contrast, women are denied such potentialities, and the Bembas acknowledge: "Mukwai ubu cende bwa mwaume to bu toba ng'anda..." (*English translation*: "A man's promiscuity or immorality does not break a home, unlike that of a woman.").

But somewhere, somehow then comes and enters the new generation of elite academic 'degreed' strong African women and all breaks hell for the men that want to tramp on the rights of women! Na Kosovo ba ibepesha fye, tata (*English translation*: "You cannot even draw a parallel with the Kosovo calamity.")!

Again, the political economy here tells much about why these reactions begin to show up. Who controls the means of production and who wields the financial and intellectual power?

There is an inherent conflict here and responsibilities are overshadowed on both ends of the man and the woman by aggressive human rights campaigns. Moods flair up and then we long to see what African customary law tells us. But I have only started telling the story.

TIMES
of ZAMBIA
forward with the nation

Monday, April 12, 1999

DID KAUNDA RULE ZAMBIA ILLEGALLY?

By

Dr. Kenneth K. Mwenda, Washington DC

THE Zambian High Court in Ndola has now passed its decision over Dr Kenneth Kaunda's citizenship. The ruling renders Dr Kenneth Buchizya Kaunda stateless.

Well, some of us, very far away from home, are not yet privileged to have a full grasp of that ruling. Nonetheless, going by the news media reports that are on cyberspace, Sound intellect prompts one to bring some preliminary re-education to the case. A brief historical prelude here would be helpful.

First, writers like this one have only met Dr Kaunda once. That was years ago when graduating from the University of Zambia (Unza) many years ago. We shook hands and that typical KK smile came from the then Chancellor. Secondly, I have never met

President Chiluba yet, although he was one of the students at the University of Warwick where I taught law for a number of years. Whilst teaching at Warwick, I had heard that there was a Zambian student who had just completed his Masters in philosophy degree in political studies.

It is our Republican President, Mr Frederick Chiluba. I always looked forward to meeting Mr Chiluba, not because I come from the same province as he does, but because he is the head of state of Zambia, a great nation (I am Zambian, too, but no one will take me to court to prove my nationality), and also because he, like many other students, was one of our Warwick University graduates.

Of course, there would have been no harm in President Chiluba hosting me to a light champagne, saying: "ba teacher... let's have a drink."

Indeed, I must put it on record that I am neither anti-Dr Kaunda nor anti-Mr Chiluba. Both are good men in their own respective ways, despite the court cases that have haunted their nationalities. Thus, my analysis here will be dictated by intellect, rather than by partisan views.

I am a writer and my will is to educate and re-educate. The Kaunda case here brings out two major issues at law; one is that of Zambian and Malawian citizenship and the other is that of ruling Zambia illegally.

Can the two issues be treated as inseparable and dependent on one another? Or, could the issues be treated as separate, but related legal issues?

In my humble view, and as I will show below, the latter view is intellectually sound and witty. The notion of an individual ruling a country legally does not 'automatically' flow from one's citizenship.

Citizenship is another issue altogether, although sometimes it can bear upon the legality of that political power. Thus, in this paper I will not dwell on the issue of Dr Kaunda's citizenship, but will strive to punch holes in the part of the judicial decision which says Dr Kaunda ruled Zambia illegally.

Those of you who have been introduced to legal theory before will appreciate the philosophy underpinning Hans Kelsen's legal theory. Kelsen argued that when a revolution takes place it is the constitution of the over-throwing regime that becomes the Grund norm in the land. All other laws are then subjected to this grund norm.

What, however, constitutes a revolution, in juristic terms, is radical transmission of power from one regime to the other. Sometimes the change can be violent, but it really need not be so. Kelsen explains carefully that the regime that takes over power must be in 'effective control' for it to claim that it has power legally. Here, let us not confuse political legitimacy with legality.

The means by which the regime conies to power are entirely irrelevant in interpreting the jurisprudential effects of the coups d'etat. Such is how a military coup d'etat, bloody or peaceful, succeeds in installing a dictator.

The courts have time and again been faced with analysing the legal implications of a coup d'etat or a revolution. Case law runs from the famous case of Edward Sallah v. Attorney General (Ghana) to Madzimbamoto's case and the Ex parte Matovu case. Although the ruling in the Edward Sallah case went against the Kelsenian legal theory, the Attorney General in that case, a former university law professor, (the case was decided after the Nkrumah regime was over-thrown), made an intelligent argument which was missed by the court. A regime that takes over power and has effective control over government can promulgate new laws.

These laws will then supersede whatever laws were enacted by the previous government, whether or not the previous government was a lawfully elected government. If we extrapolate this analysis, we find that upon attaining political independence Zambia underwent a radical change in political structuring from a white minority government to a black majority government.

Indeed, a new Republican. Constitution, the 1964 Zambian constitution, was enshrined. But what did the constitution say? If the constitution called for unitary nationality, as opposed to dual nationality, are we confined to the black letter law in analysing the legality of holding political power?

Do we just count letter after letter in the constitution and, thereafter, go to sleep feeling good that we have analysed the law? What about a foreign military invasion that circumvents the Republican constitution to acquire 'effective control'? How do we treat this?

What is clear is that Dr Kaunda's regime did not enact a new constitution to supersede the 1964 constitution. Yet, he was in effective control. Does the Kelsenian legal theory then recline from elevating Dr Kaunda's case into a legally recognisable political tenure? No, enactments are only one part of the Kelsenian legal theory.

What we are faced with here is the issue of the legality of Dr Kaunda's political tenure as opposed to legality of instruments or decisions made by the colonial regime. Thus, from 1964, Dr Kenneth Buchizya Kaunda was in effective control up until 1991 when Mr Chiluba came on the scene as 'the new kid on the block'.

Although I think that Uganda, for example, has tried to legislate against the Kelsenian legal theory, you cannot really legislate against philosophically grounded norms. Legal philosophy is only a window through which we enter to analyse the precepts of the law. It would have been helpful if the Honourable Mr Justice Chalendo Sakala, presiding in the Kaunda case, had taken on board the implications of the Kelsenian legal theory on the Kaunda case. Such an approach would have directed the judge to a much more learned view on the matter.

A good understating of the law here, especially in matters of public and constitutional law, brings into play the need to have a good understanding of both legal and extra-legal tools affecting the law. These tools include the Kelsenian legal theory. Clearly, Dr Kaunda, like Mr Chiluba today, had effective control of the government then. It matters less how the man acquired his political control, whether as a Zambian or a Malawian.

He ruled and had effective control over the state apparatus just like a soldier would have if he took over government, effectively, in a West African country. Therefore, it raises a lot of illogical difficulties at law for the learned judge to misdirect himself that Dr Kaunda ruled Zambia illegally at some point. Indeed, my humble opinion herein applies also to the sentiments raised by one of Dr Kaunda's lawyers, as reported in the newspapers – that is, the view that the judicial ruling entails that all the appointments made by Dr Kaunda whilst he was in power are therefore illegal is irrelevant.

What is relevant is a good appreciation of the legal implications of the Kelsenian legal theory as it applies to the Kaunda case. Did the man rule the country illegally? Is legality here conditioned by citizenship?

Lawyers and interested parties, let us go back to the books. The library is still open and it's not yet late.

The books of law are still there and they must be read over and over again. Indeed, no law tells us that the books are protected by a label which says 'please do not touch us.' So, let us touch the books and read them over again.

Sunday Mail

Sunday, January 31, 1999

IS CORRUPTION HELPFUL IN PROMOTING EFFICIENCY OF THE HUMAN RESOURCE?

By

Dr. Kenneth Kaoma Mwenda,
in Washington D.C., USA

AT the very outset, the term corruption must be defined, at least in a broad and universal sense. Corruption entails the impairment of integrity, virtue, or moral principle. In many jurisdictions, including Zambia, the legal meaning of 'corruption' is given structure by legislation and case law.

Even the law, in its infinite wisdom, does not depart fundamentally from the definition spelt out above. This definition is mainly articulated as a reflection of value judgment in the public eye and is thus objective enough to encompass nepotism, bribery, tribalism and all other forms of mediocre social discourse which impair integrity, virtue and morality.

What role does corruption play in enhancing or

constraining general employment opportunities in a country? You probably will have heard of fields of study such as the 'economics of crime' or the 'economics of corruption.' They are there!

Some of these studies even show that corruption can lead to efficient economic outputs in an organisation/economy.

I will merely highlight some of the notorious forms of corruption, at least for Zambia, as gathered from a number of confidential sources.

This, then, will provide food for thought on the merits and de-merits of corruption in the human resource function.

One of the commonest forms of corruption in human resource management is to recruit candidates via short-listing. At the time when the short-listing is conducted, CVs of strong candidates that seem to be threats to those of preferred individuals are shred and thrown in the dust bin!

Thereafter, extremely weak candidates, often lacking even the basic skills, are short-listed against the preferred individual. Such practice is common behavior even in big institutions where you find almost everyone is related to someone or was brought in by someone.

Another form of corruption in the human resource

function is to ask the preferred candidate - often already an employee in the organization - to draft the newspaper advert for the job. Obviously, the culprit will design the wording of the advert in a manner that simply replicates his mediocre C.V. to the exclusion of all others.

For example, an assistant director of marketing in a financial services company, who holds an MBA and a law degree, and has been promised his superior's post which has just fallen vacant, will structure the advert in a way that says 'applicants must hold at least an MBA or its equivalent, and a law degree will be an added advantage given the legal implications associated with marketing financial services!'

He may also wish to reflect his own work experience in the advert so as to get rid of any possible threats! Of course, some scholars will argue that internal recruitment has great advantages. But that is good only in as far as it is done transparently and on a fair and competitive basis. Rather than advertise the post, why not just proceed with an internal promotion?

Carpet interviews: These types of interview are a form of corruption. As I learned in Zimbabwe while working there briefly some few years back (1996), carpet interviews involve some female candidates being promised jobs (or job confirmation or job promotion or housing) in return for sexual favors.

The favor can be executed either before the interviews or immediately after the interviews. The rendezvous is for the parties to choose.

It could either be on the office carpet or on the office table. The time could range from lunch hour to after-work hours, when everyone else has left the 'building' (that is, left the place of work).

Generally, evidence indicates that female victims of carpet interviews, (now with homosexuality around, there could even be male victims) often, do not even get the job, especially if they give in before the job is offered!

The man simply comes back later with an excuse: 'You know what, the company management says they have postponed recruitment, for at least three months so that pensioners can be paid first! So, let's wait a bit for these pensioners to be paid.'

Another form of corruption, though quite rare, is where an individual is simply brought in (by powers that be) and a post is created for him or her.

Quite alright, in such cases the candidate will often have the relevant qualifications. But then, no transparent or competitive recruitment policy is pronounced or exercised. Very often such preferred individual will have 'serious' political connections from the very top.

External consultancies: This occurs where a company needs to recruit external consultants. Here, bids are invited from the public. However, the chap in charge of recruiting the consultants will make a big killing by offering the consultancy job to either a friend or his own firm!

Funny chaps! But that is how they make their money. When will they ever listen?

These are all forms of corruption. Having said that, I now leave it to the reader to evaluate the foregoing (against his or her own experiences) and see if corruption is helpful in promoting efficiency in the human resource function.

TIMES
of ZAMBIA
forward with the nation

Saturday, September 13, 1997

UNZA PART-TIME LECTURERS A PROBLEM

By

Dr. Kenneth Kaoma Mwenda
Law Lecturer, the University of Warwick, UK

THIS is my humble submission to the Unza Commission of Inquiry via your good media. The University of Zambia, one of the leading universities on the continent, now faces a major crisis.

As an alumni of the University of Zambia and having been an academic at that university in the early stages of my university teaching career, I believe there is a moral appeal to my sanity and intellect to make this my humble submission.

I have followed with a close eye the submissions on the matter. I now proceed to make my submission.

A number of institutions of higher learning in

developing countries today seem to be facing problems somewhat akin to those faced by Unza. For example, increasingly many academic staff are now seen as de facto part-time university staff whilst retaining their full- time consultant status in industry.

The spate of human rights experts in Zambia has suddenly increased and so has that of gender issues experts. There is a lot of money involved in these areas from the donor community and, no doubt, everyone wants to make a living out of it in this hard hit economy. I pray that I have not treaded on anyone's toes! I am just being honest about it.

In many African countries, earning a postgraduate degree is good enough to make you an expert or consultant! "Man, things are tough!" so it is said. But the problem does not begin there. In Zambia, the problem is a top-down related issue. I will be begin by looking at the state level, then move to the university administration level, and finally to the level of society as a whole.

As a result of what I could term poor Government policy on higher education funding, infrastructure at the two state universities in Zambia has gone down rapidly; running from books and periodicals in the library to other artifacts in general. On the other hand, the university administration has not shown much business acumen in forging links with industry and society.

This is particularly the case at University of Zambia. The institution is still run on the old myths that universities are aristocratic institutions at which only knowledge is churned out and nothing else.

The relevance of a university to society is only confined to academic debate. In addition, much of industry in Zambia does not appreciate research coming from institutions of higher learning. There is simply little value attached to research. I am Zambian, have done research in Zambia and on Zambia, and over the years been a witness to this fact.

The nexus between industry and university is simply lacking. The university is merely seen as a white elephant whose sole purpose is to chum graduates. Be warned: we don't only need professors from the natural sciences to run universities. They have the requisite academic credentials but that is not what management is all about. Times are changing fast.

A biologist professor also has to learn something about management if he has to be an effective manager. In management you do not only manage tasks, but people and human relations as well.

Indeed, good MBA's with sound academic credentials

must now be seen as imperative in giving support to top management in universities, particularly, if universities in Zambia are to be self-supporting financially.

I know that my proposals seem quite radical as there are no immediate precedents on which to fall back. But Africa's problems are unique to Africa like Europe's problems are unique to Europe. Lessons can be learned from either as much as discoveries can be made in either.

I find it hard, having studied in more than four different universities, including the University of Oxford where I graduated from – as a Rhodes Scholar – for my first Masters degree, to understand our attitude in Zambia towards education.

Just how many former Unza academic staff are outside Zambia and teaching at reputable and leading universities and holding senior positions? Don't cast the blame on lack of patriotism! That can't stand.

We all need to eat, and eat nicely in accordance with what we deserve. If politics can feed well, why can't professionalism feed well too? In societies were cultures have not yet evolved to levels at which full disagreement of opinions is warmly accepted, democracy remains a myth.

We must begin by agreeing to disagree, and

respecting each other's view first and there will be less political victimizations. Today, in Zambia many are lobbying for a seat in Plot No. 1, both from within and outside Government.

Plot No. 1 is today seen as a fundamental means through which the aspirants can feed their clans and families! It's a sad story. Let me not divert too broadly here, though it has been necessary to look at politics.

Coming back to the Unza administration, why is it that in the UK, for example, some accounting firms and other companies have co-operated with universities to fund and establish chairs (a professorship) say in business finance and economics? Yet, similar firms in Zambia have no immediate inclination to doing that.

Does Unza for example expect volunteers to come forward and set up such projects? I have deliberately avoided delving into internal politics of Unza as I am not fully vested with facts on the current affairs at the university. I have rather chosen to deal with the macro, rather than the micro issues leading to Unza functioning at below sub-optimal levels.

Turning to society in general, it is argued that the poor state of the economy has brought about a culture among the productive youth in Zambia that has little value for higher education. Indeed, many (not all) young blokes today would rather be "dealers" selling dubious cars or falling into drug related vices. For the educated, yet ostracized by the system, they turn into consultants! If not, they simply have to earn their masters or doctorate degrees and leave the university to enter politics!

That's what society has prescribed through role models' presently acquiring wealth in public offices. One then find himself or herself as a permanent secretary because in Africa we still thrive on titles! It explains why people from a particular West African country – well known for its levels of corruption and fraud – will often tell you that: "My brada (brother), I am a prince. I come from a Royal Family! You are supposed to call me Chief Ayodele!" It's the whole title syndrome.

The problem is grand and society has a great role to play in as much as the Government has. There is need for a whole cultural re- orientation towards education in many developing countries today. The state of Unza is just one such example.

I hope that my submission has been helpful. I rest and close my case.

PART - C

CHAPTER 88

POLITICAL ECONOMIC, PHILOSOPHICAL AND SOCIO-LEGAL INQUIRY THROUGH METAPHORS AND MUSES

"When the history books are written, and those in the life after us were to ask for the top ten (10) legal minds to have come out of Africa, there should be no question or contest whatsoever. The works should speak for themselves."

"If you must learn, then learn from the best. And leave the worst to the worst."

"There are some law schools where you simply go to learn the law, and others were you also learn to think critically about the law. Learning the law per se and thinking critically about the law are two different processes. Your understanding of the law in its right context and setting will often be fashioned not only by whether or not you have learned the law, but also by your ability to think critically about the law."

"It may sound harsh, but a man who does not believe in any kind of meaningful ideology or such system of ideas is no different from a boy. A man's life must be guided by certain ideals to which he aspires."

"A practitioner who is devoid of or wanting in sound theory is often a major risk to everyone around him or her in the workplace. Such people tend to be quite insecure when they come across well-accomplished professionals."

"There is enough love for everyone in the world. The problem is that we are just too impatient."

"If it is just love you want, even the broke guy or blue collar worker can do."

"Not every man that buys you lunch wants to marry you."

"He who seeks a marriage to run away from loneliness risks finding more loneliness in that marriage."

"All too often, we all start off with the very best of ideals when we are young such as the notorious romantic dreams of marrying the most handsome and most successful man, preferably one without much 'social mileage', one without any children yet, or one who is not or has never been married before, as well as marrying a fine and pretty lady, preferably one without much 'social mileage' or any children yet, and one that has never been married before, but when reality hits us as we begin to age we learn to compromise. Yet, those who truly make a difference in various spheres of life are those that, without exaggerating their potential, rarely settle for the average, preparing objective strategies continuously, with an honest, but not
illusory, open mind."

"Do not be deceived by the sophistry of a man that often postures a sense of elitism and aristocracy through his demeanour and expensive clothing. Not everyone that dresses well knows much. After all, he may even have bad breath, not forgetting the political overtones of his concealed undergarments."

"Do not be obsessed with ranking ahead of others. That is not success. Be obsessed with making a difference. That is the true hallmark of success."

"To win, you don't have to always outdo the others. You simply have to meet or exceed your targets."

"Do not be obsessed with comparing. We all can't run in the same way. But we surely gonna get there."

"Human beings are strange. Sometimes, they will even try to compare what they have just encountered with whatever they could have encountered in the past, though they may never say it, especially if it has to do with love and intimacy."

"Not everyone will tell you what they had to do to get that job or that promotion. The one common thing they will all tell you, if you were to ask them, is simply to work hard. Yet, you have been working hard and it ain't coming."

"When the lions are busy devouring the carcass, the hyenas standing in opposition will continue complaining about the lions being corrupt and undemocratic in not sharing the carcass with everyone, imploring the birds up in the trees, as voters, to support them in fighting off the lions, claiming deceitfully that if they, the hyenas, were to take over the carcass from the lions, they would share and distribute it equally to the birds. But only a bird without a song can listen to such."

"The problem with Africa is that many of our intellectuals have become political sycophants just to get ahead."

"If it means 'consulting the ancestors' before one can attempt the highest political office in the land, then it is best to wait."

"Could it be that African politicians, generally, are not good at losing elections for often a time they do not even trust their own electoral systems, repeatedly seeking the opinions of foreign observers as well as the intervention of the courts of law whenever they lose elections? Some even go to the bush to fight the victors outside the ambit of the law. When will it ever stop?"

"Politicians have to understand that the toilet seat, like the people that they exploit, is a custodian of great secrets. It knows everything about everyone. Therefore, do not upset the toilet seat."

"In Africa, it's sometimes hard to tell the difference between the concept of state presidency and that of village chieftaincy for often a time many an African leader, be it in government or opposition, wield political power as if it were an African chief presiding over a village, willfully shutting their eyes to constitutional restraints with a worrying reluctance to relinquish power even when need arises."

"When entrusted by the public with political power it is only polite and prudent not to eat, even when a chance to eat presents itself, for you risk no prosecution in the aftermath."

"The same fear that would slow you down as a child when learning how to ride a bicycle is the same fear that continues to slow you down today. When are you going to learn not to be afraid?"

"The fear of mundane matters is the beginning of self-doubt and the author of a debilitating and unhelpful worry."

"And all of us sinners, together with our friends the non-believers, shall be witnesses. Truly, therefore, there will be gnashing of teeth and wailing. It shall be too late to turn back the hands of time for all that we have lusted for and profited from on this earth will not go unnoticed. Our wicked ways and thoughts, whether hatched in the dark or not, shall be revealed."

"When out on a dinner date or at a party, I never order food or drink that I am not familiar with unless I am seated all by myself. Only then can I afford the chance of error."

"If I don't know my way, I would rather stop to ask for directions than pretend to know where I am going when, in fact, I have no clue what is to follow next."

"He who sings great praises about other people's generosity while drinking or eating from your pocket deserves no seat at your dinner table. Let him go and drink or eat from those other people."

"If you render assistance to me, I will be the first to tell the world most sincerely that you have assisted me. I have no time to pretend. And there is nothing to hide, unless you ask me not to share. In fact, I stand to gain by acknowledging your help because I know that you are likely to help me again should you hear the good things that I have said about your kindness and generosity than if I were to pretend that you have not helped me. But he who is wanting in wisdom and gratitude is often slow and reluctant to acknowledge the help he or she receives from others, thereby denying himself or herself the prospects for further assistance from those with the capacity to help again."

"He who only warms up to you when in need of something is to be treated with caution as a friend or relative for his agenda is often about what he can get out of your relationship with him than what he can share with you."

"A parent who always dresses better than his or her young children is often a nuisance to others as well."

"There is hope for a better tomorrow because of the many children from poor communities that continue to smile even when they have little to eat."

"You cannot take for granted a man who has walked a long distance to school just to get an education. He is not willing to compromise."

"The education of an African child does not always begin in the classroom. It often begins at a very young and tender age when, together with his or her parents or grandparents, the African child steps on the corn field of his or her parents or grandparents."

"You can jokingly tell a man that he looks very broke, and buy him a beer. He will still smile and drink the beer. But you cannot jokingly tell a man that he looks unintelligent or uneducated and expect him to smile even if you were to buy him a book to read. There are just certain things you do not joke about. You can joke about money because it can be shared or inherited and does eventually run out, but do not joke about education because it can never be shared or inherited and will never run out."

"Some things in life are temporal. They last only for a short period or a given time. For example, political appointments, lucrative jobs, material possessions, and many others will at some point expire and come to an end. We all cannot hold on to them forever. Other folks will have to take over. But your education is yours alone and it will never expire. And nobody can inherit or take that away from you once you have earned it genuinely. Besides, your education can even get you another political appointment, another lucrative job or other material possessions as long as you live."

"It is often futile to try to get a politician's cellphone number when he is in power. Even if you succeed, you may not reach him for his line is almost always busy. Just wait until he is out of power. You can reach him anytime and so easily even in the dead of the night. He will still pick up his phone."

"When a politician is in power, his phone will not stop ringing, with one incoming call after another, until he is out of power. He should not be surprised when the phone suddenly stops ringing; for the deafening silence has nothing to do with the phone, but him."

"That we are drinking beer together or sharing a meal does not mean we are now contemporaries in age and thought, notwithstanding that we may both get inebriated by the same beer."

"A man without principle and foresight easily gets intoxicated with power, thinking he can easily step into the master's shoes just because he has been close to the master."

"For the most part, the friends that you accumulate with power or elevated social status are not really your true friends. Rather, they are simply your associates, colleagues or acquaintances. Your true friends are usually those that were or have been there with you when you had nothing."

"There is often a difference between a friend, an acquaintance and a colleague. But in this world of political correctness we sometimes choose, conveniently and deliberately, not to draw a distinction, and thus often end up with a very poor sense of who our true friends are."

“That you are my good friend does not mean I should hate the good reasoning of your nemesis. He may have his hidden agenda against you, but not against me. Your battles with him are not my battles. So, if he has a valid point as he pushes his hidden agenda, I cannot shy away from that valid point. But that does not mean I have betrayed you. This is something that you must understand.”

“The grief of a man can never be measured in the amount of tears that one sheds. It's a very personal thing, and we all express ourselves differently.”

“You must learn to create space for your own happiness. No one will create that space for you.”

“Where I come from, in Africa, when someone is asking for financial help or a favour, they usually start with an elaborate explanation of their hardship before making the request. It is rare that an African, or any other person from such similar communitarian cultural background, will start by making the request first, followed by an explanation as to why he or she is asking for help. This is so because we often believe in explaining ourselves first, especially when we are broke, so as to win the other party's sympathy before making such request.”

“Ever wondered why, in many developing countries that have several languages, there is often a certain language that is most widely spoken by those in prisons or those committing petty crimes? And it is often the same language that is most commonly used by many when uttering profanity for it has an urban touch that makes profanity sound acceptable and normal.”

“To understand the ways of a people, you must live with them for a while. It is not enough to visit them or to read about them. Thus, to understand the ways of the African, American, British or Asian people, you must leave with them. It is not enough to visit or read about them.”

“Nobody will tell you this. But a wise man does not leave a bottle or glass of beer to go to the bathroom and then return to finish off that same beer. He must always order a fresh beer.”

“Grandma taught me many things. She said to me once: 'If you must eat with them, then wait until they start eating. And you must eat only from the same plate and side of the food that they are eating from. Do not stray into uncharted territory.' But I never quite understood what she meant until I grew up.”

- *Kenneth K. Mwenda*

"Although I am most skeptical of traditional medicines that come with no standardized prescription of dosage, as a child growing up in Africa, if you had a fever grandma would boil those traditional herbs and leaves in a big metal pot and then have you sit next to the boiling pot while covered under a heavy duvet as you inhaled the steam from the pot. There was no prescription of how long you had to fight for fresh air under the suffocating duvet, yet the fever will have left you soon thereafter. Aren't there things around us that are incapable of full explanation?"

"On the few occasions that I visited my maternal grandma in the village, I never quite understood why she often insisted that I leave the village very early in the morning when everyone else was fast asleep and without saying goodbye to anyone. I often thought it cool to throw a farewell party when one was departing for lands afar, and thus could not understand the ways of the elderly until I grew up to face the real world."

"Love potions are often less than a portion of the love you need, whether you smoke them, apply them on your body or face, or put them in someone's food or tie them around your waist."

“He who has traditional African tattoos imbedded secretly in the most discreet areas or around his waist hardly takes off his shirt for those African tattoos are not like western tattoos that thrive on transparency and democratic norms of freedom of expression.”

“There comes a time when you can pretend no more and must listen to your heart. You can't live your life constantly trying to please people or seeking their approval. You can't be happy that way.”

“A lot of people are not able to reach their full potential because of fear and self-doubt, constantly worrying about what people will think or say should they take a bold step and then fail."

"A troubling dichotomy of life is when a young and intelligent nephew or niece, or son or daughter, with a really bright and promising professional future suddenly drops the ball and chooses to get married over going to school for further or additional studies, as you try, without much success, to persuade him or her to be patient with marital issues.”

"Character is one thing you can never buy. Not even education comes anywhere close to character in the realm of leadership. You can buy your way into a top university and even graduate, and you can buy yourself some electoral votes and win an election as well as buy yourself some fame and publicity. But you can never buy yourself character. That, you must earn even without the influence of money. You can never inherit character. Neither can it be bequeathed. You must earn it. In getting there, a significant amount of introspection, self-censure and restraint helps to cultivate good character in oneself."

"One who is too proud to ask for help often ends up either stealing or doing worse off things than begging. Do not ask for help with pride, but with humility. A Bemba-speaking friend often asks for help with his hands in the pocket as if it's not a big deal. And he hardly gets the help. I often tell him to be like his Ngoni cousin who knows how to be subservient to the boss to get what he wants. Whenever he tries out that humility, my Bemba-speaking friend is pretentious and exaggerates the humility just to get what he wants before uttering profanity behind the person that has just helped him. And because his Ngoni cousin is not to be trusted, as he is often playing the snitch, the boss will get to know what my Bemba-speaking friend has just said behind the boss."

"When one is beautiful, they often know it. And when one is handsome, they too often know it. That's where the problem lies. It would be easier if they both did not know."

"One who pretends to have answers to everything, like one who pretends to know everyone that matters, is not to be trusted. He or she is covering up for some inadequacy somewhere."

"There are two types of men that often get me worried until I verify what they are saying to be true. The one who speaks with so much confidence and says so many uninvited things at the same time, and the one who is so calm and collected with a low baritone voice of ease and sophistication."

"It is wise and prudent for an old man that decides to marry or date a young lady to have his heart checked first before taking any steps."

"Rationality is often wanting in a man engulfed with the burning passions of lust for he sees nothing more important in life than his insatiable pursuit of matters of the flesh. Such a man cannot be entrusted with power or responsibility. He will engulf everyone around him."

"Where I come from, when an elder asks you for your opinion on a matter over which he or she already has an opinion or a view, you are simply expected to affirm and concur. If you begin to philosophize your own philosophy, you do so at your own peril. And this line of thinking has influenced and permeated our politics. It is perhaps our notion of democracy to expect everyone to go along with our viewpoint."

"Do not tell a lie or compromise the truth for the sake of getting ahead or protecting your self-interest."

"A notable reason why we have many problems in the developing world is because intellectuals, especially those in the political arena, are often preoccupied with where their next meal will come from."

"I have never belonged to any political party or sectional grouping. When one belongs to such, he or she risks being compromised by what is known as 'group-think', and thus weakening the prospects for an objective assessment of issues, as the lenses through which the person looks at issues are often laced with self-interest and a certain ideological bias that views anything to the contrary as a personal attack."

"People from communitarian and collectivist inspired cultures often walk around with a heavy cultural tag around their necks. And the tag often weighs them down. It is a tag of the extended family whose dichotomy lies in the ambivalence of disappointing and demanding relatives, on the one hand, and warm, supportive and pleasant relatives, on the other. The former, often in search of appeasements and bequests, are usually slow with gratitude, yet never hesitant to ask for more. The latter, by contrast, are rare, but when you find them or have them on your side then you know you are blessed."

"What some parents do not seem to realize or understand is that children also get embarrassed and disappointed with the bad behaviour of a parent."

"In the olden days, the bride's parents in much of contemporary Africa as well as in other developing nations would be concerned about the values of integrity and dignity espoused by the family that their daughter was about to marry into as well as how well-behaved or well-cultivated the groom was. Today, even a thug, a criminal or a far much older man can be welcomed for a son-in-law as long as such a being has his pockets full of money. We are living in strange times. Many parents no longer ask their daughters: who are his parents or what type of people are they? Rather, the first question is: what does he do, and what does he own?"

"In the modern world, many couples choose to cohabit without marrying. But cohabitation and marriage are two different things. Cohabitation is an arrangement whereas marriage is a relationship."

"A wise lady knows how not to expose, at the dinner table or before others, the ignorance or lack of sophistication of her man."

"There is not much to be gained out of dating a violent or abusive man. She who is in love with a violent or abusive man is a prisoner of pain."

“An insecure man, for whatever reason, tends to be violent towards women. Violence is a manifestation of some underlying insecurity.”

“A young maid or babysitter is advised not to look very pretty at work, although she may be cute, and must take instructions only from the madame of the house who is better placed to supervise her work as well as to determine and pay her wages.”

“She who 'robs' a married man through a love supreme robs also his family for the finances of the man belong to the family, and the family and him are one.”

“The problem with going out on a date with someone you've been thinking about is that both parties know full well what is at stake yet neither has the courage to mention it. They would rather pretend like little children playing with a small toothless puppy until it bites.”

“The shyness of a lady offers her no protection against the lies of a man.”

"A man that whispers in the ears of a fine single lady his plans to leave his wife usually never does, and often ends up impregnating the wife again, claiming that it was a mistake."

"When a politician is out of power, he will not hesitate to tell you that he is a 'former' this and that. You have to be patient with him. He often has nothing much to his name but a fading political past. So, he has to say something even when there is no need to."

"When you unmask power, you often find that it is nothing but egos being thrown around."

"Make no mistake: when I am silent, it is not that I do not know. Rather, I am thinking. For, he who thinks more talks less."

"It is wise not to forget your humble beginnings no matter how high you rise. He who loses sight of where he is coming from is often bound to meet his waterloo sooner than later for his attitude places limitations on the altitudes he can reach."

"Teaching is a profession. Notwithstanding the view that good academic infrastructure is vital to support teaching, not everyone can or should be allowed to teach. Those that are charged with the responsibility of teaching must be well-schooled in the scientific methods of teaching and learning as well as in the methodological aspects of curriculum design and assessing the taught. Only good teaching will produce effective learning. It is not enough that one is qualified as a lawyer or a PhD to enable him or her walk in a class and start teaching. It calls for more than that. Otherwise, we will continue seeing declining standards of higher education, with glaringly poor academic results and questionable standards of those coming out of these institutions."

"It is quite interesting to see how, at ZIALE (Bar admission course for lawyers in Zambia), the high failure rate of students is often, and almost always, blamed on the quality of the students. Nobody ever stops to ask or talk about the quality of some lecturers that are teaching at ZIALE!

We cannot pretend that everyone teaching at ZIALE is top notch lecturing material. That could be part of the problem. Not every legal practitioner is capable of lecturing and imparting knowledge skillfully in a higher learning environment. Some don't even have postgraduate advanced training, and continue to claim that a person does not need such training to teach at ZIALE because all that the students need to get are practical skills and not academic skills. But there are some illogical difficulties with that line of reasoning. Indeed, then let the students study in law firms as apprentices, and don't waste their time taking them to a school called ZIALE."

"The problem with love is that very few people have experienced it. Some just imagine it while others try to pretend to experience it."

"When Christians are dating, like sinners, there is no such thing as dating free of sinful thoughts. The very reason that certain actions are avoided confirms the sinful thoughts behind that avoidance."

"When undergoing routine annual medical check-ups, for many people, both men and women, it is usually hard to block out what you think is going through the mind of the attendant physician, especially if he or she is of the opposite sex, when he or she suddenly begins to exam your private parts. But society teaches us not to get upset and to pretend that it is just a job being done even though we may feel violated."

"Fornication is no lighter sin than adultery, and those that are single but remain indulgent in the former should not comfort themselves for even manslaughter is a felony just like murder."

"The arrogance of a man or woman with ten or fifteen masters degrees will not add up to a single PhD."

"Economics is one discipline that has suffered so much intrusion from outsiders. When mathematicians and physicists began to invade the field of economics, they brought with them highly quantitative methods of economic analysis. And everyone is now claiming to be an economist primarily because the field of economics is ubiquitous and cuts across all spheres of life. But the questions remain: where does economics begin and end, and who is an economist? Otherwise, we risk having the unsuspecting public misled."

"I don't mean to jettison patriarchy or to be a male chauvinist. But why do some First Ladies think that they can be the next President after their husband leaves power? Is it because some of these First Ladies have been whispering some little sweet nothings in the ears of their husband that they think that they too can rule? Yesterday, it was some dictators grooming their sons to take over. People gotta be serious."

"I have never taken pride in things that I have not worked for and earned on merit. Maybe that is a weakness. I don't know. But there are some people that feel very entitled even to things that they have not worked for. You just have to look at a number of our African politicians to see the calibre of some of the people who think they can run for presidency. We have a long way to go."

"In a sense, marriage is the upholding of the rule of law in the fight against celibacy and moral tresspass."

"I can only believe in a God whose name, when mentioned or called upon, other gods and spirits tremble and fear. Why believe in something that is afraid of another?"

"When you are appointed to any office, you should never forget that the one who has the power to appoint you often has the power to disappoint you."

"It is wise to dance whilst the song is still playing because every song must come to an end. Nothing lasts forever."

"Religion without an erudite enlightenment that accommodates objective secular views is dangerous. It often leads to extremism."

"As a man, you either go to work to put food on the table or go to the gym to bring home some chunky muscles for the night. Even better if you can bring home both. You don't have much of a choice."

"A wise lady knows that on a dinner date a man that eats oysters with a purpose is up to no good."

"Ambition is good. But over-ambition, like an exaggerated sense of self-importance, when pitted against reality, leaves an ugly face."

"A broke husband is still a husband. He could be put to some other good use."

"It is polite conversation and acceptable etiquette not to ask tough questions."

- *Kenneth K. Mwenda*

“Lawyers and prostitutes have one thing in common: they both love to bill their clients no matter what time of the day.”

“The truth has a tendency to undress even those that are well dressed.”

“It takes a long time to develop sound ideas, and a longer time to get those ideas vetted and accepted by professional peers. Yet, it takes a very short time to be famous with crazy ideas that seem to shake the world, albeit not having been run through the rigours of a peer review system.”

“It is a tragedy for one to claim to have professed knowledge when one's work can hardly be found in the world's leading libraries.”

“For some people, a business card has lost its originally intended meaning. It is no longer a card for business purposes but one for social elevation and aristocratic posturing.”

"The most impactful advert I ever saw of an MBA degree program read something like this: 'It is not the letters after your name that matter, but the name after those letters...'."

"Worldwide, many people are entering the legal profession. One thing is clear, though. We live in a world of prejudice and bias. For lawyers, like medical doctors or MBA graduates, it matters a lot where you studied. Even if you started off in the wrong place, you must end up in the right place."

"Do not give a man a $100 note if he has a limited appreciation of the value of money for he may just squander the $100 without realizing its actual value. Give him instead a pair of shoes or clothes worth only $20. For the latter, he can visualize, see, touch and feel the shoe or clothes, and will thus always be grateful and will remember you for your generosity."

"He who values a pair of shoes as a gift or a present over an autographed copy of a prized book from the hands of the author is often wanting in matters of erudition and enlightenment."

"The world is constantly changing. We can no longer afford to raise our children as in the olden times. We must know who their friends are as well as who their friend's parents are and what type of people they are. And we must know where our children hang out and who they hang out with. The era of the State of Nature and absolute laissez-faire in raising children is long gone. We must spend more time with our children and families."

"It is not good for a man to commit sin repeatedly in his heart every time he sees a beautiful lady or his neighbour's beautiful wife for such man might exhaust the mercies of The Lord."

"Of some pastors and clerics today, the world has seen some of the worst sinners hiding behind the cloak of faith, with their eyes cast on the tithing of the poor and the beautiful women in church. If we are to protect the flock of God, we must remain vigilant and watchful of the wolves in sheep's clothing."

"When sinners congregate on Sunday it is called worship."

"It's a good strategy not to make known all your options for surprise can overwhelm even adversity."

"He who often buys advanced electronic gadgets that he does not even know how to use often relies on his children to help him operate them."

"When some people begin to age, they turn to God because they don't know how tomorrow might turn out."

"If you can't believe anyone, at least believe in yourself to make a difference."

"You either step forward to tell your story or give the world enough good works to speak for you. Otherwise, nobody is gonna tell your story the way you know it."

"Under the Constitution, conjugal rights attract neither rights nor duties, and they are never a constitutionally mandated entitlement. Rather, conjugal rights are simply a moral privilege for those who qualify to assert such privileges within the precincts of the general law."

"When some employees quit work, many leave not because they do not like the company. They leave because of bad bosses."

"Everyone is happy as the weekend approaches, except one whose spouse has a concubine."

"People never cease to amaze me. Many want to be the only ones who own this or that. And they will go to the greatest extreme to maintain that exclusivity. But nobody wants to be the only one who owns poverty."

"Some in the audience said: 'From his good looks alone we cannot eat. But from his wallet, we can feed.' And I spoke lightly to them, 'Of his good character, you shall find honour and integrity, and many other blessings shall follow.'..."

"Sometimes the really beautiful ones are not as confident or as flamboyant as the not so beautiful ones. And sometimes the knowledgeable ones are not as loud or noisy as the not so knowledgeable ones, and the really wealthy are not as pompous or showy as the not so wealthy ones. Why is it like that?"

"When the elections are close, politicians will be your best friend and can even stop to talk to you and show you their greatest care and concern. But you must understand that it may be last time you will be getting their undivided attention until the next elections."

"It is wise for a lady before whom a man is flaunting his wealth to ask him how much he owes other people."

"There were many bright kids in school. We competed fiercely, and we all were very capable. The only difference is that some fell in love too soon. There is something about such hurriedness that sometimes stands in the way of people."

"Her greatest power lies in his greatest weakness."

“Even if she is so beautiful, do not look back. Just keep walking the road ahead. Otherwise, you will not reach your destination.”

“The problem with sin is that most sins don't take more than five minutes to commit. There is no hard work involved in committing sin. That's why sinning is very cheap.”

“He who sins early at dawn, before the sun even comes out, is capable of sinning at anytime of the day.”

“The path to excellence has many roadblocks, but no speed limits. Don't let the roadblocks slow you down.”

“That you have come to a full stop with life's issues does not mean that you stop reading. Just take a breath and continue with the next sentence.”

“Most manners begin under the watchful eye of the elders at the dinner table.”

"There are those who strive to make a difference and those who fear to make a difference. And then there are those that get inspired by the difference and those that often despise and loath those that make the difference. We can choose to be one or more of these persons depending on our social DNA and the baggage we bring along with us in our thoughts."

"When a couple with many children says, 'the Lord has blessed us with many children...', it is not as if they just stood there watching the Lord bless them with the many children. God gives us the means to help ourselves, but not to abuse those means."

"He who sleeps in the nude is to be avoided for his intentions are often unclear."

"Because children are so trusting, they often get very disappointed when they discover that, out of all people, Daddy or Mommy is telling a lie."

"Sometimes children know, but out of respect they won't say."

- *Kenneth K. Mwenda*

"Children like to ask questions. And parents are often eager to explain until the children begin to ask questions about some unspoken truth."

"When Daddy returns from a long trip, a well-cultivated child knows that he has to wait until Daddy is rested before asking Daddy for his little gift. 'If only mother could do the same and give daddy some space..', the child complains."

"A boyfriend of no fixed abode is a flight risk."
"To love someone with dependents is to love her dependents too."

"She who only sees a wedding dress upon entering a relationship misses an opportunity to love."

"A man without well-worked out muscles does not wear a muscle shirt, unless he is up to something."

"Do you ever find yourself not greeting your neighbour or workmate simply because your views and the other person's views are different? Do you ever look away and not say hello when your eyes meet with those of an innocent stranger on the streets? Why do you do that? And do you ever get to wait for the other person to greet you first before you can greet them, otherwise you will just ignore them? Do you ever find yourself judging others based on what you think they should hav...e done? And are you slow and reluctant to compliment your friends when they appear to do better than you or are dressed better than you? Do you often pretend that you have not noticed when your friend is looking good or has done well? What is it that makes you behave that way? Have you ever asked yourself that, despite calling yourself a Christian or religious person, and going to Church on Sunday, you have a lot of work to do about yourself?"

"Do not be deceived. Beauty can be found even amongst the poor. It only awaits nurturing."

"There is no doubt that the levels of economic development of any society has a telling on the levels and degrees of superstition and mysticism. When you have seen one ghost, you have seen them all. Likewise, the traditions and cultural norms of many institutions are closely tied to poverty. Even the church has not been spared when it comes to archaic traditions."

"In my culture, the nicely fried head of a tilapia (bream) fish as well as the nicely roasted gizzard of a chicken are reserved only for the man of the house. Such is African mysticism. It took me a long time to figure out until I looked closely to draw some comparative and figurative analogy of what else resembles the same. Only the man of the house would know..."

"When someone appreciates you for who you are, and not just for what you are, you will know without a doubt. You don't have to claim friends, especially those people that are very famous who we do not even know that well yet we are busy trying to claim or pretending to know. True friends will give no excuses and will give you their loyal time and attention."

"In these hard-pressed economic times, marriage has now become a business. You cannot afford not to be strategic."

"He who marries and remarries often, like one who changes churches now and again, lacks the moral conviction to lead or advise others."

"Do not marry a wife or husband that you will be constantly hiding from people or giving excuses for."

"While bedroom problems, like unflinching boredom, can weigh down someone's life and confidence, the bedroom, like a pro-active boardroom, can be a congenial habitat for sourcing great ideas and sustainable solutions to intractable problems: choose your partner and battles wisely."

"The problem with wearing tight clothes and short miniskirts is that, like submitting oneself religiously to anti-aging creams and hair dyeing lotions, your very true date of birth remains unchanged, no matter how tight your clothes may fit or how generously you may apply those creams and lotions."

"An African that cannot dance well often lacks confidence for there is power in the rhythm and melody of the African dance."

"If you are in love with her, do not worry about her toes. They don't matter. Just focus on what matters."

"You can never be inadequate unless and until you choose to be inadequate."

"It is good that the law does not convict us for our thoughts, but for our actions. Otherwise, half the world would be in prison."

"A young man that keeps staring at the good looks of an elderly lady risks losing his mind should he insist."

"An African who occasionally casts his gaze to the floor while talking to an elder does so out of respect, and not out of guilt, though often misunderstood in the Western world as a mark of guilt."

"When an African elder declines meekly an invitation to partake at the dinner table, he often does not mean so unless and until he declines a second and third time."

“It does not take much to figure out a man from the way he approaches his food or drink.”

“The premise of my intellectual and humane engagement with a fellow human being starts from the fact that he or she has decent and good manners, and not whether he or she is smart, wealthy or well-connected.”

“I have sat across the table in the same room with some of the most powerful men and women in the world. And I have seen and met some of the poorest people on earth. With the former, you learn to master and read their thoughts. With the latter, it is wise to seek to understand their hearts.”

“He who is misled by fame and beauty often risks being lonely at sunset.”

“We can eat neither love nor faith. But we still need both, especially when we are broke.”

"Questions are born of the mind, but conviction belongs to the heart. Do not let your thoughts trouble you for you can neither explain to me why you sometimes fall in love nor why you sometimes dream."

"Over the years that I have mentored many young people, I have learned many things. But one thing stands out: it is good to have a mentor, but even more important, it will help you a lot to get yourself a sponsor; that is, someone who knows someone and who will put in a good word for you. And going beyond that, irrespective of what people might say about cronyism, the presence of a godfather or a godmother tends to assure someone of better career prospects until the godfather or godmother leaves, sometimes leaving you vulnerable like an orphan. But you must quickly find another godfather or godmother to adopt you for your survival, otherwise the others waiting out there might eat you alive."

"The problem with Prince Charming is that he is not always what he promises to be or who he says he is."

"I may not be perfect, but my silent prayer is my last hope for He knew me even before I was formed."

"I do not need a bulgy wallet or crotch to marry the King's daughter for the King treasures my counsel."

"Do not let them define you through your own fears. You have to discover yourself to define your path."

"The moment you yield to that inner fear that keeps holding you down with the incessant and troubling thought, 'What will they think if I try?', you have given the haters something to joy about."

"Every day, I ask myself: why are human beings so cruel to one another? The world is being ravaged by war, crime, hatred, cruelty, greed, hunger, and poverty. What have we done to this world?"

"When a beggar receives free food from a Good Samaritan, he says to the other beggar asking him for some food: 'You have to work hard in life to bring food to the table, ya know...'."

- *Kenneth K. Mwenda*

"I don't mind the brand of the shoe that you are wearing, but I do mind the odour of your undressed feet for what comes out of you matters more than your impressive external appearance."

"Do not be deceived. In the midst of your silent fears, I know your weakness. But I will not strike at you for you are not my enemy, but my brother and sister."

"Do not feel betrayed by your bad teeth. It is the edifying words from thy mouth that matter."

"Let not the monster of your thoughts be the driver of your motives. But let the light of your heart take charge."

"He who does not shave his armpit rarely raises his hand."

"That 'it is not every battle that we should fight', and that 'one must choose his battles', is only the beginning of the inquiry. Sometimes, and even more important, we must learn to play the fool before those that are too ambitious yet less endowed in thought and capacity. Sooner or later, they will be exposed by their unrestrained ambitions."

"As far as I know, a man has only one head to reason with. If he tries reasoning with anything else, he may be courting trouble."

"Your temper will not change anything. But your reasoning can."

"It helps to sleep well if you do not tell lies for you need not rehearse or remember what you said the previous day."

"Do not just sit there waiting on your friend to make a mistake so that you can talk about it. We actually have many of your mistakes to talk about."

"If gossip were to be a profitable business, many folks would be rich."

"Today's world requires us to think differently. We have to think global, as opposed to holding onto parochial and local-based value systems. The solutions to the many challenges facing the world are no longer the preserve of monolithic or singular disciplinary approaches to problem-solving. Globalization has blurred the boundaries of excessive specialization and disciplinary silos, making interdisciplinary and multidisciplinary approaches to problem-solving unavoidable. A lawyer can no longer be just a lawyer in today's world. His skills must be harnessed and anchored into cognate and related disciplines. And so it is with all other professions. Otherwise, one risks being functionally illiterate despite his many qualifications or high levels of specialization."

"When you come out of the tunnel, it helps you to see the horizon better for there is very little light for hope and vision in the tunnel."

"If your education or schooling, or your socialization among the elites or the modest, has succeeded in altering or changing your behaviour into a right-thinking member of society, then I agree that it has been a worthwhile investment. Otherwise, let us just talk about a beer."

"Do not labour to prove someone wrong or to make a point to those you harbour a grudge against. He who is psychologically entrapped in such is often left unsatisfied, constantly wanting to drive a point home even when nobody is contesting. To find true happiness and fulfillment, keep course on your own goals and terms, and others will follow."

"First, I tried Facebook. Some people were busy posting pictures of their shoes, cars, houses, you name it. So, I went to twitter. Some people there were busy twitting that they were now in the toilet. I couldn't stand it. I left for LinkedIn. What I found there was that most people were busy posting their CVs. How vain! I could not believe it. So, I went to Whatsapp. Some people there were busy indulging in suspicious conversations and sharing some videos of bad taste. Again, I couldn't stand it. I moved on to try academia.edu. Most people there were busy posting their scholarly publications. How boring. So, I decided to go to bed this time..., at least there I can post some kisses to my wife."

"The reason why you sometimes feel as though your prayers are not being answered is because God knows you too well, and He even knows what you are up to."

“She, whose beauty is without makeup, does not fear the rain for she glows with beauty under the streaming waters of the rain.”

“You can only tell the true beauty of a woman when she wakes up in the morning without enhancements. Anything else is speculative.”

“A well-cultivated African stag does not take a bride without the counsel and blessings of the elders; for ignoring such is often at one's own peril.”

“To help me understand you better and to avoid you surprising me, I am often inclined to observe your body language and physical expressions first, and then your buttery sweet words next.”

“The name of a man does not continue to linger on the tongue of a lady whenever she opens her mouth to speak, irrespective of whether or not she speaks good of him, unless she has a soft spot for him in her heart.”

Until you know enough about a person, do not underestimate him. He may be the deal breaker at your next job interview or your new boss."

"We shall be saved not by the seemingly impressive words we utter in the presence of others, but by our honest and selfless actions and thoughts."

"He who walks along the corridors of life with some weighty baggage of bitterness against others or the world, or with ill-intent and malice towards others, is far from the goodness of the Lord, irrespective of the many Bible verses he may post on social media or elsewhere."

"I don't know about you. But for me, the smile of a child is one of the greatest blessings to humanity for it comes with the fullness of God's love; never assuming, hardly ever rehearsed and with no ulterior motive or hidden agenda, totally disarming the audience with unconditional love."

"But for your fear and self-doubt, you could have achieved more. There is no such thing as a genius. What you perceive as a genius is simply a manifestation of someone's hard work when you were probably fast asleep."

"The minds of many a youth are pregnant with great ideas. The youths need us as their midwives in the delivery of their ideas. Do not stand in their way, but help them."

"Very often, we know what is right. But we are just too scared to do what is right, or are busy worrying about what people might think."

"Our condition is a condition naturally of self-preservation. Even when we love, our condition of love is often premised on self-preservation. And such love can never be a wholesome love."

"You do not have to ask his wife to know that a short man is not necessarily a small man."

"Do not question a man when he has no clothes on for his faculties only return when his clothes are back on."

“The look in a man's eyes often betrays his thoughts, irrespective of the sweetness of his tongue.”

“Whether you are on a date or are doing business, many people simply tell you what they think you need to hear, holding back their unfiltered thoughts. But, then, you don’t want to know what they are thinking, or where or how far they have taken you with them in their unfiltered thoughts.”

“While waiting to make it big, you'll know that you are getting older when some of the people that manage your professional work-life, or those that govern your country or locality, are younger than you.”

“When an African elder is wrong, you do not tell him to his face. You wait until it is nightfall and everyone has left before asking him to consider kindly, at his own discretion, your somewhat ‘misguided’ view.”

“As an African child growing up in Africa, I learned early in school that when a bigger number was subtracted from a smaller number, such as 1- 2, the answer was always: 'It can't...' Indeed, that was my view of the world then. When I progressed to high school, my view of the world changed. It was no longer 'It can't'. Rather, 1 - 2 became 'negative one' (-1). And when I progressed to university, my view of the world changed further. I learned that 2 + 2 is not always 4. Rather, it can also be 5, thus defining the concept of synergy in management. My view of the world keeps changing every other day. And so, the world means different things to different people depending on the lenses that one is wearing or the prism through which we choose to view the world."

"Like the rainbow, the human race is one. Yet, we waste a lot of time discriminating amongst ourselves on which colour of the rainbow is the brightest. All the colours of the rainbow, like the colours of human race, have one indistinguishable source. No single colour came from somewhere else."

"Do not feel embarrassed to tell her that you are broke. She who makes a face at the sound of the word 'broke', like one who is quick to ask 'why and how can you be broke?', is often an enemy of the wallet."

"A lot of young people are impatient. They want to get to the top quickly. But by what means? And they want to change the world soonest. But the world is slow to change. So, they end up rebelling or taking the wrong route."

"When an African elder is reprimanding a child for any wrongful conduct, and the elder says to the child, 'What do you have to say for yourself?', it is not a license for the child to start defending himself or to embark spiritedly on defending his wrongful conduct. The elder simply seeks to ensure that the child understands and concurs with the course of action taken. And so it is with our African politics. In reality, when the president speaks, he has spoken. You do not question the authorities."

"The best way to lose a friend is to tell him or her the truth, especially if the person is not open-minded enough to receive feedback."

"In politics, there is no such thing as the candid truth. It all depends on the season and the reason. And that is the difference between a politician and an intellectual."

"For what other greater purpose was mankind created than to honour God and fulfill God's divine mission? Mankind was not created for himself, but for the good, glory and honour of The Lord. But the free will that we each have been given allows us to do what is right or wrong."

"When I pray, it is not because I am afraid or troubled. I pray out of conviction, and not out of fear."

"St Jude, my patron saint, and faithful friend of our Lord Jesus Christ, may your prayers open the way and harden not our hearts but increase our faith."
"It is not good for a man to be very handsome or very rich for trouble often follows such men."

"He who is broke is often left alone and will not be bothered by anyone."

"That you would loath to walk the path of booby traps and snares, do not therefore lay booby traps or snares for others for you do not know the strength or type of arsenals they carry. Our strength lies not in entrapping or undermining others, but in making them equally important and better off."

“When someone takes credit for the hard work that you have done, do not get upset. It is because they respect your contribution and intellect even though they may not acknowledge or say it. People don't steal things they don't value.”

“The wealth of a man does not define his worth. Rather, it is the richness of the values and principles for which he stands that define his true worth.”

“Not all corporate decisions are made in the Boardroom. Some are made in the Bedroom.”
“A man can fail anything without losing his pride, but not in the bedroom.”

“If you can't sleep at night and think you are having a hard time, try asking a polygamist or a debtor whose uncompromising creditors are knocking hard at his doorpost.”

“If one were to encounter poverty in one's life, we pray that it may not be poverty of the mind, but a surmountable encounter with limited resources of this mundane world.”

- Kenneth K. Mwenda

“Human beings have a tendency to show their teeth even when they don't mean it. And because animals have a tendency to show their teeth when they intend to attack or harm you, perhaps, in that respect, we share some similarities.”

“It is wise not to lend help to a married woman, financially or otherwise, except in an emergency or with the full knowledge of her husband.”

“There is no strength or honour in taking off your clothes mischievously, and anything gained out of such has no honour or dignity.”

“We all have one problem or another. The difference lies in our ability to not let it show.”

“She who waits on a married man to leave his wife will wait a lifetime.”

“Sunday is a day when many a sinner come out of their woodwork, seeking forgiveness from God,

Jehovah, the Father, yet never abandoning their sinful ways fully and remaining tenaciously resolute to the illusory idea of seeking forgiveness habitually without giving themselves a promise of abatement."

"It is not polite for us as Africans, no matter how much we try to twist the cultural argument, for an African bride to ask for specific expensive gifts from her in-laws for her wedding, or to invite prominent public figures with the prime motive and reason for the same. Let those who care and love us show their care and love without our subtle machination and shenanigans to impose undue influence on them."

"An African guest does not often warn you about his intended visit. He just shows up at your place like a thief in the night without an invitation, and says no word about his departure date or plans. Yet, you are expected to embrace his warm smile and to welcome him all the same."

"If, by any means, we were to understand the protection of human rights of children to include the restriction on all parents from disciplining their children with a cane, notwithstanding the reasonableness or the proportionality of the punitive measures applied, then how many lawsuits would we have today before the judicial organs of many developing countries, recognizing that until recently such means of instilling discipline were not alien to our indigenous cultures as well as to the cultures of some conservative western societies? But we are told today by many human rights advocates, inspired by a Eurocentric persuasion, that smacking a child, even in the slightest manner, is no good way to discipline him or her, meaning that perhaps our parents were wrong in their own humble way of raising us."

"She who undresses the King with her beauty overthrows the King momentarily. And he who is clothed with power and authority loses that power and authority when he strips naked and remains in that state for he cannot exercise such power or authority while in the vestment of nudity."

"That there are hardly any civil rights in the institution of marriage, but rather moral responsibilities is a concept that many a younger generation cannot fathom. In marriage, you do not go about asserting egoistically your individual rights. Your rights are easily realizable and attainable when individual and collective responsibilities are honored. Thus, a good marriage, and one's suitability for such, is not about attitude but about fine manners. One who is without good manners, or one who is wanting in etiquette and politeness, risks settling for less, or falling short of the standards of a well-cultivated spouse."

"Judge me by my actions, my love for others and my service to humanity. Do not judge me by standards that are alien to my existence."

"You may not like what I say, or even like me, but you know for a fact that much of what I say and stand for is true."

"Do not celebrate when your friend is down for you have never even been up there where he has been. At least, he has been there."

"For many a folk, the availability or provision of money or material things is a test of true friendship. Friends won with money or material things are not true friends. Likewise, a love won with money or material things is not a genuine love. And a wiseman knows and appreciates the limitations of money's worth, worrying not over that which reveals itself when money is either absent or not forthcoming."

"A village boy walks miles on end to school with some of his friends. The other boys in the village choose to stay away from school, mocking and laughing at their friends that: 'Look at them, they think they are the smart ones. Even if they walk showing off the books in their hands they don't even do that well in school. We, who remain at home, are even better off...'. So it is with religion. Not everyone that goes to church does well as a Christian. But that does not make the critics better off either. The critics must find their own feet on which to stand instead of criticizing."

"The Lord, God, Jehovah, hears our silent prayers too. We all don't have to shout or scream in tongues to be heard. We can pray quietly even when nobody else, but God, is watching us. For the Lord sees even the nakedness of our hearts."

"If you were to ask me, I have accomplished nothing that can make me so assured in life until I earn my salvation before my God...then, and only then, shall I celebrate truly."

"It doesn't take a genius to know that there is something good about doing good to others, and that there is something bad about doing bad to others."

"Even if you are a non-believer or an atheist, you will agree that there is something philosophical that connects the dots between pertinent values of morality and ethics, on the one hand, and those of a deity, such as God, on the other. Why are many desirable values of morality and ethics in the secular world so closely related to the laws of God when many philosophers in the early days were not even Christians?"

"For some reason, whenever I visit a friend's or colleague's home, my curiosity is always directed at the bookshelf, and never at what is in the carport or the type of furniture in the home. There are just certain things that tell you something about a person and his or her values. And when such things are missing, you begin to wonder."

"It is a truism that the Internet is a world of jewels and junk, and not a court of public opinion. A wise man knows full well that he ought not to judge others by what they post on social media for many a time those that are quick to judge lack the courage to post their own thoughts. Many a society have evolved historically on the ideas of seemingly eccentric people that said things like the world is not flat like a table but oval when such thoughts were considered crazy."

"The thunder of a wise man is neither in his groin nor material possessions, but in his edifying thoughts."

"Whatever a tall man can do, a short man can do as well. So, why are we quick to judge others based on race, looks, height, creed, religion, ethnicity or tribe?"

"It is much easier for children to trust and to forgive than it is for adults to do so."

"While love, like the ability to forgive, is divine, hating is primitive. Hating creates no opportunities, but only threats for the hater. Love makes you stronger while your hate makes you even weaker. In love, there is happiness and emotional strength, while in hating there is only emotional weakness, visible sadness, anger and bitterness. That there have been so many haters since this world has been going round means that there have been so many sad, bitter, angry and primitive people in this world. Just don't be one of them."

"When you are talking to people, and they are quiet, it is not always that they are busy paying attention to what you are saying. Sometimes, they will be turned off or are bored, and may thus not bother with what you are saying. But quite often, they will be busy concentrating just to find faults in what you are saying so that they can nail you!"

“Even in his seemingly docile or quiet state, man is capable of the most terrifying and weird thoughts. You do not want to go into a man's thoughts without praying.”

“The flight of a frightened man offers no comfort to his problems for they await his return, or he might meet them again along the way.”

“He who falls in love so often is a danger to himself for he has little left of his heart.”

"LORD, Your love conquers even the hatred of sinners. Secure in me, Lord, not the laws of men for I have much knowledge of that, but Your holy statutes for which I seek a firm understanding that they may be written onto my heart to please only You alone.”

"There is hardly any room in a man's wallet to secure firmly a marriage certificate."

"When your conscious is well nourished, you are shielded from envy and are less likely to harm others."

"The path of a righteous man is like a fountain of water from which to drink."

"He who tells lies forgets easily what he said."

"If you think you can pull a fast one by getting to the top faster by using an elevator, as your friend climbs the staircase, that elevator almost always breaks down on the second floor. Your friend will be waiting for you at the top of the staircase while you are trapped in the elevator."

"A broke brother knows best the meaning of a dollar."

“He who has smoked weed before knows the importance of keeping a secret.”

“Sometimes, pride is all that remains of expired and aged beauty. But knowledge and wisdom can serve you a lifetime.”

“The world is such a cold place. Many people in the world are lonely. And that is why they turn to social media to find companionship and camaraderie. Only in Heaven will they throw away their keyboard.”

“Stress, evading hopes, worry, uncertainty, fear, anxiety, financial distress and debts, as well as aging, unplanned retirements, marital problems, the lack of steady income, unpreparedness for academic exams, unconfessed sins, unyielding lies, the lack of intimacy and genuine love, ubu shimbe (i.e. bachelorhood or spinsterhood), office problems, bad neighbours or relatives, and hunger often rob people of sleep. Just check how many people are still awake on social media!”

“We are all different in the way we relax. Some relax by appreciating and supporting some postings on

Facebook, without bias or prejudice, notwithstanding any controversy, while others spend much of their time criticizing or frowning upon what they see or read on Facebook. Facebook may be the wrong place for the latter folks."

"While the learned and competently skilled often underrate their own abilities due to a complex manifested through a lack of self-confidence, the average minds, by contrast, seize the opportunity since the intelligent ones are doubting themselves. In psychology, it is called the Dunning-Kruger effect. Charles Darwin once said, 'Ignorance more frequently begets confidence than does knowledge.' And, Bertrand Russell made a closely related remark, observing that, 'One of the painful things about our time is that those who feel certainty are stupid, and those with any imagination and understanding are filled with doubt and indecision.'..."

"No matter how much, or how hard, an aged man exercises, age may fail his tired muscles from ever growing so much for the prime of his youthful six-pack abs is no more. He can only lower his cholesterol."

"This world is faced with so many problems because some people think that only they know God best.

Like some folks without an iota or trace of God in them, or those without much moral restraint, too much religion and dogma can be dangerous; for, religion and God are not always the same. We must pray to God, and not to religion."

"It is unwise to cause an ungodly sight to others by exposing one's legs, especially where, with age, one's legs are no longer that well configured."

"The truth of the matter is that, in whatever you set out to be, you should never settle for less. Think global, and not local or regional. Otherwise, you may never be happy or content with life. If I had wanted to make lots of money and become rich, I would not rest until I become one of the richest men in the world. But that's not what I am all about. We all have different gifts, and must discover these gifts. If you have to be the best cook or best husband, then be one of ...the best cooks or best husbands in the world. If you have to win, then win big, and not small. Never settle for less. For me, the road that I have chosen to travel is not an easy one. One has to contend with the demands and sacrifices of time and effort. It can be a lonely road, but one must travel it to the best and fullest of his or her abilities, without fear or favour. And I must say that I feel much happier in my small material world in comparison to the worries of a wealthy man with stolen wealth."

"If the other man wore his pants upside down, I would have reason to fear him. But we all wear our pants the same way."

"To win, you must keep your eyes on the prize no matter how far you may be from the prize...you will eventually get there."

"When a man or woman takes off his or her shoes, the roughness or coarseness of the feet often tell a story about his or her struggles, notwithstanding any pretension, or that he or she now has money."

"She who eats and wipes off her dinner plate clean, like one who orders a sumptuous meal or an exorbitant drink that far exceeds her usual station in life, wins no love but risks not being invited on another dinner date."

"That your host has been kind enough to serve you a whole bottle of fine wine or whiskey does not mean that it is now yours to take home or to drink it all by yourself."

“I learned very early that there is a marked difference between the kind of hand luggage or cabin case that you carry with you when boarding a plane, especially when flying First Class or Business Class, and the kind that you carry when boarding a local bus. It can be quite irritating on the plane when sitting next to someone with so many plastic-shopping bags, trying desperately and 'tutu-ishly' to load them all under his seat as well as in the overhead. Some folks like to travel heavy, wanting to carry with them to the motherland everything that they can lay their hands on.”

“Life is dynamic. At different stages in our life, we all acquire new friends and new enemies.”

“The uninvited guest at your party will often be the most talkative and with the broadest smile, warming up unnecessarily to your company.”

“In some cultures, it is acceptable and lawful for a mother to breastfeed her child in public, while in other cultures breastfeeding in public is not only frowned upon, but has also been criminalized as indecent exposure. In some cultures, it is acceptable and lawful for a man to have a sexual relationship with a fellow man, while in other cultures such acts are not only frowned upon, but have also been criminalized as sodomy. In some cultures, it is acceptable and lawful for... a man to marry several wives, while in other cultures such conduct is not only considered primitive, but has also been criminalized as bigamy. In some cultures, it is acceptable and lawful for an adult man to indulge in public masturbation on the beach as a fundamental human right, while in other cultures such conduct is not only frowned upon, but has also been criminalized as indecent exposure. Yet we are all human beings, albeit with different emphases on life."

"It's not always about money. You will know a man by his manners and etiquette. Some undergo potty training at a tender and young age, while others simply learn bad manners from their elders by peeing and spitting on the streets. Some are taught at a tender and young age to hold their mouth when yawning, and not to insult or use foul language, while others yawn with their mouth wide open in wanton disregard of those around them. Some are taught how to laugh lightly at a good ...joke when in the presence of people, while others have only known uncontrolled loud and wild laughter all their lives. Some are taught the importance of not only giving, but also saying 'thank you', or saying 'sorry', while others only know how to get and receive. Some are taught table manners and how to conduct a decent conversation at the dinner table, whilst others only know how to gossip and spread rumours at the dinner table. When young, some are taught that the last day of school term is a time to celebrate each other's achievements, whilst others only know that that is the best time for promoting school fights and bullying the good students. We are all brought up differently, and our behaviours are sometimes shaped by these experiences."

"While love, like the ability to forgive, is divine, hating is primitive. Hating creates no opportunities, but only threats for the hater. Love makes you stronger while your hate makes you even weaker. In love, there is happiness and emotional strength, while in hating there is only emotional weakness, visible sadness, anger and bitterness. That there have been so many haters since this world has been going round means that there have been so many sad, bitter, angry and primitive people in this world. Just don't be one of them."

"It's not the type of train you take that matters, but the company next to you will determine how fast you need to get to where you are going, or if you are in no hurry and are enjoying the conversation."

"The courage of a naked man is confined to the night, to the darkness of life and to the savory pit of secrecy in conjugal hegemony for he cannot walk the light of day without attempting to conceal his state of being. Do not be like a naked man in the concealed thoughts abiding in the darkness of your heart. Edify your thoughts so that you may have the courage to walk the light of day without attempting to conceal anything."

"Do not put your faith in men for they are quick to disappoint, but stay steadfast in the faith of The Lord. You can lose your friends, lose your possessions, and even lose your fame, but you can never lose God."

"When all the people that you look up to, or those that you consider to be close to you, are no longer there for you then you know that you only have God to look up to."

"One who is a prisoner of pride and attitude cannot escape the delusional sense of self-importance for s/he reasons not with objectivity but with the overwhelming burden of issues."

"Everyone who loves is a fool for love because love does not have much pedigree in logic, reason or analysis."

"The silent depths of a man's thoughts in whose abyss the guarded fears and vulnerabilities reside lie not in his mind but in his heart. To know him, you must get to his heart."

"If I asked for money, it might affect our friendship. But I only ask of the very least: remember me in your prayers."

"What we do when we think nobody is watching is WHO we are, and what we do when we think someone is watching is WHAT we are. Taking me for WHO I am, and not WHAT I am."

"To count your blessings, count the number of relatives and friends that are still around you, faithfully and truthfully, in your time of crisis."

"Why are we often impatient when it comes to making money?"

"Books alone are not enough. Neither is experience on its own (without sound intellect) sufficient. Some people may be book-smart but not street-smart.

Others may be street-smart, but not book-smart. It is important to strike a balance between the two extremes."

"Don't thank me for anything. None is of my making. Pray for me instead because your prayers make me strong and help me to come through to my calling with His Grace and His Love."

"Do not strike your enemy whilst he is half asleep. That is not character. It's cowardice."

"Those who make a difference have a different attitude to life for they choose, by their conscious actions, to be amazing than to be amazed."

"One who appears depressed or overwhelmed with life's problems does not realize that everyone out there is going through the same or similar situations, until he attends to the inebriated solemn speech of others labouring under a drunken stupor, for there are no great secrets with alcohol."

"One who loves does not live for himself for love does not grow weary; it is an act of selfless greatness in giving than receiving, it is an act of saying Thank You than asking or demanding without gratitude, it is an anti-thesis of hatred, envy or jealousy, for love is a priceless and edifying moral responsibility for which God calls us to live to the best of our abilities and intent."

"A wise elder says to the aspiring bride: do not rush for the flash for who you fall in love with, and not what you fall in love with, will help to determine the happiness of your marriage... It is no good living in a grand castle or holding gracefully to the steering wheel of a Maserati while tears flow ceaselessly from the eyes..."

"We are born of the divine love of God, with an unassuming humility that does not hate or discriminate. We only learn to hate or discriminate when we come into this world. We must rediscover who we truly are..."

"Many people are in the habit of saying, 'I will fix him...' You cannot succeed in life by conspiring to 'fix' someone. People are not 'fixable'. Only objects and issues can be fixed."

- Kenneth K. Mwenda

"Do not be afraid of age as you grow older. We all cannot hold on to our youth forever. Age is something that worries many people, especially when they begin to look out of shape or no longer look as cute as they used to look, or when they no longer have the stamina or physique to attend to certain calls of adult life. Embrace age and life as if you are still youthful. At the end of the day, what matters most is where you are headed after this life, or, for the non-believer, what legacy you will leave behind on this earth. Some folks leave behind nothing but problems. Others leave behind a great legacy of ideas for posterity to prosper from, while some others leave only bad and sad memories. Life is a journey. Travel it well and be kind to the strangers you meet on the way..."

"Over the years that I have mentored many young people, I have come to realize that trouble hardly follows you. Rather, you are the one who follows trouble. Trouble is not intrinsic to our human life. By contrast, we are the ones that have a tendency to invite trouble into our lives. If you sit quietly all by yourself without causing a mayhem or distraction, or even attracting the attention of others to yourself, there would be no trouble. Trouble is something that we go out there to seek. And because we are often restless and quite eager for something that gives us a kick of adrenalin, we end up inviting trouble into our lives."

"You worry so much about nothing really. And you are so anxious over a future you do not even know that well. Yet, you have difficulties believing that there must be someone beyond mankind who made mankind from the very beginning. You would rather say that you believe in empiricism and science, without asking why science has thus far not been able to invent (not clone) mankind or even a single planet. Science only tells us what happens when the sun goes down and the moon come...s out, but not where the sun came from initially, or why it behaves the way it does to give way to the moon. With faith, even the lions will not roar, and the waters will remain calm. We panic, and are often restless, because of our little faith and the overwhelming weight of our sins on our conscience. We are not like little children without sin. Accept God's unconditional love to find that peace of mind that surpasses all human understanding..."

"The legacy of a truly outstanding lawyer is not so much about how many criminals or suspects one has managed to free from the wrath of the law by his or her sheer cunningness, or about how many boilerplate or template-inspired legal agreements a man or woman has drafted or negotiated in his or her lifetime. Neither is it about any politically engineered office or title that one holds or has held by virtue of a mere political appoint...ment or dictate. Far from it: for every qualified lawyer can be equal to such task. When there are too many lawyers in town, people will first ask where or under whom did one study the law. Some will also ask how long it took for one to pass the Bar or to become a lawyer. Others would equally want to know where and at what level did one practice or teach the law. But more importantly, I opine, verily and truly, what defines the ultimate test and legacy of an eminent leader in the law is the indelible and distinguished contribution that one makes to the development of the law for the benefit of posterity and those that will ever come in contact with such contribution."

"You know that you truly need God's divine intervention as well as your sustained prayers when: (a) you go for a job interview only to find that your ex-girlfriend who you disappointed badly is sitting on the interview panel; or (b) the guy whose advances you turned done rudely is now your new boss."

"It is utter dishonesty to conceal from, or not to disclose truthfully and fully to, the one you are marrying the number of girlfriends or boyfriends you have serviced in the past as well as their names. Even employers expect us to disclose the number of jobs we have previously held as well as the names of those companies. No company wants to hire without a proper background check on the references."

"The problem with the African in the diaspora is that he cannot just let go of Africa even if he holds a foreign passport in his hands. The African in the diaspora is constantly tip-toeing in the shadows of Africa to pip and see what's going on there. He will do anything and everything just to know what's going on there. And so, he runs to social media and the Internet just to sneak in and find out what is going on in Africa."

"It is often difficult to explain to someone asking for some money when he says, 'Can you borrow me some money?', that you cannot BORROW him any money, but can only LOAN or LEND him the same."

"We must pray not because our lives are stuck in a tunnel full of smoke, as we search for an escape route. We must pray even when there is no smoke or tunnel."

"There is something about being cool that isn't cool. When I was younger, somewhere around elementary or primary school, most of the guys that I thought were cool turned out not to be cool. And I have seen repeatedly the pattern of this coolness not being cool at the end of the day."

"Even if the Good Lord were to grant me kindly the gift of material wealth, I pray that you do not judge me by that wealth, but by my ideas and related works, and how they both have contributed to the uplifting of others for the betterment of humanity."

"If you must study law, I pray that you do not end up as a criminal."

"When we are training our lawyers, we are not training them to go and make money. Rather, we are aiming at improving the delivery of justice and strengthening the foundations of democracy, governance and the rule of law. But we are not getting there fast enough. Something seems to be standing in the way – the aggressive pursuit of money by those to whom society looks up for the virtues of fairness and equity."

"One who is content with routine must expect a routine life, and nothing exceptional."

"There are two things that many people crave for which can help to make or break you. Forget education, at least, for now. The two things are money or marriage, or both. For some, money or marriage is the beginning of problems. For others, money or marriage marks an end to their problems. It just depends on how you approach them."

"There are two types of people that are dangerous to follow blindly, and these are the educated and the religious. Whereas it is easy to dismiss someone who is not educated, including an uneducated politician, as not knowing what he is talking about, as well as to dismiss a sinner or the non-believer as not having the moral pedigree to inform our conscience, we are often quick to listen to those that claim to be educated and learned or those that claim to be religious and righteous. We never stop to think that they too could be dead wrong or that they simply could be clothing some of their half-truths with the authority and power-base that society ascribes to them. That is why it's dangerous to follow the educated and the religious blindly. We must keep asking them questions so that they can explain themselves fully."

"If I were to go back in time some twenty-five (25) years or so as a young graduate from the University of Zambia, and were asked to make a choice between Oxford and Harvard, I would still choose Oxford over Harvard. There is something that you get out of xford that you don't find easily at any other school, not even in continental Europe. The Clintons know better."

"If I must upgrade, the upgrade must make sense. I don't believe in upgrading for the sake of upgrading or simply because everyone else around me is upgrading. I may appear to be slow until you wake up to find me ahead."

"In the western world, it is hard to keep up with notion of beauty. It is as if beauty is an evolving subject. Today, the focus can be on those that are slim and slender as the epitome of good looks. Tomorrow, everyone will be saluting those with an endowed posterior, with clothing companies beginning to make garments that reveal an endowed posterior supported by curvy handles. By contrast, in Africa, we have one standard that holds true for the most part."

"While a bonus has to be earned by those to whom it will be given, the African concept of 'mbasela', that is, some extras in addition to what one has paid for, should not be confused for a bonus. Imbasela is never earned and it calls for no hard work. It is simply the institutionalization of opportunism by the buyer. And so, imbasela has no justifiable place in a modern free market economy."

"In a democracy, people are free to make choices. But one who picks prostitutes is to be feared. He is not your friend for in the end he will want to pick you!"

"One who is in a hurry to begin dating at a young and tender age often struggles later to acknowledge some questionable characters that he or she dated before he or she found fame or attained a higher station in life."

"There are two things that many people crave for which can help to make or break you. Forget education, at least, for now. The two things are money or marriage. For some, money or marriage is the beginning of problems. For others, money or marriage marks an end to their problems. It just depends on how you approach either of the two or both of them."

"The problem with the practice of endorsing a presidential candidate is that the individual or person making the endorsement must himself or herself be a notable political factor to sway public opinion. It is folly for a presidential candidate to get excited with the endorsements received from some people who have no political clout or influence whatsoever. Likewise, those making the endorsements need not cry foul when the candidate they are endorsing wins the elections, but does not offer them a job or some business contracts. Indeed, great and unfathomable anguish has been known visit and preoccupy those who have campaigned vigorously or endorsed a presidential candidate that later abandoned them upon winning an election."

"When I first arrived in Europe from Africa, almost three decades ago now, I bought myself, among other things, some dinner candles. My Caucasian housemates from Europe and America were very impressed that I appeared a romantic at heart, not knowing that I bought the candles just in case there was load-shedding (i.e. electricity power outages); which never happened, anyhow!"

"To offer an interview to a distinguished and eminent professor who has applied for an academic position, or such other lofty job, is doing the professor grave injustice. The professor applied for the job, and not the interview."

"No matter how many Bible verses you may quote or how deep you are in speaking in tongues, or whether you are a deaconess, pastor, bishop, prophet or prophetess, the one fundamental truth about life is that, in the absence of artificial insemination, the public knows fully well what you were up to for you to get pregnant. You might as well lower your voice."

"One who is courageous enough to wear a mini skirt or mini dress, despite her advanced age or tired looking legs, might as well be courageous enough not to cross her legs painstakingly while she is seated. It does not help also to sit fidgeting at an angle to avoid facing the audience directly. She wore that short skirt or dress knowing fully well what she intended to achieve. She might as well go ahead and expose everything."

"A man of great honor does not lose his distinguished thoughts at the sight of a beautiful lady. He maintains decorum, without allowing war to rage in his heart or to torment his crotch."

"We often stigmatize those who are addicted to drugs and alcohol, without realizing that a great many of the people that are found on social media and elsewhere do have an addiction to pornography or some sort of sexual romantic fantasy. I kid you not, many do suffer from a void somewhere, constantly wanting to unlock the puzzle or to fill the gap through some kind of mystery. Others are just seeking attention or fame, and thus are addicted to some attention seeking behavior."

"The eyes of a lustful man will often give him away. And he tends to fall short on his breath."

"When all the mini skirts and mini dresses have been worn, and there is nothing else left to excite the men, some people will just begin to undress."

"A man without decent thoughts must not come before a fine lady or seek her company. For, his racing thoughts are not only a mayhem to oneself but also a menace to society. And society cannot learn from such undignified thoughts."

“We all can choose to be anyone or someone. It all depends on how far we can act on our dreams, that is, if we have any at all.”

“In life, you can't keep running all the time. At some point, you must stand your ground and fight back. To live a restless life full of fear or anxiety, and devoid of hope, aspirations and dreams, is to deny yourself of the full potential that God has imbedded in you.”

“Many of you feel unappreciated by your employers, workmates, friends, neighbors, relatives, spouses, children and colleagues. But you must understand something. If they don't show you the respect you feel you deserve or give you the opportunity to realize your full potential, you must create your own opportunities and move closer to those who truly appreciate you. It's that simple. Don't sit there and wait, thinking that they will change their wicked, perverted and distorted mindsets.”

“Each time you pray, you upset the guy with a bone chew against God. But understand something: you must upset him so much that he leaves you alone. Nobody messes with those who upset them.”

"Human beings are all made in the likeliness of God. Intrinsically, they are interlinked to Godliness in one way or another. They cannot therefore deny the one who represents their likeliness in the same way that they cannot deny their own offsprings who represent their likeliness. That no human being was ever made in the likeliness of the guy that continues to fight God almost always upsets that guy, with much envy and chagrin. But the problem is that if that very guy wants to compete with God he had better understand that when God gets angry there will be nobody to stop God."

"Over the years, I have come to understand that one of the most effective strategies of negotiation is to make the other party realize that you have some very damaging information about him or her. And you just have to look at the said party straight in the eye from across the floor or the table for him or her not to misbehave. Sometimes, you just have to clear your throat lightly, as he or she is trying to say something before he or she withdraws into quietness."

"A priest who is consecrated to the Lord cannot by himself or whomsoever he may call upon contract himself out of priesthood. Neither can any higher earthly authority by itself decree such a man to be no longer a servant of God. Only God has the final say. Let the priest repent from his sinful ways and go back to the Lord."

"Do not run away when those who know your bad habits show up, thinking that your lies or mischief won't catch up with you. They are headed to where you are going."

"If there is anything that should be guarded and protected from the intruding eyes of others, it's our sexual organs. They remain, no doubt, very private. Yet, for some people, these same private parts are more easily accessible even to the young, while the mere password to their cellphone is so highly guarded and protected as private."

"A large faction of the generation of our parents in Zambia often spoke nostalgically of the great times that they spent at such famed schools as the then Munali College in Zambia before proceeding to either Makerere University in Uganda, the University of Fort Hare in South Africa, the University of Ibadan in Nigeria, the University of Ghana in Ghana, or the University of East Africa in Tanzania. Others never went beyond Munali, but kept parroting Munali, none the less. For the young ladies, the brightest often attended Chipembi Girls High School back in the day. Those were the schools.

Today, we cannot have some pockets of political leadership whose highest intellectual pedigree or point of reference is their primary school days at Mamba or Bwacha Primary School. Not even stories of Macha Secondary School in Southern Province are extraordinary any more. The world has changed so much. Some young folks with an Oxford education will fellowship with me on the famed BCL at Oxford. Others with a Harvard education will share their perspectives on the LLM or MPA degree programs at Harvard. And many Rhodes Scholars have traversed the green lawns of Oxford and walked through those heavy wooden doors at Oxford. Also, Yale, Columbia, Cmabridge, Princeton, Stanford, MIT, Imperial College, Warwick, London Business School, Sorbone, INSEAD, as well as many other prestigious schools continue to graduate bright and dynamic African professionals.

The story of today is no longer about Mpatamato Secondary School in Luanshya, Matero Boys' Secondary School in Lusaka, or Masala Boys' in Ndola. Neither is it about Mpelembe Secondary School in Kitwe because those names do not often show up on the CV, unless that is the highest pedigree one has attained."

"You cannot compare Pele to Maradona, or Ali to Tyson. Every soccer player or boxer is different. Neither can you compare Jordan to other top basketball players in the NBA. Every player is different. Not even two intellectual heavyweights are the same. They each have a different writing style or outlook to issues. Comparing them would be doing them injustice.

In essence, you must have your own style and identity. And the signature must be your own, and not that of someone else. It is that aspect of originality that sets you apart from the rest. You can only sustain your leadership in whatever form of endeavor you choose by leading, and not by following."

"Brethren and sisters, do not throw stones and sticks at a sinful man. Rather, pray for him so that he may turn away from his sinful ways. For, none of you is righteous. It is for this reason that our Lord Jesus Christ challenged the elderly Pharisees who were attempting to stone the lady accused of a moral wrong, asking them: 'Bushe, pali imwe bonse apa, ni ani usha tola po ihule?' (English translation: 'Let the one who has never picked up a prostitute be the first to throw a stone at this woman.'). And they all walked away in shame and guilt to the surprise of their most dignified wives who had followed behind spiritedly to witness the stoning of the accused lady."

"I tell you solemnly, my brethren and sisters, be weary of one who does not express his or her opinions. You are better off with someone who expresses his or her views than a person who pretends to be in agreement with you all the time or one who remains silent, saying nothing."

"Some people talk too much. Even when you have not solicited their opinion or advice, they will be busy telling you what you should be wearing or not wearing, what you should be buying or not buying, who you should be talking to or not talking to, how you should be living or enjoying your life, what you should be saying or not saying, what you should be writing on or not writing on, what you should be doing or not doing, and so forth. They do not realize that you, in turn, do not treat them that way. You respect their space."

"Some people live their lives as if they need the permission of others to be happy. If you can walk on water, then please do so even if they keep talking that you should have been swimming instead. They will always have something to say anyhow, especially if they themselves cannot walk on water."

"The problem with seeking the approval of men is that you don't really know why they are saying yes. Not everyone that says yes agrees with you."

"Many people who behave as though they have a lot of money don't even have half the money that they want to make you believe they have. And many people who want to sound to the public as though they are very learned and knowledgeable don't even have half the education or knowledge that they want to make you believe they have. Even those who only took their first flight abroad the other day want to talk as though they have been flying all their life. And many who come from the rural areas tend to overdo things when they finally settle into city life, trying so much to urbanize as city elites but the rough edges and cuttings of where they are coming from often show."

"The King himself is usually not very loud. Rather, it is the King's children, wife, messenger or servant and those that are remotely related to him that tend to make the loudest noise, often quoting the authority of the King, as if the King and they are one and the same indivisible body."

"Of everything that I have and own, my ideas and my faith are my greatest possessions. Nobody else can steal them from me. Each person's faith is his or hers alone. Each person's ideas are his or hers alone. But the car that you drive and the clothes that you wear, or the houses that you own, shall be left behind and inherited by others. Sometimes, we don't even have to wait that far before the bailiffs pounce on them! But your ideas and faith can never be touched by the bailiffs!!! They are yours forever."

"We must respect those who teach our children in schools and other learning environments. Theirs is the work of building a future. Sadly, we often want to respect those with money even though they are not related to us and do not know us. We talk of them so highly as if they matter so much to everyone. Quite often, these people will not even share their money with us, yet we continue to throw ourselves at them. A society that does not respect ideas, but material things, cannot expect to see much development sooner."

"Do not thrive in the shadow of a fellow mortal man for he has no lasting shadow. Thrive in the shadow of the Lord so that you can stand firm in every season."

"Sometimes it is hard to explain to someone your age whose father is your friend or close professional colleague that you are not in the same peer league as he is, despite being of the same physical age. Neither is someone your age, who is a friend of your older brother, a peer of yours, notwithstanding that you are of the same age. Young folks of today don't seem to get it. It ain't about money, but respect."

"In the olden days, we used to think that many older folks in the workplaces or other walks of life were quite insecure to recognize young talent and give a chance to the young. Today, the greatest resistance comes from some of our very own friends, brothers and sisters who have known us for years, including our immediate neighbors as well as those that were once with us in class or in the same peerage or cohort at school. While others will clap, they won't. Indeed, resistance does not come from afar or from those who came years before or after us. It comes from those that we once shared a meal with or drank beers alongside. And that is why our Lord, Jesus Christ, was betrayed not by someone from afar, or someone much younger or older, but by one of his twelve disciples who knew Him well and was from within His circles."

"In cultures where people are able to express themselves fully and responsibly, as well as where talent is often recognized and appreciated, society tends to develop faster than where people are constantly cynical about progress and progressive elements, thus leaving a vast majority overly fearful about what others will say or think regarding what they would like to do. You cannot innovate with fear or worry."

"There are many things that happen in African football that you will not understand if you have never played African football or soccer before. You don't just pick up someone else's soccer boots in the team and wear them. It may not be safe to do that. Simply stick to your boots. Unlike European football where you depend mainly on the technique and physical-mental fitness of the players, African football offers more than meets the eye. Perhaps, that is why it has taken us such a long time to get anywhere close to winning the World Cup. We sometimes rely on wrong and unscientific variables to influence a scientific outcome."

"An accused person should never think that by wearing talismans and charms around the waist he will mesmerize the judges into giving an easy verdict for an acquittal (i.e. acquittals are often referred to by the laity as 'washout'). The judges themselves have better and more sophisticated talismans and charms hidden in their impeccable knowledge of the law. And that's what makes it interesting."

“The generation of our children, born in the computer age, are a more refined species of human beings than us. To a large extent, they are almost entirely free of superstition. Unlike you and I, they see no reason why someone should not announce his or her travel plans, especially in the village. They believe that one should throw a farewell party with other villagers amicably when leaving.

Yet, you are often afraid to bid farewell to some of your relatives when leaving the village. You even fear to share the good news that your wife is pregnant, leaving it to the people to discover for themselves when the pregnancy begins to show. And when the child is born, you have to consult your elders for a name, praying that the child does not begin to cry, signaling that the ancestors have rejected the name and want the baby given a different name. No doubt, the generation of your children does not think like that. Rather, it believes in looking at a book of names and choosing a name for the baby in a civilized way, and that thereafter the mother can breastfeed the baby even if there are some suspiciously looking women around who are also breastfeeding their babies with some kind of necklace-missile dangling around that baby’s neck.”

“Aren’t there things around us that are incapable of explanation? In Africa, while you are fast asleep, you'll sometimes dream of someone trying to choke and suffocate you, and thus find yourself gasping for air and struggling to scream or breath, until suddenly the chokehold is released before you wake up from the nightmare, panicking and not knowing what has just happened. Sometimes, as you try to find your sleep, you hear footsteps on the roof as if someone is running on top of the roof. At the other times, the footsteps can be heard near your bedroom window. And you begin to pray for divine intervention from God above. Aren't there things around us that are incapable of explanation? Sometimes a woman dreams of her neighbour, a man, making love to her yet the two are not even in love, and the same man will be the first to say good morning when day breaks the next day.

And if you see an owl or black cat in some societies and cultures, you must chase it away to avoid any problems. If an owl is making noise outside at night, you must come out of the house to hurl unpalatable insults at it, while chasing it away and issuing threats that you will not take any nonsense from anyone of the underworld.

By contrast, in Europe and North America, you find yourself sometimes dreaming of snow and a white Christmas or a tooth fairy. People's experiences are thus shaped in part by the environment, and not necessarily by destiny. We just have to change the environment sometimes to have a different experience."

"Sometimes, depending on what you have smoked, you will see different things. Also, depending on what you have read, you will understand issues differently. And depending on how much you are offered, you will view morality and ethics differently."

"Ici fukushi nga ca kwi kata, wi ponta!!! Elo, wi ya mu ci pyu. Pantu na mailo uka bwela. Ici Bemba ci sosa a citi, 'Ta ba nyela mu mpoto pa ku ya.'" (English translation: "No matter how upset you are, do not insult anyone, throw profanity at them or walk out on them with uncontrolled anger. Tomorrow, you might need the assistance of the same people you are insulting. As we say in the Bemba language, do not shit in the cooking pot when leaving because you may need to cook from that same pot on your return.").

"When everyone else in the top ranks of your political party has been given a cabinet position and only you have been left out, the best thing to do is form your own political party and begin to insult the political party that left you out. They call it mature politics."

"It is wise for a man or woman to refrain from indulging in expensive habits or acquiring a fine taste of good life that he or she can neither maintain nor sustain. To keep insisting unscrupulously that you only drink a certain fine brand of whiskey when you can hardly afford the cheaper one, and are busy waiting on someone else to buy you a drink, is not only embarrassing but extremely discourteous. People will see that you are desperate from the glow in your eyes when you are served with the drink even if you try to maintain some superficial decorum as if all is well."

"A town mouse and a bush mouse are two different things. When you put a bush mouse on the golf course, he will be busy looking for peanuts. When you take a town mouse to the village after retirement, he may not last long. A town mouse loves his cheese and wine, with good life in the city. But the bush mouse now also wants that same lifestyle even though he does not know how to hold a glass of wine. It makes life so stressful when people have to race and hustle for the same things much of the time. Nobody wants to sit in their place."

“If you were to rescue a man or woman from drowning in a river, you are likely to be met with one of the following five responses: (a) utter silence as if nothing happened, and it's just business as usual; (b) a casual remark from the rescued person that after all he or she was just about to swim to safety when you threw him or her the life jacket, or when you dragged him or her out of the water; (c) some irresponsible and ungrateful statement by the rescued person that he or she does not like people going around and telling people how they helped him or her, despite that rescued person not showing you gratitude in the first place; (d) once rescued or while being rescued, the person may turnaround thanklessly to try and drown you in the water instead; or (e) humility and appreciation from the rescued person, thanking you most sincerely for your selfless effort. One of these five responses is very rare. However, it remains the most dignified response.”

“Because of a deep-rooted culture of pretense and hypocrisy amog some church people today, especially the holier than thou brothers and sisters, there is a tendency for such people to rush into marriage as soon as they realize or discover that the man has impregnated the supposedly Christian sister out of wedlock, with a view of concealing and covering up their sinful act given that they have been too judgmental of others. What is more sinful, if I may ask, to eat pork, whether on Saturday or not, to get blood transfusion against dictates of the church, or to indulge clandestinely in illicit premarital sex while pretending to speak in tongues at church on Sunday? It is therefore not surprising that many firstborn children in some Christian families are born way before eight or nine months after the wedding date. The church has been besieged by hypocrisy!!!"

"To keep pacing up and down the street where a young lady you are after stays was often the preferred mode of signaling to the young lady that you are waiting for her by the roadside. There were no cellphones, social media or internet back then. Some guys would send a small kid from the neighbourhood to call the young lady for them, but things would turn very sour should the kid break the news innocently to the young lady in the presence of that young lady's parents or older brothers. So, other guys would opt to whistle repeatedly for an agreed number of times or throw a little small stone on the roof of the house where the young lady was staying to signal to her that her man was around. Whichever way, it was always risky, especially if the young lady had very rough older brothers or uncles. But that threat never deterred most guys since there was no social media to facilitate such mischievous endeavors. You just had to have the courage, and live with the consequences. For, there is no sweet without sweat."

“The primary schools that you attended back then are very different from your son or daughter’s primary school today. You grew up believing that the last day of the semester or academic term was all about fighting and settling scores against your nemesis. Sometimes, you would be so terrified to go to school on that last day, feigning sickness just to avoid the bullies at school. But the generation of your son or daughter is different. They are more eager to go to school at the close of the semester or academic term not to fight, but to celebrate achievements. They are growing up in an era where they celebrate and appreciate achievements, whereas you grew up in an era where bullies would beat up the top achievers in class, accusing them falsely of boasting, especially if they spoke better English or understood issues easily while the bully struggled to comprehend.”

“The middle class, when managed properly, can be a promising engine of economic growth, especially that it has aspirations of getting wealthier, and not getting poorer. But when managed poorly, the middle class can pursue selfish interests to enrich itself materially through compromised integrity. Unlike the rich or the poor, who often have an identifiable social class ideology or culture, the middle class tends to be very fragmented. A common problem with the middle class is... that it belongs neither to the wretched of the earth (i.e. the poor) nor to the upper crust of society (i.e. the rich), and often has a foot in either camp through, say, relatives or friends. Sometimes, the middle class will have graduated from poverty, or downgraded from wealth, to come and rest midway in the chasm of middle-ness. It can, therefore, be opportunistic or progressive, depending on where it stands to gain."

"If you believe that your friend who was born and raised in Africa, and only went to Britain to pursue his or her undergraduate studies for three or four years, is justified in putting up a contrived British accent, then what are you going to say about those of us who not only studied there but also taught British and immigrant students like your friend in that same country, Britain?"

"It is bad training, as was the case when you were growing up, to ask someone young to kill a chicken or goat. It prepares them for violence. You must buy processed chicken or goat meat from the butchers to avoid training potential terrorists."

"Irrespective of whether you are alone or not, or are in the bush, cornfield or elsewhere, if you must get naked, it must be for a dignified reason or noble cause, with utmost decorum."

“To laugh at your friend when he or she is not doing well does not make you any better than him or her. You are still in the same place and at the same spot. You have not advanced a single inch because you are busy looking at what others are doing, forgetting that, by doing so, you are losing focus and not making any progress. Your eyes must be on the finish-line, and not on the guy in the next lane.”

“If stuff is going good for you, they ain’t happy. They gonna be sulking all day, insulting and striking their breasts in protest but with nobody to hear them like the Pharisees did each time they heard that our Lord Jesus Christ had performed another miracle and drawn a large crowd.

But if stuff ain’t going good for you, they gonna be dancing, laughing and rejoicing all day, pretending to be sympathetic when they call you yet busy trying to find out how worse things have gotten. And they surely gonna talk all night on the phone. What kind of people are they who only get excited when stuff ain’t going good for others? Stay the course and work harder to keep them sulking more and more. That's the option they’ve chosen.”

"We are all gifted differently. And our paths are often not the same. Some start off at a very fast pace, but lose steam halfway before the finish line. Others start off slowly but pick up momentum halfway before the finish line. Some make it straight into law school and graduate as lawyers, while others have had to become lawyers after doing other things and then returning to school as mature-age students. Some make it straight into the school of medicine, while others have had to go through the other path of biochemistry before being admitted eventually to medical school. Some make it straight to study economics whilst others have had to become more closely associated with economics after their postgraduate studies. Whichever way, we are all not cut out the same, and must appreciate diversity. Some start their PhD studies and never finish. Others start to write a book that never gets to be published. We are all cut out differently. That's just how life is."

"A man that, acting uncaringly and with a clear lack of seriousness, does not provide for his wife or girlfriend should not complain when some other guy provides for her. He just has to pull up his socks before the other guy takes over his position on the soccer field."

"In cultures where people have to lobby for political appointments from the powers-that-be to serve in or hold public office, it is not uncommon to see many professionals make fools of themselves just to get those jobs. Do not be deceived, such people, though pretending and holding out to be men of integrity, will often do almost anything just to get that job."

"The nice thing about any heavy snowstorm is that even the very rich and powerful people get affected. It does not discriminate or choose. Each man or woman gets his or her share no matter where you live, what type of mansion you own or what type of car you drive."

"You need not get offended or feel belittled when your fellow African brother or sister says he or she speaks only English or French, and none of the native African dialectics. Even amongst the Caribbean folks, as well as amongst the Hispanics and Asians, there are folks who behave like that, claiming not to know how to speak their native dialect. All you have to do to get them back to reality is insult them with profanity in the native dialect, and then apologize should they get offended, politely reminding them that,

'Oh, I thought you hardly understood a word of our native dialect. What happened? I am really sorry. I didn't meant to. It's just that I was so sure that you wouldn't understand a thing or two.'"

"Do not ask a man the name of the lady that left him. And do not ask a lady the name of the guy that walked out on her. You must pretend not to know anything. It is safer that way."

"Do not look down on poor people. Being poor does not mean that their brains are also poor. You can learn something from the boy on the street if only you took time to listen to him. But if all you do is chase after the so-called big names who don't even have time for you, be rest assured that you will never be happy in playing second fiddle as you wait patiently to eat their leftovers, and warm up to their dry and boring jokes with a contrived smile."

"The greatest criticism that I have about the bench in some developing countries, especially at the highest court of appeal, is not on allegations or rumors of corrupt practices by some men and women of the wig, but rather on the glaring absence of intellectual and thought leadership, leading to some poorly reasoned and written judgements."

“When one has never studied or taught at a reputable university in a particular country or region, abroad or locally, there is often a tendency to think that doctoral degree programs or such other qualifications offered in those lands afar are not as rigorous intellectually as where the person got his or her doctorate. Such type of intellectual myopia and dishonesty often leads to intellectual violence.

By parity of reasoning, one who has written or published little scholarly work, if any at all, cannot sit to dissect one who is busy writing and churning out serious peer-reviewed scholarly work, asserting that one need not write just for the sake of publishing. That's intellectual dishonesty. The question will always arise: before you say anything negative about someone, please show us your published scholarly work so that we can compare the two of you.”

“The men and women of God, the church pastors, the bishops, the prophets and the prophetesses, cannot just come to social media for the purpose advertising a religious business or for recruiting new members into their congregation. They must show more Godly love to the people they befriend in many other ways, and not just advertising their church or sermons. That is not the way of a Christian. It ain’t about the numbers of crowds that you can draw or the tithes that you can attract.”

- *Kenneth K. Mwenda*

"Do not stop your friend from dancing just because you can't dance. And to look away when your friend is dancing will not slow down the swiftness of her dance. You might as well just ask her to teach you how to dance."

"For some people, the obsession to be in the limelight and to be seen to be happening often blinds them from reality. When they see someone younger on television or in the newspaper, they think it's a question of just getting up there and making some noise, without realizing that some people spend many years studying what they are talking about. In life, there are simply no shortcuts to success or to becoming a celebrity, especially if it has to do with knowledge, intellect and technical competence. Even sportsmen practice for hours everyday just to establish their position in a particular sport. You can't come up from nowhere to outshine those that know more than you do. It does not work like that. You have to stand in the queue, otherwise you are just a charlatan to be ignored safely."

"To describe yourself or hold out as someone you are not professionally, especially if you have not even studied whatever you are claiming to be, is not only dishonest but also disingenuous. Those with the good training of the eye can see through your lies and how far you are struggling with an identity crisis."

"In many societies, money can win you influence and affluence, but knowledge and wisdom can win you respect. Those with money are sometimes feared, but not respected, especially for the things that they can do with their money or how they acquired it. But with knowledge comes respect and power to influence and persuade without causing fear. Ultimately, the authority imbedded in knowledge is immutable as long as it is not abused."

"Where a donor or person tells you that he can only provide you with the actual goods or machinery, and not the money, needed to carry out your project activities, it is a simple statement that he cannot entrust you with money. Read the writing on the wall. And you have no right to question his decision not to put any of his money in your bank account."

"To inflate figures of expected financial expenditures when asking for financial help is nothing but utter dishonesty, especially where the person providing you with that assistance works out the figures and discovers that you have cooked up the numbers to make some mark-up profit off him. In future, you may not get any such help not because the person is bad, but rather because of your own dishonesty which you thought he might not uncover."

- *Kenneth K. Mwenda*

"For most people, amongst their former boyfriends, they only mention the one who is more accomplished or well-regarded in society. The riffraff former boyfriend is never mentioned. Even the men don't mention the humble prostitute, office cleaner or housemaid that provided them with an escape service from a debilitating emotional crisis of conjugal deprivation."

"One who takes casually to a friend losing a parent only gets to know how it feels when it is his or her turn to lose a parent."

"The problem with anger is that it does not produce results. It only produces emotions."

"It is hard for a person to forgive if he or she cannot forget and let go of the past. To pretend that you have forgiven someone when you are constantly replaying the past in your head each time you see or hear about the other person is nothing but a mockery of your own internal justice system (IJS). You, alone, can fix your IJS."

"People sometimes struggle to reconcile what got them so excited about a man or lady that they thought was so beautiful or handsome some twenty or so years ago. We all change in physical appearance. Some grow fat, and look very different from the slim and slender chic that they used to be. Others become plump, and their curves disappear into excessive tummy fat, and they cannot wear shorts anymore. For those that did not end up with such a 'transformed' man or lady, they are lucky. They must continue to thank God for steering them away from the calamity of fading looks! But for those that ended up with a man or lady that is now transformed in looks or income, prayers are with you to strengthen you against the tide of the changing circumstances!"

"No matter how far away I may be, no matter where the road may lead me, I will always love you. You are not only my love, my wife, the mother of my beloved son, my gal', my best friend, but are also my mother, my sister, and my guardian angel, ever and always providing me with wise counsel to see beyond the horizon when I sometimes can't see clearly enough. And that's just the truth of my heart."

"Whatever comes from the generosity of a humble man that works hard to make a living is worth more than the lavish and extravagant abundance that you will receive from the stolen wealth or abused public funds of a dubious man. It is wise to drink the palm wine of a poor man than to indulge in some expensive and rare brand of wine from someone who abuses state funds and resources to keep up appearances."

"The most dangerous diva is a broke diva! She will put up all manner of show, with seemingly sophisticated but contrived lies, just to make an impression and keep up appearances. Yet, at the end of the day, she cannot pay her bills or settle her debts, constantly looking for a man to bail her out."

"If you must love, it is best to love with your heart genuinely. Those who look only at a man's or woman's bank account will never love you. Love is not about lifting off someone's financial burdens or solving their socio-economic hardships. Love is not about filling a void to satisfy someone's ends meet. Love has no price. It's about honesty, sincerity, and truthfulness, as opposed to shrewdness, craftiness, and exploitative mannerisms disguised as the way of a diva."

"The problem with loving someone you can't have, yet are busy pretending not to be attracted to, is that you will end up hating the person for nothing, especially when you see him with his love or hear that he is in love with someone else. You are better off admitting to yourself, quietly and magnanimously, the unsettling emotional vulnerabilities that have befallen you."

"If we are to develop a generation of future leaders, the girl-child and the boy-child must learn from proper role models, and not from overzealous persons masquerading as role models through all manner of egoistic and self-interested activism."

"There is nothing wrong in a man being proud of his wife and talking about his wife proudly. But there is everything wrong in a man not being proud of his wife and confining her to the backstage."

"A lady that, out of envy, gets upset or irritated whenever a man talks about his wife or buys his wife a lovely gift is not only insecure but also knows her own weakness in relation to the man's wife."

"When the elders are seated quietly in a pub, enjoying their beer, you must not pretend to be the one buying them the beers when they give you some money and ask that you bring them some cold beers from the barman."

"When we were growing up, a number of our parents appeared to be very wise because they could predict easily our childish prank. And as we grow older, some people's behaviour and conduct remain easily predictable because they just have not grown up."

"To educate a thief, you sometimes need not arrest him. Simply deny him of any future prospects and opportunity to access those very resources he has stolen."

"To tell a lie using dishonest ways of the street, thinking and believing that you have outsmarted someone, when that someone can easily see through and predict your shenanigans even before you attempt to pull one, is nothing but a mere vanity of your troubled ego. It serves only to lower your standing in the eyes of the right thinking members of society. It does not uplift you."

"When the neglected and abandoned stepbrother or stepsister, born out of wedlock, say, from your father's other woman, or one born within wedlock through your father's previous marriage, becomes very successful, he or she gets embraced quickly as a family member even by your own mother."

"Those individuals that subscribe to tribal politics and tribal affinity only have to look at their own lives. There have been unforgettable moments in your life when the person that threw you a lifejacket to enable you to swim to safety was not from your tribe. And there have been certain painful moments when someone from your own tribe who you thought would help you or fight for you just walked away as if he or she had not noticed or seen your predicament. You must wake up from the slumber. Not everyone who has given you a chance or supported you in various ways is from your tribe. The concept of tribe is a fiction, and not a reality. If you insist on that tribal card, you will be very disappointed when your so-called 'own people' abandon you in the end."

"One thing about unconscious bias is that many people are not even aware of it. They can't seem to understand why they tend to form quick negative or bad impressions of others, pontificating often with anguish to those listening that, 'Na li ka pata kalya... Na ka pata fye. Ka li tumpa' (English translation: 'I hate that chap. I just hate him or her. He or she is silly'), without really explaining to the listener what it is that is so silly about the other person or group of persons. Racism, bigotry, tribalism, ethnic prejudice, gender bias, religious extremism and many other forms of discrimination often stem from unconscious bias and are fueled by the environment that we are exposed to. We must continue to ask ourselves about things that we may not be fully aware of or that might seem to be outside our control. We all can make some progress if only we are willing to try."

"People often talk about morality and ethics as if they are one and the same thing. An immoral person is not necessarily unethical in his or her conduct. Neither can we say that an unethical person is necessarily immoral in his or her conduct. Although the boundary between ethics and morality is not always clear, many notable philosophers have spent several years of ink studying the same. Put simply, if the issue is about value judgements between what is right or wrong in human behaviour or conduct, then it is likely to be an issue of moral values whereas if it is an issue between what is good or bad then it is likely to be about ethical choices. Indeed, what is wrong may not always be bad, and what is right may not always be good. And if it is about value judgements between what is beautiful or elegant and what is ugly or a displeasing sight, then it is likely to be about aesthetic values. Sometimes, though, these issues get so intertwined that our moral choices cannot be delinked from our ethical standing or our view of the aesthetic world."

"You must not be afraid to stand shoulder to shoulder with the best that there is out there in the world. But to reach those heights, it takes great discipline, hard work and character. Those that choose to walk on tiptoe, constantly sneaking behind you to see what you are up to or criticizing you behind closed doors and in dark corners, never walk more than a mile. They lack what it takes to get there."

"An act of greatness lies in those rare moments when you have nothing to gain or profit from what you give. It is an act of sacrifice born out of love."

"Different societies or cultures have different emphases. Where I come from in Africa, nobody is expected to talk when plucking the feathers of a slaughtered chicken placed nicely in a big dish or pot of boiling water, fearing that if anyone were to talk some new feathers would begin to grow, thus making the task at hand impossible to accomplish in good time for a sumptuous meal. We all grew up believing firmly in such mysticism and mythology, although the beliefs helped us to focus on the work. Yet, in the American food industry, machines are used to pluck the chicken feathers and the workers operating these machines continue to talk, with no new feathers springing out of the chickens. And productivity remains high."

"When a handsome, well educated and prosperous man is a bachelor or divorced, it does not mean that all and sundry should now pursue him to try their luck at converting him into a husband. That is where some sisters get it wrong. There is a reason why he is not married. And you don't even know why he remains single, but are busy trying to change his marital status. Did he ask you to change his marital status?"

"To be obsessed with dating or marrying only guys that have come from abroad because they have some put-on American or British accent, with some fancy polished looks, is nothing but utopia. Sooner or later, the guy will become local, and the excitement about his coming from England or America will disappear. And that is when reality sets in."

"You can't sit and wait on a man hoping that one day he will change his mind from simply dating you to marrying you even when you can see that he is quite reluctant to marry. Very few ladies ever get married that way; that is, out of a man's sympathy. Smell the coffee and move on. Your clock is ticking, and you can't force a man to marry you. Even ladies that are forced into marriage often end up running away. You can't force matters."

“Those that come from a humble family background but are so obsessed with marrying into some elitist family ‘name’ usually end up as underdogs in their marriages, often discovering only too late that they married a ‘finished’ or ‘expired’ name.”

“Some people are so obsessed with wanting to get things that are way beyond or above their level or pedigree. A person is in the seventh grade at primary school yet wants to date someone at university level, and is busy looking down on her fellow classmates. Even where a person can hardly string a sentence or two in English or French, he or she is busy trying to date a lawyer or a medical doctor. Sometimes people are just too ambitious for nothing. Life is much easier when when you are honest and truthful with yourself. If you cannot afford to fly every time, then just get on a long distance bus. If you can't afford to rent a home in a good and expensive neighbourhood, then just rent one where the commoners live. Why do people often struggle with themselves? If you have no training or schooling in journalism do not go on television pretending to know what you are doing or talking about unless you are an interviewee who is fully competent in his or her field.”

“Most people that swindle others are simply cheap characters, pretending to be some diva, businessman, entrepreneur, businesswoman, public personality, television star, philanthropist, motivator, and so forth. But the truth of the matter is that an accomplished and respected person with a name to protect, and one who has earned his or her respect, will not swindle anyone or steal someone's money. Neither will the person try to take credit for things that he or she has not worked for.”

“It is hard to trust a person who has swindled you or others. Such a person does not deserve any honor, but contempt. Swindling, like fraud, is a very dishonorable act for which any reasonable person cannot walk with his or her head high. Swindling has shame written all over it.”

“To swindle someone out of money by making false promises that you know very well you do not intend to fulfill is a criminal offense for which you can be arrested no matter how smart you think you are. That you have not been arrested is not because you are smart or clever, but rather because the person you have swindled is kind enough not to embarrass you by reporting you to the police and exposing your cheap shenanigans and manipulative schemes.”

"For women, your young children are much more likely to tell you that they love you than their father would, irrespective of whether or not you are single or married to him. Some men don't even know how to react when their young children tell them that, 'Daddy, I love you.' They just blush, and mumble something inaudible before walking away. Others simply use wrong expressions, saying: 'Same to you.'"

"If you do not want people to say, 'Without me, her wedding would have been a flop...I had to step in at the last minute!', then you had better finance your wedding without asking for financial or material contributions from people. Otherwise, they have a right to say what they are saying if, indeed, they did give you some financial or material contributions, notwithstanding their exaggerations."

"You can never go far in life if you are too proud to the point of not wanting to acknowledge the role played by those that have been there for you. Sooner or later, you may need their help again or may need them to help your children or grandchildren. So, don't block those blessings with pride."

"Because of pride, some people have difficulties acknowledging that a friend, colleague or a relative bailed them out of their hardship. They would rather pretend that they had everything under control, yet things were spinning out of control."

"Those that are too proud to say 'thank you' when someone helps them out, or when an opportunity, invitation or gift is extended to them, are often too proud to say 'sorry' when they are in the wrong or have hurt the feelings of others. The two often go together; that is, ungratefulness and foolish pride."

"When a Christian is cornered and discovered for his or her sinful ways, it is no good saying, 'Let he who is without sin be the first to cast a stone.' That you have held out to the world to be a Christian is the very reason you should be held to a higher standard of morality and ethics than those who have not done so. Even for a surgeon, he or she will be held to a higher standard of care than an ordinary medical doctor with no specialization in surgery. The question would be: what could have a reasonable surgeon of his or her standing done? The same can be said of priests, pastors, bishops, apostles, prophets, prophetesses and others with grandiose clerical titles and responsibilities in the church. They are to be held to a higher standard of care than the people they lead because they have held out to the world to be the most highly committed servants of God."

"I don't trust every Christian or religious person, be it a priest, bishop, pastor, apostle, prophet, prophetess or whatever, because not everyone is a CHRISTIAN. In fact, it is best to exercise caution with some seemingly Godly people. Even some Pharisees were like them. I would rather put my trust in God."

"If we all could see what lies in some people's hearts, we would have fewer friends."

"There is no need to feel upset or envious whenever others cheer your friend. You must just learn to cheer as well to avoid feeling that way."

"There are several ways in which to win or lose a friend. Most of the arguments here apply to social media networking as well. Psychologists that specialize in relationships have spent a lot of ink on these issues. Some of the notable ways to win friendship include maintaining mutual respect, effective communication, respecting each others' privacy, loyalty, reciprocity in kindness and generosity, acknowledging and complimenting one anothers' successes without feeling envious or jealousy, asking your friend for guidance or advice without feeling too proud to ask, honesty, integrity, trust, truthfulness, faithfulness, empathy, genuine care and concern as well as some degree of politeness.

Friendship is often lost where someone does not want to be told the truth or where there is mistrust, the withholding or hiding of valuable information by one party, promiscuity, infidelity, betrayal, treachery, arrogance, attitude, pomposity, lies, pretense, boasting, envy, jealousy, gossip, poor or lack of communication, self-righteousness, lack of reciprocity in kindness and generosity, unnecessary competition between or amongst friends, feeling outshone by a friend, irritable behaviours such as loudness and being too nosy, including telling someone what they should choose, do or how they should dress when they have not asked you for such advice, as well as wanting to know everything about a person's life, struggling with poor hygiene, bad odors, economic hardship, constant begging, long distance friendships with lack of or rare communication, stubbornness and not wanting to admit mistakes, including foolish pride of not wanting to compliment others or acknowledge their good deeds or works simply because you don't want them to shine or outshine you, and would rather see their thunder extinguished."

"Today, knowledge is no longer arranged or organized in silos. The many problems facing the world are of an interdisciplinary and multidisciplinary nature. Therefore, resolving such issues requires a holistic and meta-paradigmatic approach. At university, I started off with an immersion in the social sciences, with courses taken in political science, philosophy, psychology, development studies, economics, sociology and other cognate disciplines before turning to law.

After law, I turned to business administration, with courses taken in human resources management, marketing, financial management, strategic management, organizational behavior, creative problem-solving, systems management, financial analysis, operations management, leadership, and many other fields. It is not a question of a Jack of all trades. Rather, it is most helpful for one to read beyond his or her comfort zone and primary field of specialization to be able to have a good grounding in other related disciplines as well.

For a medical doctor to step into political leadership as a head of state, he or she must read a bit about the constitution and politics. The same could be said of an engineer or a biochemist. We all have to step out of our comfort zone, especially when we move into leadership and managerial roles."

"It may not be wise to have your wife, fiancée or girlfriend as a Facebook friend. When other 'people' begin to like your postings or photos, she may not take too kindly to it. Also, for you, as a man, you may have difficulties reconciling her reluctance to like most of your postings when other people are seen to be appreciating them, notwithstanding that you are not in a popularity contest. Your wife, fiancée or girlfriend, however, is traditionally expected to be your loyal cheerleader, and not your critic! If she can't support you, then who will?"

"To try to compete with someone who does not know that you are busy competing with him is not only a waste of time but misplaced energy as well. You are better off learning from him than trying to challenge him. You will be more upset to the point of even suffering from constipation when you discover that you still cannot match him despite your shenanigans to outdo him."

"Do not be surprised that not everyone is going to be happy when you are happy. There are many people out there who are only too happy when you are down or sad. You can even see it in their eyes and from the way they look at you in real life or on social media. Their stare is too loud to hide. And there are fewer people out there who will be happy for you whenever you are happy. In short, you will be wasting your time to wait on some people to be happy for you. As long as you are happy, and have not done anyone any wrong, you have every right to live your life to the fullest and to the max."

"There are some people who claim to know almost all prominent personalities in town, including some 'finished' celebrities. Others go further to claim family ties. That you have seen previously someone on television or in the newspapers does not mean that you know him. You simply know of him, but do not know him. Neither is someone you have just met and greeted through a friend or at some function your friend. Simply say that you have met him or her before. Do not embellish your social CV to appear well-connected and all important. And neither is a young lady that has just been greeted by a celebrity or public figure going to claim that the man is after her so as to jettison her claim to fame amongst her peers. He was just saying hello."

"If you want to hang out with the rich folks or the so-called 'people who matter in society', whereas you yourself are not even rich and hardly ever matter to them, then you should be prepared to suck up to those guys as well as lift their bags in order to remain in the circle of their friends. And your opinion may not count on anything that matters. If anything, it is your job to ensure that you make them smile and that they are happy. Also, you must laugh to their dry jokes even if those jokes are not funny."

"The problem with many educated people is that they are too shy to say that they know more about what some pretender is pretending to know, thus allowing the wannabes and charlatans to occupy the space. Rich people don't do that. They never allow the poor people to occupy the space. Rather, most rich folks claim their space, with no apology. Educated people can learn something from the rich."

"You cannot become somebody by simply following somebody. As a simple follower, you are just anybody. The difference between a 'somebody' and an 'anybody' lies not in how much empty noise a person makes, but rather in the preparation and hard work that you undergo to get to where you are or want to be."

"The thing about playing some sports is that you must be of a certain level of income or be able to afford the right type of sports attire. You just don't show up as a wannabe, with a low income or dressed in some torn socks and worn out attire. It is all about social class. Some people don't just get it!"

"Intellectuals should not be afraid to think. They must, to the greatest extent possible, think even the unimaginable, and must not hold back from exploring the craziest ideas out there. In the midst of all those crazy ideas sometimes comes a gem of intellectual brilliance. All we need is courage to go where those without courage are too afraid to go. And that is why I believe that salvation is not for Christians alone, but for many others as well. We all don't know the final truth, although we think that we have all the answers."

"We must not be afraid to ask tough questions. The problem with many religious people is that they are too afraid to ask controversial questions or to think for themselves. For the most part, they choose conveniently to think only as far as their pastor or church will allow them to think.

Closely related to this, where I come from in Africa, like many other conservative cultures of the emerging world, people are generally too afraid to confront the elephant in the room. They often talk only as far as they believe that they are not offending any taboo. Yet, many injustices have been perpetrated under the banner of taboo and swept underneath the carpet. The concept of taboo is neither scientific, progressive nor objective.

And so, we must not be afraid, for example, to talk about sex or to educate the young ones about the perils and pitfalls of reckless sexual behavior. We must face the elephant in the room. And there is nothing unchristian about this approach. Otherwise, it would be like a Caucasian person who is too afraid to talk about racism and slavery with black people, fearing that they will get upset. You cannot avoid the elephant in the room."

"A notable social function of marriage is not only to raise a family but also to legitimize and moralize sex. For the most part, any sexual activity or engagement that occurs outside the institution and framework of marriage is deemed by many societies as immoral, uncouth, dirty, unholy, sinful, and unwelcome. Through the institution of marriage, humanity gets a moral permit to indulge in sexual activity without the moral compass of society tilting against the winds of fidelity. Without marriage, the eyebrows of onlookers will continue to rise, with the court of public opinion pronouncing judgements constantly of the highest order. As one elderly Bemba-speaking auntie would tell his adventurous nieces, 'Ala, mule upwa ko pakuti mwa chindamika ko ubu chende.' (English translation: "You had better get married so that when your now disgraceful sexual life is done with your husband only it will become more honorable.")."

"Sex is like a cold or flu. At some point, you have to blow your nose when you feel congested in your nostrils. It's where and how you blow your nose that matters."

"A man that has just been circumcised or who is nursing the wounds of circumcision is well served not to look at a beautiful woman lustfully. For, if he were to act otherwise, it would be at his own peril."

"Those in the habit of condemning prostitutes often misdirect themselves. Leave the prostitutes alone. The problem is not with the prostitutes but with those men; that is, the husbands, the widowed and the divorced as well as the seemingly smooth bachelors, that go to solicit the services of prostitutes. If we can cage such men, there will be no prostitution."

"A beauty queen must understand that as time goes by there will always be some younger beauty queen who might steal her thunder if she does not maintain her cutting edge. Some people have difficulties accepting that some hardworking young people can eventually surpass them or do even better, especially if such people have always enjoyed public praises and a lofty position as the forerunners or pioneers in a given field. So, instead of becoming threatened and resentful to upcoming young talent, it is wise simply to nurture such talent and be part of their success story. That way, you won't feel left out!"

"When I played soccer in my youth, I often took it for granted that everyone should be good at soccer. When I started writing my scholarly work, again I often took it for granted that anyone with a Masters degree or PhD should be able to write and publish. But not everyone with a PhD has published or ends up getting published. And when you are an excellent teacher, you take it for granted that anyone with the right qualifications should be able to teach. The same is true if you have a beautiful voice as a musician. It is hard to understand why others can't sing that well.

Whatever you are good at, you will have difficulties at some point to understand why others are struggling over the same. But God gives us different talents. Not everyone can write or sing that well. And not everyone can play soccer that well or solve complex mathematical equations. Also, not everyone can rule, lead or govern properly. And not everyone is an excellent manager. Likewise, not everyone is an excellent husband or wife. Neither is everyone a romantic lover. Whatever talent you have, do not put it to waste. Not everyone has it. And in case you did not know something, many out there crave for it. So, do not sit on your diamonds."

"You cannot neglect a talent that God has given you. Not everyone is born or gifted with your talent. We are all gifted differently. Some are politicians, others are thinkers. There are also those that just watch and do nothing about their life. Whichever way, whether as a musician, lawyer, economist, physician, sportsperson, bureaucrat, clergy, husband or wife, you must avoid neglecting your talent. God gave you that talent for a reason."

"In mature democracies, many senior judicial officers or judges are chosen from amongst the brightest, most experienced, mature, sober and highly dignified persons. In emerging democracies, some judges are appointed from amongst close allies and friends of the appointing authorities as well as from a cohort of political cheerleaders. That's one of the greatest challenges of our democracy."
"In an intellectual discourse, it is not your age, but the power of your reasoning, that matters. The moment you import age, logic disappears."

"People don't get it. There is a lot of power in buying beers. You call the shots and set the tempo for the jokes at the pub. Whoever is drinking on you must respect that divine rule. That's the democracy of beer drinking. The votes come from the wallet."

“You cannot afford to get upset with the person buying you your next meal or paying your rent. You must control your temper to not end up on an empty stomach or sleep outside. That’s just how it is.”

“That a person has not given you what you want does not mean that he or she is a bad person. By contrast, you are the bad person because you are failing to reason. The other person does not owe you anything, unless there is a legal obligation to provide you with what you are asking for.”

“You cannot hate and love someone at the same time. There are some people who will cheer on anyone who is your critic or nemesis just because they feel very resentful towards you for not having bankrolled their agenda or for not unfolding your pocket or wallet in their favour. At the same time, they will crawl back to you asking for help and receiving everything that you give them. Such people are not only unprincipled, but also lack the intelligence to win. They often remain losers if they do not change their attitude. You can't love and hate someone at the same time.”

“There are some people who for reasons only known to themselves will try by all means to avoid mentioning your professional rank, prefix or rightful salutation just because of their own pride. If the other person has now been ordained as a priest, such people will try by all means to avoid addressing him as, 'Fr', and will just proceed straight into a sentence without the usual prefix as if the conversation has been going on for a while. It is not unusual for this type of insecurity to come from some proud colleagues that were once ahead of you in the profession or a few notorious ones that were just about your peers. Even where such people fall sick and are being attended to by a young physician that they have known since childhood, they will try by all means not to call the physician, 'Dr', opting instead just to start the sentence by explaining how they are feeling. For women, it is not unusual at kitchen parties and such other social gatherings for some elderly ladies that are not married to avoid by all means addressing a young lady that is married as 'Mrs'. The sentence will just start without a prefix even though the two are not on a first name basis.

Similarly, a military officer who remains at the rank of captain from the time that he trained you to be a lieutenant might have difficulties addressing you as colonel once you get promoted to the rank of colonel. He may simply want to start his sentence without any 'Sir' or 'Col' prefix so as to make it appear as if the conversation has been going on for a while. But the truth is that it is not about people getting obsessed with titles. Far from it. Rather, the person avoiding to offer these courtesies is the one struggling within himself.

- *Kenneth K. Mwenda*

Likewise, some men struggle to call someone that marries their widowed or divorced mother as 'Dad'. The same is true for those ladies that have difficulties addressing as 'Mum' the young lady that their divorced or widowed father marries. And in my native country, not every lecturer that taught you at undergraduate or was your senior when you joined the academy will swallow their pride to address you correctly by the rightful academic salutation if you surpass them in scholarly standing and rank. Some would rather omit your name altogether, much to their chagrin. Pride is such a terrible thing."

"Some people appear to be very rude when praying, as they shout and scream loudly as if they are threatening God. How can your prayers be answered like that? You have to show humility before God. In my culture, for example, when you are asking for a favour from the elders, you don't shout on top of your voice. By contrast, you are expected to lower and soften your voice as you go down on your knees to seek their favour.

By parity of reasoning, if we can be so humble to fellow mortals, we ought then to do better before God. Pray with respect and humility, and not with noise and rudeness. And if your heart is half in the world, you must bring it back to God for He sees what lies in your heart and your mind."

"Lord, I know that many out there are busy asking You for various things. It is all about what they want. Some have received and never looked back. Others are yet to receive but doubt You. Lord, God, Jehovah Almighty, the God of Abraham, the God of Moses, and the God of Elijah, I am not worthy to stand before You or demand anything of You. But through Your Son, Our Lord Jesus Christ, You have shown us Your mercy. And I thank You for sparing this sinful and ungrateful world from Your anger. For, we are created primarily to serve and praise You, though we often focus on asking and demanding for things from You, O Lord. It is always about ourselves, and hardly about You. Have mercy on us."

"Many people work simply because they need the paycheck. If it were not for the same, they would not be working. Many people go to school because they expect to get a fat paycheck in the near future. Some people get married because the man or woman they are marrying gets a fat paycheck. And the fatter the paycheck, the more the relatives and friends. There is just something about that paycheck that enslaves everyone. God help us!"

"That a man pulls out from a dirty looking sack some old dried hooves of an impala or kudu to make you believe that the game meat that he is selling you is that of a kudu or an impala does not mean you are getting what he is promising you. I have no doubts that many of us who love game meat have eaten many strange things far removed from what we were told had been sold to us. Even dog meat tastes good, so they say. And so, I can't say that I have never tried it, though I want to believe that I have never."

"Some things look similar. But there is a big difference in the outlook to life between a parent who grew up eating ichi waya (i.e. crudely roasted hard grains of maize) whilst struggling with life in the school of hard knocks and his modern son who eats nicely oiled popcorns whilst watching a movie from the comfort of a living room sofa. Indeed, a nicely homemade pancake cannot compare to street fritters sold from a shomeka (i.e. big metal basin used often for washing baby napkins). Often times, the two taste differently, and the pancake, unlike the fritters, will usually not soil your pockets with oil. The world sees the two differently until someone begins to prepare them under similar conditions. And so it is with life. If you don't polish up in manners and presentation, it may not be that easy to find yourself a fine and well-cultivated lady or man."

"To wait on someone to fail so that you can rejoice is nothing but mere foolishness. At least, he has been there while you have not. So, what is there for you to celebrate? Some people celebrate even where their friend's marriage is on the rocks as if that will make them any better. If you are ugly, you still remain ugly notwithstanding what your friend is going through. If you are broke, you still remain broke even if someone you don't like loses elections. In short, mind your own business."

"The problem with that beautiful woman you are not married to but keep admiring is that she may not be as beautiful as she looks. You really do not know what she looks like without a wig or make-up. And you have not yet encountered her on one of her bad days. Besides, you don't even know how she will treat you when you are broke and have no money. At least, you do know how your dear wife handles and deals with these kinds of situations. So, from a risk management point of view, you are better off with someone on whom you have sufficient, timely, valuable and reliable information than where information is scanty and in short supply."

"St. Augustine was fond of young ladies, and his most remembered prayer is when he prayed to God to give him just one last chance to have one additional young lady before he could cease and abate his sinful ways. But it never ended there. It kept repeating itself every time he saw another pretty lady, praying again the same prayer until finally he was saved by the power of his faith in God.

- *Kenneth K. Mwenda*

In whatever walk of life, and in whatever we do or like to do, we all have some bit of St. Augustine in us. Time and time again, we promise ourselves that it should be the last time we will ever touch alcohol, smoke cigarettes, eat unhealthy food, insult with grave profanity, and so forth, but we suffer regrettable relapses like a patient in rehab. May God look kindly on our pitiful selves and grant us pardon for our faulty and sinful ways."

"It is not my job or duty to soothe anyone's ego when I write. Rather, if you are open to the truth, you will have little difficulty with my reasoning. I follow the truth through the dark valleys and the thorny patches of life as much as I do through the gorgeous sunny days of blissful love. But nobody wants to walk through the dark valleys and the thorny patches. Neither do they want to be led to the cliff of life for introspection. They all want to play safe, as if all is well. And that's where the problem is."

"You cannot lead on tiptoe from behind. As a leader, you must come out from obscurity even if you are to lead from behind. And there will be times when you have to make tough decisions or say things that will not sit well with some people. You must be prepared to lose some friends as well as retain others while gaining new ones. Leaders are never content with the status quo. They seek new and better horizons all the time even for those that they inspire and motivate. You can never be an effective leader if you cannot inspire and motivate others. Leadership is not only about the self, but about others too. A leader is one who loves people genuinely because leadership is about people. Those who harbor hate can never lead that long. Sooner or later, they will run out of steam because the person that they hate will have advanced so far that they can no longer touch him or see her."

"People ask questions for various reasons. Some ask questions to let you know that they are smart or that you do not know what you are talking about. Others ask questions just to cause trouble or to show you that they actually know more than you do. It could also be a genuine and sincere question to seek clarity or information. Or, it could be a veiled innuendo to embarrass you or throw you under the bus in the presence of your superiors or colleagues. People ask questions for various reasons. Whatever the motive of your question, it is wise to ask only intelligent questions. Do not ask stupid or redundant questions."

"To assume that the practice of law is confined only to what goes in a law firm or to the mundane aspects of litigation in a court room is nothing but an unfortunate misdirection of oneself. In the absence of proper guidance from statutory or regulatory documents, we are left to turn to the common law as well as to developments in parallel jurisdictions for guidance on a fuller understanding of what constitutes the term 'practice of law'. Some lawyers carry out legal work in international organizations or corporate settings. You cannot discount that experience as not constituting the 'practice of law'. From a scholarly point of view, the analysis here ought to go deeper than the superficial construct of the English language dictionary.

Accountants and medical doctors too have not been spared. That a person qualified in accounting is not working as an auditor does not mean that he or she is not a practicing accountant. Auditing is not the only way in which a person can practice accounting. Some accountants are involved in policy and strategy formulation on pertinent aspects of finance and accounting, working closely with the firm's finance and accounting departments. Others simply count church tithings and donations. It is still accounting!

By parity of reasoning, that a qualified medical doctor is not carrying out clinical work in a hospital does not mean that he or she is not practicing medicine. The practice of medicine goes deeper, and can extend to community medicine and public health. The renewal of a practicing license per se does not provide us with a fuller understanding of what it means to practice a profession. Someone can renew his or her practicing license, and then start doing strange things with his or her life. The world is changing, with many transferable skills in various professions being deployed to closely aligned areas of the professions. We must respect that."

"To get upset simply because someone is wearing the same outfit or pair of shoes as yours is nothing but a pitiful conundrum of your insecurities. Why should it matter? She also paid for them as you did."

"Some people get very upset when they see you with someone they hate or have issues with. And they take it very personal, as if you have betrayed them or some sort. Yet, you are not part of their problem with that person, and have at no time discussed them with the said person. But just the thought of seeing you talk to the other person eats them up. And they can punish you for that."

"Some people will not greet you when they are in the company of someone they consider very important. Even if you try to look at them with a view of saying hello, they will not look back at you, focussing instead solely at the important person they are with. And they will be laughing the loudest, as they talk with the boss or foreign investor, just to show you that they are very close to him or her. But when things go wrong, the same people will be the first to run to you to complain about that person and how he or she mistreated them or messed up."

"There was always that strikingly cute young lady in high school or university that refused to date any local guy, maintaining that her boyfriend was in the UK or USA. But when she would later emigrate to the UK or USA, her standards changed, maintaining that she only dated foreigners, and not her nationals, without realizing that her fellow nationals were also foreigners in that foreign land.

After dating a few foreigners, mainly unscrupulous fraudsters, and getting demystified with the whole fuss about dating a foreigner, she would then change again to say she cannot date a black or African man. And it would go on like that, as she waited endlessly for a spectacular man from Mars or Venus."

"At some point, the engineer educated abroad was often treated better than the locally educated engineer during the parastatal era of the Zambia Consolidated Copper Mines Ltd (ZCCM). The mines would offer the foreign trained engineer better housing accommodation, with subtly better prospects for career development as well. And some young single ladies from the immediate neighbourhoods would give their attention to the UK or US trained engineers than the local fellas from the University of Zambia. This issue persisted for a while. But why do we often think of things from abroad as better than their equivalents from home?"

"The problem with the classical model of education is that you are taught to get the best education out there and to go to the best schools in order to get the best job. In the real world, that theory holds true only to a certain extent. Your good education and the schools that you attend will only help you to start the race, especially where recruitment and selection are not tainted with nepotism or corrupt practices, but not to maintain the lead once you are in there. When the race is on, it does not matter so much which school you attended, how hard you are working or how fast you are running. Other obscure criteria take the center-stage. Who you know and who you suck up to often become the determining factors of how high you can climb up the corporate ladder."

"Some men end up marrying or dating a lady that turned them down disrespectfully when they were struggling with life's hardships or before they got established in social or business circles. Such men never learn! A man that was once turned down badly cannot suddenly become the lady's sweetheart simply because his economic fortunes now appear promising. Sooner or later, she will leave."

"A marriage should not be boring. A boring marriage is a recipe for disaster."

"A man that gets upset every time his wife or girlfriend greets another man warmly, especially if the man she's greeted is of a higher station in life, must remember that she has not just told him about the other fellas that are busy sending her unsolicited social media messages. He cannot afford to be mad with every one of them."

"A man that does not provide for his woman often worries when he hears her talk about how her friend's man provides for the friend. He will be quick to dismiss such a man as irresponsible and hopeless even if he has never met him and does not know him."

"One who easily suffers boredom in marriage is a serious threat to herself. For, her restlessness may lead her into harm's way."

"Nowhere in the world is boredom accepted as a ground for divorce. Those who choose to marry must understand this principle fully well."

1061

"The reason why some young people today don't fancy going to school is because some teachers and professors make school look boring. School should be as much fun for the youths as anything cool out there. Educationists need to understand the psychology of a number of our youths. Many youths don't like boring things. Therefore, we must make schools a fun but safe place to be without necessarily compromising on the educational standards. Our youths must be incentivized to look forward every morning to the next lecture or class, as they acquire valuable skills.

When people everywhere in schools look very serious, some youths will shift their cool to hip-hop. We must keep that cool in the schools while promoting effective learning. The world must begin to celebrate some Oscar type of awards on television for outstanding academic performance before we lose our youths to the sports, musical and Hollywood celebrity world. We must embrace the concept of academic celebrities to keep our youths in schools. The youths must begin to understand that it is cool to go to school just as they see hip-hop and rap music as a cool thing."

- *Kenneth K. Mwenda*

A NATION THAT STOOD TALL ABOVE OTHERS AND GAVE ITS BEST TO THE LIBERATION OF SOUTHERN AFRICA FROM COLONIAL RULE AND APARTHEID.

If there is a nation that has been so pivotal in the liberation of the Southern Africa region from colonial rule, Zambia stands tall, followed by Tanzania. When South Africa was battling the cancer of apartheid, the Zambian people showed empathy and welcomed South Africa's main liberation party, ANC, to set up its base and headquarters in Lusaka, Zambia. And Zambia's President, Kenneth Kaunda, continued to press relentlessly for the unconditional release of President Nelson Mandela from prison.

When Namibia was fighting for its political independence, her main liberation party, SWAPO, was welcomed by the Zambian people to set up its headquarters in Lusaka, Zambia. When Zimbabwe was fighting the oppressive white minority rule under Ian Smith, one of the two main liberation movements, ZAPU, found a home in Lusaka, Zambia. FRELIMO, the ruling party of Mozambique also had a great ally in Zambia for that country's liberation. The people of Zambia have never turned their back on those under the yoke of colonialism and apartheid.

In Zambia, we have treated those of our brothers and sisters we hosted from the neighboring countries without an iota of xenophobia or discrimination. We treated them with respect. Even when the Biafra war broke out in Nigeria, we welcomed in Zambia several Igbo scholars and intellectuals from Nigeria. And as the turmoil of military rule continued in countries such as Ghana, Zambia opened its doors to many Ghanaian exiles. The former president of Uganda, Milton Obote, lived peacefully and died while in political exile in Lusaka, Zambia. Zambia's foreign policy in that respect has remained consistent. We have provided home and support, including educational opportunities, to our brothers and sisters from many other neighboring countries such as Rwanda and Burundi during and after the tragic genocide. When Malawi's founding president, Dr Hastings Kamuzu Banda, was clamping down on the opposition, many Malawians fled their home country and quickly settled in Zambia and have remained there ever since.

And so, when the history books of Africa are written by those historians who care to write and tell the truth, let them say, for example, why Nelson Mandela chose Zambia as the first foreign country he would visit after being released from prison. He did not choose America, Britain or Russia. He went to Lusaka, Zambia, shortly after he came out of prison. Even the Palestinian leader, Yasser Arafat flew down to Lusaka, Zambia, to meet Mandela there. When Mozambican president Samora Machel died, he was flying from Zambia after some high level political discussions. Zambia has an indelible place in the politics of Africa! And that is the rich political heritage of the Zambian people whose first president, Dr. Kenneth Kaunda, had parents of Malawian origin but was warmly accepted by the people of Zambia without any ethnic resentment as you sometimes see in other regions or countries. There was no movement or political agitation in Zambia to try to paint Kenneth Kaunda as having been born in Malawi as some sections of the public in the western world have tried falsely to paint the first African-American president of the United States of America as having been born in Kenya. As recent as the 2000s, the Zambian people upheld their constitution again to permit a Zambian Caucasian or white man to take office as acting president to the astonishment of many the world over. That is who we are. In other parts of the world, that would have been an issue.

RECONCILING RELIGIOSITY WITH SUPERSTITION

Is it permissible within religious circles for a Christian or any other religious person to believe, say, in the works of an African traditional herbsman or a witchdoctor?

Or, should some Christians be allowed to continue holding the Bible during daytime while they sneak out secretly at night to consult the occult for prospects for marriage, fertility, lucrative jobs, lawyers winning court cases, accused and guilty persons being acqui...tted under unclear circumstances via 'wash-out' verdicts, visas to go abroad, promotions at work and successful business ventures, as well as prospects for political victory in elections and political appointments?

How does a Christian reconcile these competing values? Or, as someone recently said, does the fact that even some white people believe in some kind of occult for their professional and business success make it OK for many an educated, modernized and ambitious African to embrace such beliefs?

UNDERSTANDING THE MEANING OF WEDDING TEARS:

I always thought that many brides the world-over tend to shed tears of joy when getting married because of the intensity of love between the couple. But an African-American friend of mine said to me recently that:

"It is not necessarily true in all parts of the world, including places like Europe and Africa. Some brides shed tears simply because they cannot fathom the idea or believe it that there is a man out there who can commit to marriage, especially when many of their friends, aunties or sisters are not married. It's that shock and disbelief that someone out there can actually be true and commit to marriage that leads to those tears because very few men today want to settle down and marry, if the man does not already have children with other women..."

SPELL-CHECKING TEXT BEFORE SENDING:

English is an interesting language. Certain words mean different things to different people. It is always best to try to spell check to avoid making common errors such as where one inadvertently omits the letter 'l' in trying to type the word 'public', as in the sentence:

"The boy is too young to be found in pubic places at night."

FRIDAY LAMENTATIONS:

Little John races back hurriedly into the house from outside where he has been playing, trying desperately to get to the toilet. They live in a small house with only one toilet. Little John is very pressed and wants to pee. But, the toilet door is locked, and it has been locked for a while now. This is the third unsuccessful attempt by Little John to relieve himself, but the toilet door remains locked. As Little John paces up and down the living room, whi...le waiting, he is visibly anxious and agitated, and begins to complain irritably:

"Aweee mwe, ifi bantu fya pano pa ng'anda fya li temwa uku ko kola mu chimbusu!!!" (English translation: "Damn it, people at this house like to take their time in the toilet! Can whoever is in there hurry up, please!")

To which his older brother watching TV, interjects politely:

"Iwe, ni ba tata bali mo..." (English translation: "It's dad who is in there...")

Both Little John and his brother suddenly hear the old man clear his throat audibly from the toilet, and Little John, still seemingly upset, goes:

"Oweee, sorry!!! Yaba!!!" (English translation: "OK, I am sorry. But I need to pee!")

THE PLIGHT OF THE AFRICAN IN THE DIASPORA

The African in the diaspora belongs neither here nor there. We must be patient with him. He may have changed his national passports to secure some fortunes, but he knows fully well that that is not an end in itself. The African in the diaspora may have made some investments in Africa, but he is also not completely welcome amongst his own there. They keep reminding him, 'You have been gone too long. You abandoned your country. Go back.... What do you want here now?'

The African in the diaspora must find an antidote to cure his nostalgia for Africa even if he pretends that he is now westernized. He misses the old Africa he knew, but then the times have changed and moved on. He reminisces all too often on social media and other Internet forums about the good old times, struggling to accept that those times are long gone and will never return. For him, it is as though time stands still. His sentimental attachment to aspirations for a better Africa often leaves him feeling disappointed whenever he sets foot on the African soil. He wonders when things are going to get better. His heart is sometimes broken for a better Africa. In the diaspora, he is also constantly reminded that he is a black man with a thick accent who should go back where he came from. The ambivalence in which the African in the diaspora finds himself draws on a dichotomy of love and nostalgia, on the one hand, and bewilderment, rejection and uncertainty, on the other. We must be patient with the African in the diaspora. He has picked up so many new tastes of life and other expensive habits that are alien to Africa. He may not have an acceptable place in today's Africa, and neither does he have such a place in the Western world.

SELF-CENSURE BEFORE STEPPING FORWARD TO TAKE UP LEADERSHIP.

Legend has it in the Zambia soccer fraternity that when one great late Samuel Zoom Ndhlovu was coach of the Zambia national soccer team, he would at times pile a hip of jerseys in the dressing room, and invite all the players to a self-censure team selection process before the game began. Ba Zoom, as he was fondly known, would say:

"Aleni bane, ba goalkeeper tu kwete banga? Uwu lemona kwati mwaume sana a bule po iii-jersey lya kwa goalkeeper (English translation: "OK guys, how many goalkeepers do we have in camp? Whoever amongst you feels is the best goalkeeper should step forward to pick up the goalkeeper's jersey.")."

All the players knew amongst themselves who was the deserving guy to step forward to pick up a jersey for each position. And as soon as one great Charles Musonda, then playing for Anderlecht in Belgium, or one great Kalusha Bwalya, then playing for PSV Eindhoven in Netherlands, would arrive in Zambia after some flight connection delays in Europe, the other players who had picked up Charles or

Kalusha's jersey would on their own volition step forward to alert the coach, humbly saying:
"Ba coach, abene ba chi fulo baisa...iii-jersey ili (English translation: "Coach, I am less worthy. The man himself who should be playing in this position is here.")."

There was self-censure, bane. On your own, you would just do some introspection before stepping forward to claim a jersey.

At some point, during the days of one great late Godfrey Ucar Chitalu, who is another soccer icon in Zambia, some guy, whose name I will not mention, mustered some courage and stepped forward to pick up the No. 10 jersey customarily worn by the Great Ucar. And Ucar was seated quietly in the far corner of the room, busy polishing his soccer boots and not paying much attention, when all the other soccer players burst out laughing at this pretentious player who thought he could pick Ucar's jersey and play in Ucar's position. All the players exclaimed in unison:

"Imwe, bikeni po iii-jersey lya bene! Abene abo bekele apo... (English translation: "Comrade, don't even think about it. Put back that jersey. It belongs to the Great Ucar seated there. You are too small to fit in his shoes.")."

Now, if only our people could understand and learn from this process of self-censure. We all need to examine ourselves thoughtfully before we begin to entertain fanciful ideas of political ambition. It is evident today that some politicians are going nowhere with their presidential ambitions, yet they are busy raising small storms in a teacup. But for what?

HUMAN RIGHTS VERSUS HUMAN RESPONSIBILITIES

What does one say to someone who, retired and aged, but loaded with a hefty pension, begins to father children in old age with a young wife or young girlfriend? These are some of the social problems that we are seeing today. Even some Heads of State and other politicians tend to do the same. We need to be giving some thoughtful consideration to a number of these issues. How does a grandfather go around having babies? Why would someone behave that way when they know very well that they are too old to be there to raise the child they are fathering? Is it because of human rights that anyone can do as he or she wills? And is that human rights argument alone sufficient to convince us?

IT IS GOOD NOT TO BE TOO ASSUMING

The husband, enjoying some nicely roasted steak prepared by his wife, calls out his wife who is in the kitchen:

> "Where did you buy this meat?"

The wife quickly responds in a high-pitched voice:

> *"Why? What's wrong?"*

Her husband smiles and continues:

> "It is actually very good meat."

Only then does the wife relax, saying:

> *"Oh, Ok. I thought that maybe you didn't like the food..."*

THE STATE AND THE PRIVATE SECTOR IN DEVELOPING COUNTRIES.

One thing that intrigues me about much of African private riches is that, for the most part, they have arisen out of, or resulted and benefitted from, the State. There are very few exceptions. Many serving or former Heads of State, Cabinet Ministers, and some Permanent Secretaries, for example, including some of their relatives, or those private citizens with huge government contracts are typical examples of such wealth accumulation. It is rare that African riches have no direct or indirect link to the State. And this seems to be the ca

se even in some other developing regions of the world. The question that I continue to ask is: Can Africa's rich men survive without the government or any form of State structure to milk from? Do we have the Bill Gates and Steve Jobs type of entrepreneurs who can start, grow and sustain their business empires relying mainly on the private sector, with minimal leanings, if any, indirect or otherwise, on the government or State for survival?

THE FOOTPRINTS OF THE SUN

The footprints of the sun are in Africa. We must follow the sun. In 1991, the world was watching, while not sure what to expect of the first One-Party State in Africa to have turned to multi-party politics, as Zambia went to the polls. To the bewilderment of the critics and cynics, we excelled as an African nation becoming the first One-Party State in Africa to demonstrate a smooth transfer of power from a defeated incumbent to a victorious leader f...rom the opposition. We have never looked back, always scoring a first when it comes to political tolerance and democratic civility in accepting the general will of the people at the electoral polls.

- *Kenneth K. Mwenda*

Even though we may seek a new constitution today, we have always operated within the limits of the current law in as far as the change of government is concerned. That is who we are, and that is who we shall continue to be. Even when we obtained our political independence we did not shy away from supporting, and even hosting, the liberation movements in much of Southern Africa. For us, we would not accept our own freedom if our brothers and sisters were not free. And we embraced, and continue embrace, our first republican president whose parents were not of Zambian origin. That is who we are. Even now, we continue to surprise the world that seems to struggle to understand that our acting republican president is Caucasian. It is our political maturity that has blessed us with such heart of inclusivity and diversity. We have even had Asian cabinet ministers. That's just who we are: a warm people. Tell the world to watch for the footprints of the sun in Zambia.

ABOUT THE AUTHOR

Prof. Kenneth K. Mwenda
PhD, LLD, DSc(Econ)

http://www.kennethmwenda.com

A distinguished thought leader and public intellectual, **Prof. Kenneth K. Mwenda** read law at Oxford as a Rhodes Scholar. He has also taught law at top universities in the United States of America (US), the United Kingdom (UK) and South Africa. A Fellow of the British Royal Society of Arts (FRSA), Prof Mwenda is a recipient of several international academic awards, including a competitive fellowship from Yale University Law School in the US. Most recently, he gave the 2015 Distinguished Lecture at the University of Nairobi Law School in Kenya, and was appointed as Extraordinary Professor of Law in the Faculty of Law at the University of Pretoria, South Africa. He has also held previously the position of Extraordinary Professor of Law at the Centre for Human Rights, the University of Pretoria. Based in Washington DC, Prof. Mwenda is the Program Manager and Executive Head of the World Bank's Voice Secondment Program, a major capacity-building initiative of the Board of Executive Directors of the World Bank.

Prof. Mwenda has had a stellar academic career as well as an outstanding professional life as a leading international development practitioner, travelling to more than thirty countries worldwide. His is a fine blend of theory and practice, with many years of international experience in both academia and international development. Prof Mwenda has maintained a parallel academic and professional life, publishing academic books and other scholarly work in top journals and law reviews as well as holding various senior academic appointments at leading universities internationally, while serving with the World Bank. A member of the editorial boards of several scholarly journals, including the *Journal of*

International Banking Regulation and the *Africa Finance Journal*, he is also an occasional editor of the *Journal of African Business*, and was until recently the joint Editor-in-Chief of the World Bank's *Law, Justice and Development Book Series*.

With sustained thought leadership in academia, in addition to valuable experience in international development practice, Prof Mwenda is a widely recognized authority in his field of expertise as well as a highly sought-after speaker that has been interviewed and quoted by numerous print and broadcast media, including the *New York Times* (US), the *Voice of America* (VOA, US), *CCTV* (US), the *Times* (UK), the *British Broadcasting Corporation* (BBC, UK), and *Sky TV* (UK). In 2008, after a rigorous and thorough examination of Prof Mwenda's selected scholarly books and peer-refereed journal articles by a distinguished panel of top international legal scholars, Prof Mwenda was admitted by Rhodes University, a leading university in South Africa, to the rarely awarded Higher Doctorate degree of Doctor of Laws (LLD). It was the first time ever in the rich academic history of that university that such an award was being conferred in the Faculty of Law! Six years later, in 2014, after another rigorous and thorough examination of Prof Mwenda's other substantial portfolio of scholarly books and peer-refereed journal articles by a distinguished panel of eminent international scholars, Prof Mwenda was admitted by the University of Hull, a leading British university, to the rarely awarded Higher Doctorate degree of Doctor of Science in Economics (DSc(Econ)). It is important to stress that in the entire English speaking world, Prof. Mwenda is arguably the only senior legal scholar to have earned two Higher Doctorate degrees in two different disciplines! Higher Doctorates, it should be emphasized, are never the immediate step after a PhD. Rather, they are reserved for those internationally recognized senior scholars that have made exceedingly significant contributions to a science or body of knowledge through exceptionally insightful and distinctive scholarly publications, earning them recognition as international authorities in the field of research that forms the basis of the degree.

Further, Prof. Mwenda holds a PhD in Law from a leading British university, the University of Warwick. At the World Bank, he has served additionally as Senior Legal Counsel in the Legal Vice-Presidency as well as Senior Legal Counsel in the World Bank's Integrity Vice-Presidency. All in all, Prof. Mwenda has written more than twenty-five (25) scholarly books and over ninety (90) articles in leading law reviews and academic journals. Prior to joining the World Bank, he served as an Assistant Professor of Law at the Faculty of Law, the University of Warwick, in the UK. Prof Mwenda has also taught as Adjunct Professor of Law at American University Washington College of Law (WCL) in Washington DC. His scholarly work is cited frequently as authority not only in academia, but also by the courts of law, most recently by the Supreme Court for the Republic of Zambia in the case of *Ventriglia and Ventriglia v. Eastern and Southern Africa Trade and Development Bank and*

Robert Simeza SCZ NO. 13 OF 2010 (Appeal No. 11/ 2009). His other scholarly work has been seminal in some of the research work and country assessments carried out by the International Monetary Fund (IMF), the World Bank, the Asian Development Bank (ADB) and the Inter-American Development Bank (IADB).

In addition, Prof. Mwenda holds, *inter alia*, the prestigious BCL degree from the University of Oxford (UK) and an MBA degree from the University of Hull (UK), with subsequent executive leadership training from Cornell and Georgetown Universities, respectively. His first professional law degree, a Bachelor of Laws (LLB), is from the University of Zambia where he graduated in 1990 in the top one percent (1%) of his class. He was admitted to the Bar in Zambia in 1991, as the best Bar admission student. Prof. Mwenda is a US Certified Anti-Money Laundering Specialist (CAMS) as well as a Fellow of the British International Compliance Association (FICA). He has served as Visiting Full Professor of Law at a number of leading universities in Europe and South Africa, including the University of Miskolc in Hungary, the University of Cape Town (UCT), the University of Western Cape (UWC) and the University of Zambia. He has also given many lead lectures and presentations at major US universities, including George Washington University, the University of Maryland, Duke University, Temple University, and the University of South Florida.

- *Kenneth K. Mwenda*

OTHER BOOKS BY THIS AUTHOR

2016

Kenneth K. Mwenda, **Public Intellectualism and Socio-Political Inquiry through Metaphor and Musing**, Vol. 4, (Toronto, Canada: Africa in Canada Press, 2016).

2016

Kenneth K. Mwenda, **Public Intellectualism and Socio-Political Inquiry through Metaphor and Musing**, Vol. 3, (Toronto, Canada: Africa in Canada Press, 2016).

2016

Kenneth K. Mwenda, **Public Intellectualism and Socio-Political Inquiry through Metaphor and Musing**, Vol. 2, (Toronto, Canada: Africa in Canada Press, 2016).

2015

Kenneth K. Mwenda, **Understanding Securities Law and Regulation in Zambia**, (Cape Town, South Africa: Juta Academic Publishers, 2015).

2015

Kenneth K. Mwenda, **Public Intellectualism and Socio-Political Inquiry through Metaphor and Musing**, Vol. 1, (Toronto, Canada: Africa in Canada Press, 2015).

2011

Kenneth K. Mwenda, **Public International Law and the Regulation of Diplomatic Immunity in the Fight against Corruption**, (Pretoria, South Africa: Pretoria University Law Press (PULP), 2011).

2011

Kenneth K. Mwenda, **Contemporary Issues in Zambian and English Company Law: A Comparative Study**, (Amherst, NY: Teneo Press, 2011).

2010

Kenneth K. Mwenda, **Legal Aspects of Banking Regulation: Common Law Perspectives from Zambia**, (Pretoria, South Africa: Pretoria University Law Press (PULP), 2010).

2010

Kenneth K. Mwenda, W. Fischer, H. A. Amankwah and D. Goulding, **German Hyperinflation 1922/1923 – A Law and Economics Approach**, (Cologne, Germany: Josef Eul Verlag, 2010).

2009

Kenneth K. Mwenda and G.N. Muuka (eds), **The Challenge of Change in Africa's Higher Education in the 21st Century**, (Amherst, NY: Cambria Press, 2009).

- *Kenneth K. Mwenda*

2007

Kenneth K. Mwenda, **Comparing American and British Legal Education Systems: Lessons for Commonwealth African Law Schools**, (Amherst, NY: Cambria Press, 2007).

2007

Kenneth K. Mwenda and W. Fischer (eds), **Country of Origin – A Law and Economics Approach to the Concept of 'Made in Australia'**, (Cologne, Germany: Josef Eul Verlag, 2007).

2007

Kenneth K. Mwenda, **Legal Aspects of Combating Corruption: the Case of Zambia**, (Amherst, NY: Cambria Press, 2007).

2006

Kenneth K. Mwenda, **Legal Aspects of Financial Services Regulation and the Concept of a Unified Regulator**, (Washington DC: The World Bank, 2006).

2006

Kenneth K. Mwenda, **Combating Financial Crime: Legal, Regulatory and Institutional Frameworks**, (Lewiston, NY: The Edwin Mellen Press, 2006).

2006

Kenneth K. Mwenda, **The Legal Administration of Financial Services in Common Law Jurisdictions: with special attention to the dual regulation system in Zambia**, (Lewiston, NY: The Edwin Mellen Press, 2006).

2006

Kenneth K. Mwenda and V. Mosoti (eds), **Contemporary Issues in International Economic Law**, (Cologne, Germany: Josef Eul Verlag, 2006).

2006

H. Kyambalesa and M.C. Houngnikpo; with contributions from Kenneth K. Mwenda and G.N. Muuka, **Economic Integration and Development in Africa**, (Aldershot, UK: Ashgate Publishing Co., 2006).

2005

Kenneth K. Mwenda, **Anti-Money Laundering Law and Practice: Lessons from Zambia**, (Lusaka, Zambia: University of Zambia (UNZA) Press, 2005).

2003

Kenneth K. Mwenda, and D.A. Ailola, (eds), **Frontiers of Legal Knowledge: Business and Economic Law in Context**, (Durham, NC: Carolina Academic Press, 2003).

2003

Kenneth K. Mwenda, **Principles of Arbitration Law**, (Parkland, FL: Brown Walker Press, 2003).

2002

Kenneth K. Mwenda (ed), **Banking and Micro-finance Regulation and Supervision: Lessons from Zambia**, (Parkland, FL: Brown Walker Press, 2002).

2001

Kenneth K. Mwenda, **Zambia's Stock Exchange and Privatisation Programme: Corporate Finance Law in Emerging Markets**, (Lewiston, NY: The Edwin Mellen Press, 2001).

2000

Kenneth K. Mwenda, **Banking Supervision and Systemic Bank Restructuring: An International and Comparative Legal Perspective**, (London, UK: Routledge-Cavendish Publishing, 2000).

2000

Kenneth K. Mwenda, **The Dynamics of Market Integration: African Stock Exchanges in the New Millennium**, (Parkland, FL: Brown Walker Press, 2000).

2000

Kenneth K. Mwenda, **Contemporary Issues in Corporate Finance and Investment Law**, (Washington DC: Penn Press, 2000).

1999

Kenneth K. Mwenda, **Legal Aspects of Corporate Capital and Finance**, (Washington DC: Penn Press, 1999).

Thank you!

FOR YOUR READERSHIP

- *Kenneth K. Mwenda*

FEEDBACK

Now that you have read the book ...

Was it interesting?

Did you enjoy what you wanted to read?
Was there any room for improvement?

Let us know at:

http://www.kennethmwenda.com/feedback

Your feedback is highly appreciated.

Thank you!

\- *Kenneth K. Mwenda*

www.ingramcontent.com/pod-product-compliance
Lightning Source LLC
Chambersburg PA
CBHW070344030726
47504CB00001B/60
9781988251073